LOSERS AND WINNERS

*The Pursuit of Equality
and Social Justice
in Higher Education*

Paul Anisef • **Norman Okihiro**
In collaboration with **Carl James**

Butterworths
Toronto

Losers and Winners: The Pursuit of Equality
and Social Justice in Higher Education
© 1982–Butterworth & Co. (Canada) Ltd.

This study is based on research funded under contract by the
Ministry of Colleges and Universities, Ontario. It reflects the
views of the authors and not necessarily those of the Ministry.

Printed and bound in Canada
5 4 3 2 1   2 3 4 5 6 7 8 9/8

Canadian Cataloguing in Publication Data

Anisef, Paul, 1942–
    Losers and winners : the pursuit of equality and social
justice in higher education

Includes index.
Bibliography: p.
ISBN 0-409-81111-4

1.   Educational equalization - Ontario.   2.   Education,
Higher - Ontario.   3.   Right to education - Ontario.
I.   Okihiro, Norman R. (Norman Ryukichi), 1948-
II.   James, Carl.   III.   Title.

LC213.3.C3206 1982   378.713   C82-095067-X

39,605

The Butterworth Group of Companies

Canada:
Butterworth & Co. (Canada) Ltd., Toronto and Vancouver

United Kingdom:
Butterworth & Co. (Publishers) Ltd., London

Australia:
Butterworths Pty. Ltd., Sydney

New Zealand:
Butterworths of New Zealand Ltd., Wellington

South Africa:
Butterworth & Co. (South Africa) Ltd., Durban

United States:
Butterworth (Publishers) Inc. Boston
Butterworth (Legal Publishers) Inc., Seattle
Mason Publishing Company, St. Paul

Contents

Appendices

List of Tables, Charts and Figures

Preface

Schools are perhaps the most ubiquitous and visible of govern-
ment-supported institutions. Parents, children, and taxpayers at
large have a lot at stake in them. Indeed, when asked about the
public education system, most people will respond with strong
opinions. Education, by its very nature, tends to make us
emotionally responsive rather than indifferent.

One area of concern regarding public education in Canada is
that of existing educational opportunities at the post-secondary
level. Is post-secondary education equally available for all who
desire it? Or are there bases of discrimination that actually
result in unequal educational opportunities? Who winds up going
to university or community college? Are these institutions representative in composition of the larger society, or are they elitist?
Have patterns of post-secondary participation changed over time?
How?

These questions and others are the foundation for our en-
quiry in this book. The authors share an intense personal and
research interest in accessibility to higher education and its
parent concept, equality of educational opportunity. This
interest has been spurred on by empirical studies initiated by
Anisef on educational aspirations of Ontario Grade 12 students in
1973 and culminating with analysis of educational and occupational
outcomes in Is the Die Cast? Educational Achievements and Work
Destination of Ontario's Youth, published by the Ontario
Ministries of Education and of Colleges and Universities in 1980.
These studies have raised important questions regarding the
province's opportunity structure and changes in accessibility
which may have accompanied policy shifts (e.g., shifts in student
assistance plans).

With these questions in mind, an in-depth review of relevant
literature was undertaken. The review unearthed these important
facts. First, somewhat to our dismay, key concepts like equality
of educational opportunity seemed to change definition with changing times. Even more crucial than this, however, was the remarkable fact that no regular and reliable monitoring strategy for
identifying accessibility trends had ever been developed in
Canada or elsewhere.

ix

Our mandate seemed clear. First, it would be necessary to unravel the complex meanings of accessibility and equality of educational opportunity. To do this, we would need to trace their historical significance, both in the social science literature and in public debates. Chapters 1 through 3 are directed to this objective. Secondly, we would have to develop a reliable strategy for monitoring accessibility at the post-secondary level. After some consideration, the Census was selected and its use is fully described in Chapter 5.

We chose a social-stratification perspective for discussing and understanding accessibility. This perspective emphasizes that our freedom to choose among social alternatives is frequently constrained by structural inequalities in our society (e.g., social class, race, and sex differences). For this reason we offer an explanation of the sources of structural inequality in Chapter 4.

The social-stratification perspective is based on the key assumption that the learning process (i.e., socialization) helps sustain structural inequalities. We also believe, however, that this same process can be employed in reverse to equalize opportunities for young persons. We suggest, for example, that schools, working co-operatively with parents, and early financial incentives can be strategically used for creating a more equal society. These ideas are formulated as recommendations and presented in Chapter 6. These recommendations do not necessarily reflect current government policy or thinking on these issues; rather their intent is to stimulate public debate and to provide more social science input and updated solutions for the 1980s.

We believe that there is an especially critical need to re-evaluate accessibility priorities as we enter the increasingly sober 1980s. There is, for instance, a growing trepidation that the gains in equality of educational opportunity, realized in the 1960s and 1970s, will be eroded by the end of the present decade. It is our conviction that more rather than less needs to be done to convert post-secondary education from a fantasy to a viable alternative for relatively disadvantaged adolescents in Ontario.

In this book we have attempted to identify some of the major sociological and value assumptions underlying various treatments of concepts like equality of educational opportunity. It is not less true that our own analysis is grounded in such assumptions. Here we owe a large debt to the late John Porter who presented in a brilliant series of McInnis lectures at York University in 1977, a re-appraisal of his essentially functionalist views on equality of educational opportunity (Porter, 1979: 241-280). Porter recognized that education alone could not eliminate the deeply rooted inequalities of condition that characterize Canadian society. At the same time, he never doubted that "equality of access to all educational institutions was and should continue to be an important objective of social reform" (Porter, 1979: 241).

While Porter's analyses have been strongly critical of educational policy, they did not call for the types of revolutionary changes frequently endorsed by social scientists who espouse the conflict perspective (see Appendix A). Rather, his orientation, like ours, is forcefully reformist. Thus, in Does Money Matter? a grant system is proposed that would minimize existing income differentials across families varying in socio-economic origin.

In our view, Porter's proposal needs to be extended to take into account the sources of structural inequality. Social science research documents the social psychological handicaps suffered by less advantaged groups through weaker ambitions, less crystallized aspirations, lower self-evaluations and placement in lower academic tracks or streams. Indeed, we argue, in Chapter 1 that many bright but disadvantaged adolescents selectively perceive their opportunities from a more constrained range of alternatives that their more advantaged, middle class counterparts.

At a more general level, as social scientists, we subscribe to Rawls' conception of social justice (Rawls, 1971:303). He suggests that inequalities can only be justified if they benefit the least advantaged groups. The alternative, justifying inequality on the basis that it lends to greater advantages for society as a whole, seems less palatable to us, since the disadvantaged in Canadian society insistently fall short in the race to acquire highly valued social resources (e.g., post-secondary education, prestigious professional jobs).

There are a number of people we wish to thank who helped bring this book to print. First, the Ontario Ministry of Education/Ministry of Colleges and Universities funded the research project and allowed Butterworth's to publish this revised version. Within the Ministries, a number of civil servants were helpful, but we would especially like to thank John Bonner for causing us to sharpen our ideas and more fully develop our argument. We are also very grateful to Dr. Lloyd McLeod for his good humor and ability to solve problems.

Two colleagues contributed to the early stages of our formulation. They are Professor Anton Turrittin, who took the time to read our initial chapters and comment on them, and Professor Clifford Jansen, who provided constructive criticism on Chapter 5 and helped us clarify and simplify our census strategy.

Others who deserve acknowledgement include: Debbie Armbruster who aided in collecting Hansard materials and other government documents; Steve Arvay of Sheridan College who made critical comments on our historical and conceptual approach; and Professor Gottfried Paasche who offered editorial comments on some chapters.

People in the Customer Services Division of Statistics Canada deserve credit for their general helpfulness in providing valuable information and their promptness in delivering Special Computer Runs to us. The University of Western Ontario's Social Science Computing Laboratory staff were helpful in the initial stages of analysis. Doris Rippington of Secretarial Services at York University, was responsible for the typing and revisions and should be thanked for an excellent job. Irving Kalushner developed the index and Gunar Saulitis and Socorro Roque of Butterworths smoothed the transition from report to book form.

It is usually true that the frustrations and agonies associated with manuscript writing are borne by those closest to us. This instance is not exceptional. Special thanks to Etta Anisef for suffering through some long months and offering a receptive ear and a keen editorial eye to our project. Finally the senior author would like to dedicate this book to his parents, Harry and Ann Anisef; their support and encouragement during the early years will always be remembered.

Introduction

The achievement of a post-secondary education is an important and characteristically Canadian ambition. It symbolizes so much about the very essence of this nation: that no one should be fixed or limited in terms of individual accomplishment, and that social class or background should not inhibit the opening of new doors and the broadening of horizons. In addition, higher education has a justification that goes far beyond individual rewards or general economic returns. Its true justification is associated with the development of new frontiers, with the pushing back of the boundaries of knowledge, with social improvement and human betterment, and with the building of a more sensitive and compassionate society. Much satisfaction in life is derived from the new vistas that such an experience provides and the additional responsibilities that are assumed as payment to society for providing a quality education.

Canadians should strive to be egalitarian in terms of broadening the accessibility of post-secondary education to the widest spectrum of society. The trend of higher education in Canada has been in that direction, but great care must be taken to ensure that this trend does not revert to elitism. At the same time, we should continue to insist on the highest possible standards within the post-secondary education system. Not to do so would undermine our basic case for greater public support. These two objectives, accessibility and quality education, are entirely consistent. We must make a post-secondary education available to all who can meet our standards.

The issue of accessibility to institutions of higher learning becomes more pertinent each time the economy takes a downswing. This is especially so when universities and colleges are compelled to operate in the restrictive environment created by underfunding. The proposition that, by some arithmetical yardstick, one might alleviate financial tensions in these institutions by the arbitrary reduction of admission opportunities or by changing admission requirements is disconcerting because the factors associated with equality of educational opportunity are consequently ignored. The formula for improving the effectiveness and the public credibility of post-secondary institutions is not one of reduction in the size or number of our institutions, nor of making accessibility more difficult. Instead, we should be enhancing the democratic tradition of this nation by expanding access and bringing educational opportunities to a greater number of people. Those things that can be done should be done to ensure that those in a position to benefit from, and to contribute to, post-secondary institutions have the opportunity to secure a place.

It is time we came to understand why students who deserve, and would benefit from, higher education are not enjoying the opportunity. The objective of equality of educational opportunity is one that we must continue to work at, and work at with great effort. Whereas we tend to deal with short-term conditions as a guideline to future policy and to undertake static analysis, we should be thinking in terms of our dynamic society. Guided by thorough studies and by documented trends, we can begin to recognize the importance of servicing the long-term need for continuing and adaptive education of people from all backgrounds, at all stages of their lives.

The future of our society depends directly on the quality of its human resources and on the availability of "knowledge workers" as never before. In Ontario specifically, we urgently require more, not less, investment in education if this province is to compete successfully in the world economy and to maintain its vital contribution to the life of the nation. My comments are not intended to assault governments for stupidity, shortsightedness or incoherence, which is certainly a common pastime today. Rather, I wish to make an urgent plea for all levels of government along with representatives of our institutions to recognize the vitality embodied in the goal of equality of educational opportunity. Our responsibility to collaborate on a national strategy to achieve this goal is clear. The first requirement is to understand the constraints on accessibility to higher education, and then to determine what we can do to reverse them. This study is a landmark in fulfilling that need and we, in York University, can be proud that this work has been undertaken here.

H. Ian Macdonald
President
York University

CHAPTER 1

Equality of Educational Opportunity:
A Social-Stratification Approach

OBJECTIVES

All societies endorsing liberal and democratic philosophies stress the overriding importance of providing wide opportunities for improvement and betterment. Where education is concerned, this philosophical belief is tied to the notion that all young people should be provided with opportunities that are consistent with their abilities. Moreover, socio-economic origins, locality, sex, or cultural roots should not affect the provision of opportunities. Social scientists have employed the phrase "equality of educational opportunity" in describing this generalized belief.

In this book we shall focus on one important facet of equality of educational opportunity in Ontario, that is, accessibility to post-secondary education, and we do so from conceptual, historical, empirical, and analytical perspectives. The reader should note that most of our discussion of Canadian post-secondary education refers to university, and not post-secondary non-university, education. [1]

This book has several major objectives. First, we have undertaken a lengthy review of the social science literature regarding such concepts as equality of educational opportunity and accessibility. Our view is that treatment of such concepts is influenced by the social, political, and intellectual climate of the period in which it is written. Not only are studies constantly appearing and providing new information about the state and nature of equality of educational opportunity, but the concept itself is also continuously redefined. This has contributed to confusion in the discussion and evaluation of equality of educational opportunity. In other words, when discussing educational opportunity, we are essentially tackling the thorny areas of individual and social responsibility for choices made, of human rights and social justice. These social issues change as society itself evolves.

A second major purpose of this book is to examine parliamentary minutes and reports of commissions and other bodies to show the controversy regarding the goals for post-secondary (primarily university) education in Ontario, and to determine what policies have been pursued by government. Our goal is to clarify the different ways in which the concept "equality of opportunity" has been used by researchers, policy makers, and others concerned with equality of educational opportunity. This will enable the reader to identify implicit assumptions employed by these persons, assumptions that frequently mask strong personal value biases or ideologies. Our purpose is not so much to judge or debunk these biases as to make them explicit; policies that seem to make important educational or social changes possible are rarely value-neutral.

A third objective is to examine social science research which has documented patterns of post-secondary educational participation. This includes several important Canadian studies, and seminal research done in Canada and elsewhere which relate post-secondary participation patterns to factors associated with socialization early in the life cycle. In addition, we show recent trends in post-secondary accessibility in Ontario through quantitative analysis of several kinds of census data. Our major concern is to identify key sources of inequality in post-secondary education and to delineate possible ways of solving them that have social science support. Indeed, in the final chapter, we present a number of recommendations, based on our census analysis and reading of the social science research literature, for reducing important structural inequalities in accessibility to post-secondary education identified in this report.

Throughout, we have tried to place the data on accessibility into an analytic framework, that is to say, into a social science model of social stratification in order to interpret factors associated with limited accessibility.

THE SOCIAL-STRATIFICATION PERSPECTIVE

Individuals and groups in society strive to maintain and advance their positions relative to others. As a consequence of competing for scarce resources or rewards (e.g., wealth, prestige, power), hierarchical distinctions emerge among people in a society. Social stratification consists of inherited, hierarchical distinctions among persons in a given society (Forcese, 1975:22). Another way of expressing this thought is to say that all societies are characterized by structural inequalities. Furthermore, these inequalities have multiple roots. Thus, Canada or Ontario can be described as having a complex stratification system in which hierarchical distinctions or inequalities appear in a variety of guises–class, ethnic, sexual, religious, and political.

Socio-economic status (SES) or social class is viewed by most social scientists as the single most important basis of social stratification in post-industrial societies such as Canada. Occupational position serves as a crucial factor in identifying one's position in a society's class stratification system. Education is one of the final pieces that completes this puzzle. As societies become technologically more complex and sophisticated, occupational training occurs increasingly outside the context of the family. Therefore, the amount of formal education attained by persons affects the nature of their occupational choices. For example, to become a doctor, lawyer, or engineer requires an education commitment that extends well beyond a secondary school diploma. Given the logic of this argument, amount of formal education strongly affects one's future socio-economic status.[2]

A social-stratification perspective alerts us not only to the marked hierarchical differentiation characterizing Canada, but also to inequalities in opportunity. Although it is true that opportunities for improvement or social mobility exist in Canada, there also occurs a considerable inheritance of disadvantage. To the extent that families are not able to pass on social or economic advantages to their children, equality of opportunity suffers. In the extreme case, ascribed characteristics form the sole basis of subsequent status, and no mobility or equality of opportunity is present. Families pass on to their children not only a given socio-economic status, but also a specific urban-rural residence, ethnic group membership, and gender, all of which affect a person's chances of mobility.

THE FAILURE TO REDUCE INEQUALITY

At this stage it is worthwhile to offer some general comments regarding the difficulty most societies have faced in reducing inequalities in educational opportunity.

Providing equality of educational opportunity has been an important concern in Ontario in the past several decades. The quest for equal educational opportunity, however, has not been limited to Ontario or Canada; rather, it has been embraced by many nations around the world as national policy (Medsker, 1972). There were grounds for optimism regarding the provision of equal educational opportunity during the 1960s and 1970s as governments, particularly in North America and Europe, invested heavily in expanding all levels of their educational systems. The optimism stemmed from the hope that the expansion of these systems would make education much more easily available to groups and individuals who were previously unable to attend such institutions. But success in achieving full equal educational opportunity has been judged by many educators and policy makers alike to have been limited. Marked differencies in

3

patterns of educational attainment by socio-economic origin, ethnicity, sex, and so on remain.

The limited success of the strategy of equalizing educational opportunities by expanding facilities has engendered a period of conceptual crisis and reflection regarding equality of educational opportunity. At one level, reasons for the inadequate realization of this socially desirable goal have been put forward, including observations on the intransigence of our society's stratification system and accusations about the duplicity or insincerity of those responsible for democratizing education. At another level, observers have noted that the concept of equality of educational opportunity itself has taken on different meanings and connotations for different persons in different historical circumstances.

In the following section we briefly review some of the meanings and connotations implied in divergent treatments of equality of opportunity.

MEANINGS AND ASSUMPTIONS OF EQUAL EDUCATIONAL OPPORTUNITY

The essays of the late John Porter, which appear in his last published work, provide a rich source for mapping the conflicting social philosophies or ideologies underlying equality of opportunity. Also identified are the social changes in Canadian society relevant to a discussion of education, opportunity, and equality. For instance, Porter develops the analytical distinction between equality of condition and equality of opportunity:

> The former implies that whatever is valued as good in the society—material resources, health, personal development, leisure—should be distributed among all the members of society in relatively the same amounts regardless of the social position which one occupies. Equality of opportunity, on the other hand, implies a society in which access to the structured inequality should be open to all without regard to the individuals' social class origins, their parental resources, their religious affiliations and, in more contemporary discussions, their membership in minority groups or their sex. For many, the principle of equality in a liberal society is satisfied by providing equal opportunity to seek out and compete for unequal rewards (1979: 224-45).

This quote suggests that a relatively "open society" (that is, a society where social mobility is pervasive) maximizes equality of opportunity, whereas a "closed society" minimizes this quality.

In a free market context, however, an open society may still be characterized by strong inequalities in condition. Be that as it may, the competition for scarce rewards (e.g., wealth and income) has increasingly required an emphasis on equality of educational opportunity.

A brief review of important social changes in Canada will illustrate the connection between equality of opportunity and equality of educational opportunity. This is followed by a conceptual analysis of the various ways in which the term "equality of educational opportunity" has been employed.

SOCIAL CHANGES IN CANADA AND EQUAL EDUCATIONAL OPPORTUNITY

In early nineteenth-century Canada, agriculture provided the primary economic basis for the adult working population and few ordinary people received extensive schooling (Ramu and Johnson, 1976:402-3). Indeed, few needed formal schooling to carry out the relatively simple work tasks of a rural society. Many social changes occurred, however, in the late nineteenth and early twentieth centuries, including a technological and energy revolution, the growth of modern factories and cities, and the evolution of complex work arrangements within organized bureaucratic settings. All this meant that the family's role as a major provider of vocational training diminished. In fact, the very structure of Canada's economy has altered radically: in 1901 fully 40.3 per cent of Canada's labour force was engaged in agriculture, but by 1961 this involvement had been reduced to 10.0 per cent (Ramu and Johnson, 1976:121). Large increases occurred in the demand for white-collar workers, professionals, craftsmen, and skilled technicians. These new and higher levels of occupational specialization reduced the importance of the family in training children and increased the importance of public education. Whereas in agriculturally-based Canada inequalities in condition were strongly tied to family status, the proximate basis for inequalities now shifted to the amount of formal schooling attained by Canadians. Accompanying this change was the growing perception that equality of opportunity required equality of educational opportunity. An investment in public education in the early years of the twentieth century was regarded positively for a variety of reasons. Public schools could serve the practical function of training industrial workers while, at the same time, alleviating the growth pains of cities (e.g., by curbing juvenile delinquency and helping assimilate the diverse groups of people migrating to cities [Ramu and Johnson, 1976:404-5]).

In the 1970s a discussion of equality of educational opportunity was almost automatically linked to the question of accessibility to post-secondary institutions for socially disadvantaged persons, whereas in earlier decades the democratization of education meant increasing educational participation rates at the elementary and secondary levels. The success of these earlier efforts is reflected in the increases in student participation or retention rates in Ontario over the last several decades. As late as 1960-61, the student retention rate in Grade 11 of the cohort starting in Grade 2 was only 55.7 per cent; seven years later, in 1967-68, it had jumped to 73.3 per cent (Zsigmond and Wenaas, 1970:237). By the early 1970s, approximately 90 per cent of males and females 16 years of age were attending primary and secondary school (Information Canada, 1974:70). With improvements in student participation at the elementary and secondary levels the concern for educational opportunity gradually shifted to the post-secondary level.

A number of other factors are associated with the concern at the post-secondary level. In 1965, Porter published The Vertical Mosaic, documenting the extent to which upper social classes dominated universities. Substantial rises in personal and national wealth in the 1960s, the effects of the "baby boom" (i.e., a swelling of the 18-24 age group) following World War II, and the perceived need to augment national identity through the development of an all-Canadian post-secondary system were important factors in promoting significant increases in post-secondary enrolment. In 1960-61, 163,000 full-time students were enrolled in post-secondary Canadian institutions; in the next twenty years that number more than tripled, rising to 543,400 in 1980-81 (Ramu and Johnson, 1976:406; Statistics Canada, 1981:54). In Ontario, the corresponding number in 1980-81 was 236,002 (Statistics Canada, 1981:74).

EQUAL EDUCATIONAL OPPORTUNITY:
EVOLUTION OF A CONCEPT

James Coleman (1968) and Christopher Jencks (1972) in the United States and Torsten Husén in Europe have made significant contributions to our understanding of the concept of equality of educational opportunity. Reading the works of these scholars reveals three essential ways of analysing "equality of educational opportunity". These involve examination of:

- the changing meaning of equality of educational opportunity as society evolves;

- the types of variables and constraints normally associated with equality of educational opportunity;

6

-     the ideological belief differences among those who par-
      ticipate in discussing the concept.

Stages of Equality[3]

James Coleman provides us with an evolutionary overview of the
concept (1968:30-31). He suggests four stages, including:

(1) Preindustrial society-at this stage the concept has
     little relevance for systems of formal education insofar
     as society was agriculturally based and education pri-
     marily occurred within an extended family system.

(2) Industrial society-the industrial revolution changed the
     role of the family. Given increased occupational com-
     plexity, the family could no longer act as a training
     ground for children. Children became more occupa-
     tionally mobile and schools came into prominence.

(3) The notion of equality of opportunity became prominent
     as society evolved to the post-industrial phase. The
     concept was equated with equality of exposure to a
     given curriculum and a free education for all children
     up to a certain age. It was up to the child and family
     to take advantage of abundantly available opportunities.
     The child and not the educational system was to blame
     if failure occurred.

(4) With systematic social science research after 1960 came
     recognition that the real problem was how to bring
     about more equality of academic performance. Exposure
     was not enough. Schools were seen as responsible for
     equalizing educational results. Thus, the effects of
     schools in producing comparable cognitive and achieve-
     ment performance became the focus of equal educational
     opportunity.

Coleman convincingly demonstrated in a national U.S. study
of over 645,000 pupils that variations in school resources were
less important than pupils' socio-economic and minority group
origins in explaining academic achievement. Schools appeared
simply to transmit differences among students in academic performance, not reduce them. Schools were sorters, not equalizers.
From this, the conclusion was drawn that equality of opportunity
could not be obtained from simply equalizing school resources and
facilities. If a contest mobility model was to be fairly employed in
schools, then remedial or compensatory education programs became
the necessary strategy. Through these programs children were
provided "equal opportunities for unequal treatment so far as
socially relevant differences are concerned" (Husén, 1975:40).
The social science emphasis therefore switched from equality of
initial opportunity in accessibility to equality of results.

7

Losers and Winners

This recent equality-of-results perspective explicitly recognizes the need to include group-level considerations (e.g., SES, gender, ethnicity) in measuring the relative success of schools. Wide variations in achievement or cognitive results across socio-economic groups are taken as signs of failure. Moreover, those who employ an equality-of-results perspective (e.g., Jencks, 1972) realize that young children enrolled in pre-kindergarten classes display early performance differences. These variations in performance (e.g., linquistic abilities, cognitive abilities), as we shall argue forcefully in Chapter 4, are directly related to family socialization and to one's socio-economic or cultural endowments.

In commenting on Jencks and Coleman's treatments of inequality in educational opportunity Porter made clear the ramifications of different levels of analysis:

> An important difference in the treatment of equality between Jencks and Coleman is that the former deals with large aggregates of data to demonstrate inequality between individuals, whereas the latter deals with inequality between groups and is concerned to equalize group averages. For example, we might in this country be concerned with equality among all Canadians or we might be concerned with equality among English, French, and others. Thus if all three groups had equal average income, equal average years of schooling and so forth, the Coleman model of equality would be met even though within each group inequalities existed. In the Jencks model of equality, which is fairly extreme, individuals are not classified into groups, but are all considered together, and they must all be near the average. The difference between the two approaches to measuring inequalities is met if there is no discrimination because of group membership. For example, women and men are equal in the labor force when their average rates of pay are the same. Jencks would say they must all be considered together to calculate the average and must all be near it. (Porter, 1979:254)

As we indicated earlier, equality of condition implies an equal distribution of "valued" goods to all, while equality of opportunity entails unequal reward distribution. Everyone, however has an equal chance to compete for more of what is valued. Equal representation in post-secondary education for all social groups does not necessarily imply that every individual within the group receives an equal amount of post-secondary education.

Given that equality of opportunity is probably viewed by most persons in Canada as the more appropriate societal goal, many persons have raised questions about how to measure "opportunity". Is the provision of access merely a right to try with the basis of participation being completely voluntary? (Medsker, 1972:81). In the absence of adequate measures of whether an individual has a voluntary right today, some have suggested that equality of results constitutes a more appropriate education goal than equality of opportunity[4] (Husén, 1979:75).

Variables and Constraints

A review of social science literature reveals that an extraordinary number of variables or constraints are associated with achieving equality of educational opportunity. The reader will find a concise summary of these variables useful for understanding the arguments presented in Chapters 2 and 3.

(1) One set of variables embraces the non-scholastic, physical ones, the material circumstances. Here, we are dealing with the economic resources available to the student's family, the cost required for tuition, the geographical distance from a school, and the transportation available.

(2) Another set includes the physical facilities of the school, such as the quality of its plant in general, laboratories, library, textbooks, etc.

(3) A third set of variables has to do with certain psychological aspects of the home environment, such as the level of the parents' aspirations and expectations with regard to the schooling of their children, their general attitude towards learning at home, and the amount of independence training, language training, and so on provided there.

(4) A fourth set describes the psychological aspects of the school environment in terms of teacher competence, teacher attitudes towards different categories of students, teacher expectations with regard to student performance, and student motivation.

(5) A fifth set of variables describes pedagogical conditions such as, for example, how much time is allotted in the curriculum to a subject or a topic, how much time the teacher devotes to that topic, and how much homework he/she assigns to it.

(6) A final set of variables describes the social-stratification influences on value orientations of families and children, educational and occupational aspirations, cognitive traits, and student motivation and achieve-

9

ment. Included in this set are regional stratification, gender stratification, ethnic and racial stratification, and social class stratification.

Ideological Beliefs

Ideological beliefs reflect variations in the ways individuals think of achieving "equality of educational opportunity". In fact, this phrase conjures up images of variables not unlike those described in (1) and (2) of the previous section (e.g., financial accessibility, physical presence of facilities, etc.). The contrast between "equality of opportunity" and "equality of results" evokes distinct images as well. We suggest, for example, that the former elicits a "passive" and the latter an "active" dimension. Thus, one group argues that individuals with appropriate potential need to take advantage of existing, widespread opportunities. On the other hand, those who are aware of and accept the significant impact of variables described in (3), (4), and (6) of the previous section will present arguments for more far-reaching reforms. The severest critics see education as consistently influenced by economic and political variables. Education is not seen as susceptible to basic restructuring or reform. They argue that meaningful increases in equality of opportunity or accessibility to post-secondary education will only result from a redistribution of income (Bowles and Gintis, 1976). As it stands now, they argue that schools are great sorters and not equalizers; they reinforce inequality through streaming and frequently increase inequalities to the point of students dropping out of school.

The less radical camp does not necessarily reject an "opportunity" model. It desires instead to improve the fairness of the contest. To do this, remedial or compensatory education programs are recommended. Proponents of this "equality of results" school argue that structural inequalities are experienced early in life and only early intervention can significantly reduce inequality in initial opportunities.

Persons who endorse either of the above-stated positions are themselves frequently criticized, if not condemned. Among their critics, those who conceive of education as a training ground for occupations, anticipate that inefficiency, loss of freedom, and perils to academic excellence will result from the implementation of reforms focusing on early intervention.

In the Sociology of Education these positions are tied in with the Functionalist and Conflict perspectives (cf. Murphy, 1979; Karabel and Halsey, 1977; Okihiro, 1981). The interested reader should consult Appendix A for an explication of these perspectives.

10

The ideologically distinct beliefs described above are positions on a continuum in the current debate on equality of educational opportunity. It is safe to predict that heated discussions will continue to be waged.[6] Our analysis in Chapter 2 of legislative sessions dealing with equal opportunity (1956-81) documents the ideological nature of the debates over a 25-year period.

PAST LEGACIES: SPONSORED AND CONTEST MOBILITY

At this point it is useful to introduce the concepts of sponsored and contest mobility. Sponsored mobility occurs when children are sorted early, according to criteria developed by a governing elite and streamed into occupational levels according to desired qualities. Sponsored mobility may be likened to a series of escalators, sending children to their respective floors (Harvey and Lennards, 1973:63). These floors are terminal working-class, middle-class, or upper-class destinations rather than temporary stop-offs. By contrast, in a contest mobility situation, children are encouraged to stay in the race as long as possible, competing with each other in a fair manner according to universalistic standards. The educational system is charged with the responsibility of proving ineptitude for elite positions and also with providing a climate in which curriculum choice is flexible and transfer to streams heading for post-secondary education is relatively easy.

How do these concepts help us in understanding educational opportunity in Canada? Many educational researchers maintain that, in the past, Canada exhibited a sponsored-mobility pattern with its emphasis on compulsory subjects and formal streaming of students at the secondary level of education. Clement (1975) documents, for instance, the proportionately higher social-class origins of Canadian economic elites as contrasted with their American counterparts (Murphy, 1979:115). A far greater percentage (41%) of the Canadian economic elite attended top private schools than the American elite (20%).

A crucial historical difference accounting for this contrast in mobility pattern involves the early establishment of U.S. independence from Great Britain as well as the continued colonial domination of the British value orientation (emphasizing elitism and sponsored mobility) over Canadian development (cf., Lipset, 1964). Clark (1976) argues that in Canada there has been greater control over education by the Church and provincial ministries of education, and consequently there has been the maintenance of a stronger elitist tradition in post-secondary institutions compared with the U.S. Clark further argues that a strong demand for technological skills and a highly-trained labour force accompanied Canada's role of supplying materials during

World War II. This led to large-scale economic changes and opportunities unrelated to changes in the educational system of that time. People had made it the hard way by seizing economic opportunities in the 1940s and earlier. However, by the 1950s the successful group had formed the basis of a broadened middle class who wished to maintain their families' socio-economic position by pushing their children into universities. Thus, in the middle and late 1960s an extraordinary expansion of post-secondary institutions in Ontario and the rest of Canada occurred. Elitism and sponsored mobility were viewed as obstacles and no longer tolerated. Murphy (1979) comments on this phenomenon:

> A wider choice of subjects, late separation into hier-archically ordered programs, and subjects and programs available to all were necessary to convince students that selection would be made according to individual merit and individual taste. In short, structures and content based on contest mobility and formal equality were introduced to replace those based on sponsored mobility and elitism (p. 206).

Although a fair degree of consensus exists among social investigators that Canada has moved towards a pattern of contest mobility, public education is still perceived as failing to provide greater social equality (Porter, 1979:242).

THE ARGUMENT OF THE BOOK

Throughout this book the reader will note that we adopt an explicit social-stratification perspective emphasizing inequalities as related to socio-economic and cultural background, gender, and region, as well as other social dimensions. After an extensive analysis of social science literature, and empirical research studies dealing with accessibility (see Chapter 3), we are firmly convinced that these bases of structural inequality, particularly socio-economic stratification, pose strong barriers to achieving equal educational opportunity in Ontario.

In Chapter 5 we demonstrate that there has been little con-vergence in the 1970s in university participation rates among socio-economic groups. Our data sources in this chapter are the 1971 and 1976 censuses, and socioeconomic status is defined in terms of parental levels of formal education. Claims that Ontario has moved in the direction of contest mobility in the attempt to democratize education would appear to stand in contradiction to the government's apparent failure to implement greater equality of accessibility to universities. This contradiction is more apparent than real, however, if the relationship between equality of oppor-tunity and contest mobility is considered more fully. Contest mobility requires not only succeeding in school subjects but also having the motivation and initiative to remain in school and eventually to select the school subjects that will allow advancement to post-secondary education (Murphy, 1979:207). These factors place an important responsibility both on the student and on his family. Contest mobility is thus simply a move towards a limited form of equality of educational opportunity, the form emphasizing equality of exposure (with the necessity to take advantage of existing arrangements), not equality of results.

That so little convergence in university enrolment rates among different socio-economic groups has occurred despite tremendous increases in expansion of educational facilities and student participation, illustrates the tremendous resistance of our society's stratification system to various attempts at democratization. We maintain that the crux of this resistance is to be located in the early socialization of pre-adolescents. Our review of the sources of structural inequality in Chapter 4 documents the importance of value transmission, linguistic development, and achievement orientation relative to vocational and educational outcomes. These areas are amenable to change, and schools can act as effective agents of change in providing fuller educational opportunities for economically and culturally disadvantaged children. We are essentially arguing that although opportunities may indeed be available to young persons in our province and country, they are selectively perceived. This selective perception has its roots in our initial socio-economic origins. Any genuine attempt to provide a more equitable distribution of higher education among the subgroups in society must deal with this selective perception.

From this view, it seems that more can be achieved in equalizing access by taking an equality-of-results perspective. By focusing on equality of student outcomes, consideration is given to factors affecting such outcomes, including the lack of appropriate attitudes and expectations and the structural sources of these attitudes. It is not simply assumed that provision of facilities is adequate and that people have to take advantage of opportunities for equality of opportunity. The active orientation associated with the equality-of-results perspective holds that schools can move in the direction of improving the fairness of contest mobility. Indeed, recent research (Ravitch, 1981) reveals that schools do matter relative to student cognitive and achievement scores. In our concluding chapter we offer recommendations for developing programs which are aimed at equalizing the fairness of the contest by addressing problems of inadequate socialization skills.

Chapter 2 is an attempt to unravel the history of public discussion and debate surrounding accessibility to post-secondary education within Ontario. The review covers several decades, and a number of important conclusions may be drawn. First,

Ontario has provided excellent facilities that deal with a wide range of problem areas (e.g., the handicapped, prisoners, Francophones, women, etc.). Secondly, Ontario has worked unceasingly to develop loan and grant programs for senior secondary school students planning or enrolling in post-secondary institutions. Thirdly, most of Ontario's efforts are consistent with stage three (e.g., providing opportunities) of the equality of educational opportunity model described earlier. Finally, Ontario has not seriously considered an equality-of-results perspective in discussing how to achieve more equitable accessibility for all of its residents.

Although we wholeheartedly agree with those who argue that money matters in the decision to pursue a post-secondary education, we are strongly sceptical regarding the timing of financial assistance. Most discussions and proposals reviewed in Chapter 2 emphasize the provision of loans and/or grants at the point of entrance to post-secondary education. As Chapters 3 and 4 will reveal, only a relatively small minority of young persons from economically disadvantaged families are in a position to take advantage of available assistance programs. We are not arguing that these financial structures be tampered with. On the contrary, they are fundamental to the ongoing and desirable objective of democratizing education. What we do, however, stress in this report and especially in Chapter 6 is that intervention programs, including ones involving financial incentives, be introduced at the critical stage when children and families begin actively to discuss future educational and career options. This stage occurs prior to entry into senior secondary school, the level at which most present programs are aimed. If government is to move forward in its pledge to sustain, and even increase, equal opportunities for access to higher education, intervention programs are required which have as their goal the reductions (early in life) of disadvantages associated with structural inequalities experienced.

ORGANIZATION OF THE BOOK

Chapter 2 presents a brief historical review within three areas: (1) various attempts by governmental, quasi-governmental, and academic committees and task forces to assess and resolve inequalities in educational opportunity; (2) government attempts to remove financial barriers to post-secondary education; and (3) the verbatim record of Ontario's legislative activity (Hansard) over the past 25 years (i.e., How have legislators defined equality of educational opportunity? What groups have been seen as disadvantaged?).

Losers and Winners

Six important Canadian studies, published since 1956 and dealing specifically with accessibility to post-secondary education, are reviewed in Chapter 3. These are data-based studies that illustrate the influence of structural inequalities (e.g., social class, gender, ethnicity) in the Canadian context. Data, methods, key variables, and findings are all indicated in this chapter.

Chapter 4 is an important part of our overall argument. Altering financial arrangements at the point of entry to post-secondary education is in our view an insufficient strategy for significantly reducing inequalities in access. As indicated in Chapter 2 this has been Ontario's position or strategy in developing student assistance plans. In this chapter we employ the concept 'socialization' to argue the importance of early formative years in relation to later educational aspirations, expectations, and behaviour. What is the relationship of structural inequalities (e.g., social class, gender, etc.) to value acquisition, cognitive development, and educational aspirations?

Chapter 5 presents an empirical analysis, using census data, of trends in post-secondary enrolments in Ontario from 1971 to 1976. There are several objectives in presenting this analysis. First, by comparing various socio-economic and gender groupings we empirically document inequalities in educational opportunity and changes in such inequalities. Secondly, we argue that the use of the census provides us with a reliable means for establishing trends.

In Chapter 6 we present conclusions derived from prior chapters and make specific recommendations that would alter the direction of government in two areas, namely, early financial intervention and early socialization intervention. Underlying these recommendations is the basic presumption that an attack on structural inequalities must, to be effective, start with the early formative years.

There are also three appendices to this book which are available upon request to the Ministry of Education. The first, Appendix A, presents a brief explanation of the Functionalist and Conflict perspectives generally employed in the Sociology of Education. This explanation is provided to help students of social science more fully understand the ideological assumptions associated with the treatment of equality of educational opportunity. Appendix B consists of a series of detailed notes, comments and tables concerning specific points raised in the census data analysis in Chapter 5. Appendix C contains an annotated bibliography of over fifty articles relating to issues discussed in this first chapter. This annotated bibliography will give a head start to readers interested in deepening their knowledge in this area. The Technical Report referred to in Chapter 5, describes the problems and methodology employed in analysing trends in post-secondary enrolments using census data, and is available on microfiche from the Ministry of Education/Ministry of Colleges and Universities.

Notes

1. The term "post-secondary education" usually includes a variety of educational forms, including universities, community colleges, private vocational schools, trade schools, and apprenticeship training programs. Unless otherwise specified, the bulk of our literature review for Ontario refers only to university education. It is unfortunate that scant research on non-university post-secondary education exists for Ontario. This may to some extent reflect the relative "newness" of these forms of post-secondary education. Another possibility, however, is that social science has failed to follow closely the fundamental shifts that have occurred in non-university post-secondary education within the past decade.

2. Amount of formal education is strongly correlated with occupational prestige, but less strongly correlated with the income component of social class.

3. The 1970s has witnessed the emergence of a new or fifth stage of educational opportunity. This stage may be referred to as "lifelong" or "recurrent" education. This stage is characterized by OECD examiners as "the recognition that the right to equality of educational opportunity should not remain confined to the short period of childhood and youth, but should be a lifelong recurrent principle, aimed at catching up on lost chances, and at opening up new opportunities" (Organization for Economic Co-operation and Development, 1976:39). The principle embodied in lifelong education marks a radical departure from conventional thinking in several ways. Lifelong education implies that:

    -   a second or third chance may be provided to students who "drop out" of the educational system at an early age;

    -   the stigma attached to dropping out may fade as persons resume old studies or enrol in new educational programs for the first time. The conventional notion that post-secondary education should be completed by the age of 24 will become folklore;

    -   the idea that educational programs label students as failures will also fade if recurrent education becomes the norm (Pike, 1979:36).

Lifelong education is a new phenomena in Canada. At the moment it constitutes a most desirable addition to our existing opportunity structure. However, it may be too early to assess its impact on altering the types of attitudes described above.

4. This, of course, leads to the question of what results? Opportunity for what? Gilbert and McRoberts provide one sort of answer in their definition: "Equality of opportunity is effectively the degree to which, under universalistic criteria, individuals have an equal chance to attain desired occupational roles" (1975:166). However, it is not clear that occupational training should be the most consequential outcome of education. Porter et al. (1979) include the following goals of higher education: the development of human potential, cultural enrichment, the need for highly trained persons, a more tolerant citizenry and access to high status occupations and economic rewards. Indeed, Everts, in an insightful analysis of equality of educational opportunity stresses the general indeterminacy of our educational system. Educationalists vary widely in how they see the important tasks of education:

> Some educationalists see the most important task of education to be to give each child an equal opportunity to realize his potential. Others, although acknowledging the desirability of excluding 'irrelevant' factors such as class, income, religion, race or early handicaps, would stress the necessity of maintaining high intellectual standards for all to aim to achieve or otherwise running the risk of debasing the whole education process. Yet another factor, the 'needs of society', would be included by the realist who asserts that it is dangerous to attempt to consider education apart from its connection with the occupation structure (Everts, 1973:55).

5. The discussion in this section concentrates on Canada as a whole. It should be noted, however, that the generalizations developed also apply to Ontario.

6. The nature-nurture controversy constitutes yet another aspect of the multifaceted debate concerning equal opportunity. This debate has had a "seesaw" quality, swinging first toward support for the hereditarian view, then back to support for the environmentalist perspective. Some of the implications of the controversy for policy changes in public education are expressed in the Preface to Richard Herrnstein's 1973 book IQ in the Meritocracy:

> There is evidence not only for the genetic ingredients in mental capacity but also in social status. Many of

17

the means and ends of contemporary social policy fail to take into account those biological constraints, and they may consequently misfire. Equalizing educational opportunity may have the unexpected and unwelcome effect of emphasizing the inborn intellectual differences between people. It may instead be better to diversify education. . . . Even the effort to encourage social mobility may have its penalties. The biological gap between social classes will grow if the people who rise from lower to higher status are selected for their native ability. (P. 10).

Guy Rocher would take issue with Herrnstein's position by pointing out that IQ is not intelligence per se but rather an evaluation of a mental activity by specific tests. Furthermore, such tests are more familiar and natural to children of upper social stratum and the activities being measured are those most valued and frequently transmitted within middle-class-oriented schools (Forcese and Richer, 1975:147).

The nature-nurture controversy is likely to continue and this review is not designed to either fully evaluate or settle this contentious issue. Rather, the philosophical assumptions and political implications of adopting either position should be made clear. Without conclusive evidence to the contrary, belief in the hereditarian view would provide moral support for limiting the scope in providing increases in equality of educational opportunity and accessibility to post-secondary education. For example, some persons (e.g., Jensen, 1969) suggest that compensatory education for blacks may be wasteful if genetic differences between blacks and whites are great. On the other hand, imbalances in post-secondary representation across social groups may not entirely be attributed to inequality of opportunity. As Husén indicates, "only half the variance in scholastic attainment has consistently been shown to be a result of home background, including such factors as parental education, verbal stimulation, and motivational support" (1979:83). Thus, insisting on equal subgroup participation rates to indicate equality of opportunity assumes equal I.Q. distribution among subgroups.

CHAPTER 2

Accessibility: The Public Debate

In our review of the evolution of the concept of equality of educational opportunity in Chapter 1, we saw how the concept was
influenced by predominating social, economic, and political conditions. Changes in these conditions are reflected in the nature
of the public debate concerned with equality of educational
opportunity. This chapter examines this public debate by looking
at legislative minutes[1] (Hansard), government-appointed commission reports, and government advisory body reports over the
past two decades. We are interested in a number of questions:
What groups or subgroups in society were seen as disadvantaged
in educational opportunities? What factors were seen as causing
these disadvantages? What strategies were used to implement and
obtain equal educational opportunity? How have these changed
over time?

Examination of the public debate is particularly important
because it is ultimately publicly-elected government bodies which
are responsible for the mounting and implementation of programs
geared towards achieving equality. Thus, the legislative debate[2]
itself and the analysis and recommendations of influential advisory
bodies and commissions provide key insights into past and present
policy patterns. In keeping with the analytic framework introduced in Chapter 1, we have attempted to examine the extent to
which the various positions taken fit into the stages of development of the concept of equal opportunity (especially an equality-
of-results perspective) and to make explicit underlying ideological
positions. This examination has contributed greatly to the
development of our own equality-of-results perspective and our
suggestions for reducing inequality.

It is important to note, however, that in writing Chapter 2,
it has not been our purpose to provide full documentation of the
effect of changes in the external environment on the nature of
public debate. Indeed, our examination of the various positions
taken and concerns raised is much more tenuous than that.
Instead, we have attempted to provide a framework for understanding the public debate and enough documentation to suggest
that the framework is credible. For example, in going through
Hansard, we noted instances when certain types of structural
inequalities in connection with post-secondary education were

mentioned. For our purposes, mention of such inequalities in public means that at least some legislators have brought the matter to the attention of the legislature, regardless of how much impact such a mention may have had on subsequent public policy. In brief, we have had to be selective in providing quotations and comments which support our interpretation.

Our interest in the past two decades is explained by Lawr and Gridney (1973):

> The problems that absorbed the energies of the school-men in the 1960s were, in part, inherited from the fifties. The baby boom, which had flooded the elementary schools in the previous decade, threatened to inundate the secondary schools and the universities in the next. In several provinces, immigration and urbanization aggravated the situation and put extreme pressure on city and suburban school systems. Post-war prosperity, moreover, enabled more parents to keep their children in school longer . . .
>
> The enrolment explosion alone would have caused a massive expansion of the educational system. But the sixties were also characterized by a host of new demands. For years reform-minded schoolmen had argued for a more extended secondary education for all, for better facilities for rural schools, for wider oppor-tunities at the post-secondary level, and for more pedagogical change than had yet taken place. On some issues they had been ignored by both government and public; on others change had been slow or half-hearted. But in the sixties the enthusiasm for change spread beyond the professionals to the society at large. A growing number of Canadians were convinced that Canada, along with the rest of the western world, was entering a new age characterized by rapid change, a highly developed technology, and a new commitment to democracy and social justice. The demands of the new era . . . would reshape our political and economic institutions. If the schools and colleges were to meet the needs of the new society, they too would have to change (p. 232).

Since approximately 1960, a number of dimensions of in-equality of education have been subject to public debate. Mention has already been made of regional disparities, the disadvantages of some ethnic groups, and the financial barriers faced by some students because of the social stratification of our society. Other issues identified during this period were the needs of "culturally deprived" students at the Kindergarten level, provision of free education at the post-secondary school level, and the special situation of women in post-secondary education. Also identified was the need to cater to handicapped students, be they retarded, mentally ill, deaf, blind, or crippled.

In essence, the legislators, over the years, recognized that social, cultural, physical, regional, age, gender, and financial differences of students had to be considered if they were going to make equality of educational opportunity a reality in this province. Importantly, they suggested that living in rural and poor communities, poor teaching, inexperienced teachers, large classes, poor housing, ill health, lack of awareness of educational opportunities, and early educational experiences all contributed to inequality of opportunity.

Chart 2.1 illustrates the times at which major issues or topics pertaining to educational opportunity were discussed by legislators. If, in a given year, there was some mention in Hansard of a particular subject, an "x" was placed in the appropriate box. Chart 2.1 shows that legislators have at various times recognized the social, cultural, geographic, and economic factors that contribute to inequality of educational opportunity. Some issues have received relatively constant attention (e.g., minority-group students and student assistance), whereas others have come to parliamentary attention more recently. The nature of the debates in the legislature and in the various other sources indicated previously is outlined in the remainder of the chapter.

The rest of this chapter is organized as follows. (1) The evolution of concern over various dimensions of educational inequality in Hansard is outlined, from the late 1950s to the present. The nature of this concern is suggested as being affected by changing social and economic conditions in the larger society. Opposition and government positions regarding how to deal with such inequalities are briefly reviewed. At this point we attempt to characterize evolving patterns and positions. (2) The section following reviews the highlights of a number of influential reports by government advisory bodies and quasi-official organizations which contributed to public debate of post-secondary education over the past two decades. (3) The section entitled "Dimensions on Accessibility" examines key developments in Hansard and in reports along four separate dimensions of structured inequality: social class, ethnicity, gender, and region. (4) The next section concentrates on the development of Colleges of Applied Arts and Technology as a government response to unequal opportunity in post-secondary education. (5) Since so much of the emphasis in reports and parliamentary debate has centred on financial barriers to post-secondary access, examination of the public debate on OSAP, the government's current program of student financial support, and tuition fees is presented in a separate section. (6) The final section of the chapter presents our conclusions.

THE EVOLUTION OF CONCERN IN LEGISLATIVE DEBATES

In this section we attempt to outline how legislative concern for various aspects of equality of educational opportunity has evolved, and indeed, the way in which the term itself has changed over the last twenty years or so. A more detailed analysis of treatment of structural inequalities by social class, ethnicity, gender, and region occurs in a later section. Underlying this analysis is the view that the nature of this concern has been affected by changes in the larger social system. For example, Lawr and Gridney (1973) note:

> In earlier decades, swift and substantive educational reform had not been possible because of financial difficulties. In the sixties, this obstacle was removed. Since the end of World War II Canadians had enjoyed a nearly uninterrupted period of rapid economic growth. Rising national and personal wealth made it possible for the public to underwrite the costs of the educational changes that newspapers, intellectuals, politicians, and schoolmen all claimed were necessary (p. 232).

Thus, it was only because of rising societal affluence that post-secondary expansion occurred, and with this expansion the concern over who should go to newly-created or expanded institutions became relevant.

As early as the 1950s, politicians recognized that cultural and social factors were important in providing equality of educational opportunity (see Chart 2.1). Moreover, it was suggested that the special needs of rural[3] and Native Indian children, the deaf, and the handicapped should be addressed, and ways found to motivate potential drop-outs from leaving school early. In terms of policy, however, an overwhelming amount of effort was directed at providing financial assistance (e.g., bursaries and loans) and educational facilities while the other impediments were left unaddressed. This is reflected in the statement by the Hon. Mr. Frost (Conservative) that "In Ontario we have dedicated ourselves to equality of opportunity. Education has been made available to the people by building more facilities in the various areas, and loans and grants have been provided to help finance costs" (Feb. 4, 1959: 134S).

With the advent of the 1960s, legislative debate began to reflect concern for social unrest, in particular the rise of French-Canadian nationalism and the feminist movement. The concern about inequality of educational opportunity expanded to include additional factors, as Chart 2.1 indicates.

That more social issues were identified after the mid-1960s was probably the consequence of the economic prosperity at that

22

CHART 2.1: INDICATION OF WHEN ISSUES PERTAINING TO EQUALITY OF EDUCATIONAL OPPORTUNITY OR EQUAL ACCESS TO POST-SECONDARY EDUCATION WERE DISCUSSED 1956-1980

GROUPS/ ISSUES	YEAR 19-										
	56	57	58	59	60	61*	62	63	64	65	66
Lower social-class students		X						X	X		X
Minority group students	X	X			X		X			X	X
Women											
Rural Area Concerns	X	X	X	X					X		X
Part-time Students Education											X
Special groups (handicapped, prisoners, etc.)		X			X		X				
Student Assistance	X	X	X	X	X		X		X		
CAAT concerns	X									X	X
Early Education											X
Free Education									X		X

*election years

CHART 2.1:   INDICATION OF WHEN ISSUES PERTAINING TO EQUALITY OF
(contd.)   EDUCATIONAL OPPORTUNITY OR EQUAL ACCESS TO POST-
SECONDARY EDUCATION WERE DISCUSSED 1956-1980

GROUPS/ ISSUES	YEAR 19-													
	67*	68	69	70	71*	72	73	74	75	76	77*	78	79	80
Lower social-class students	X		X	X	X			X				X	X	X
Minority group students			X	X	X	X		X	X	X				X
Women	X					X	X			X		X	X	X
Rural Area Concerns	X	X	X		X	X	X							X
Part-time Students Education				X				X	X					
Special groups (handicapped, prisoners, etc.)	X					X		X		X				
Student Assistance	X	X	X			X	X	X	X	X	X	X	X	X
CAAT concerns	X	X	X			X					X			
Early Education	X	X				X		X					X	X
Free Education	X	X				X		X	X			**	**	X

* election years
**argument around tuition fees as barriers to post-secondary education

time and of published research. Research studies (Porter, 1965; Clark et al. 1969; Porter et al., 1979; and others) were funded and became sources of evidence supporting a broader view of educational inequalities. In addition, in their effort to address the unequal opportunity of disadvantaged minorities and low-income students, and perhaps fearing that the protests in the United States might spread to Canada, politicians made recommendations that they hoped would prevent a similar situation from occurring in Ontario.

One prominent position expressed in the 1960s by the government was its commitment to ensure that "every student of ability and ambition who wishes to proceed to university will have the opportunity regardless of their financial means" (Lt.-Gov. J. K. MacKay, Speech from the Throne, Jan. 26, 1960). Later, emphasis was placed on the need for "efficiency and con-scientious" spending "so that the cost of providing equality of educational opportunity could be borne equitably by all taxpayers in the province" (Mr. Nixon [Liberal] 19 Oct. 1970: 5223). Note that this comment reflects little concern for the sources of struc-tural inequality which affect motivation early in life.

Other (mainly opposition) legislators argued that the par-ticipation rate of students from the different social-class back-grounds in post-secondary education was mainly due to early educational experiences. Thus, it was recommended that

> the money must be placed at the bottom of the scale. We are working at the other end of the scale. Our province of Ontario student aid programme, the student bursary--these are largely at the other end of the scale in their efforts to provide an opportunity for those who do not have the economic advantages of others who are in the system. But the point remains, that if the young person is not shored up in terms of motivation in the early years, then the game is up.

> He never does go on to university and he may very well not go to a college of applied arts and technology. That is what I mean by a recognition of the responsibility of this department to give grants to special classes, preschool classes for those who are culturally deprived (Mr. Pitman [NDP], June 4, 1968: 3905).

In some cases, analysis of factors associated with dis-advantages learned early in life was quite detailed. For example, in 1966 Mr. MacDonald (NDP) stated:

> If the culturally deprived child is going to be rescued from the limitations of his early environment and educa-tional opportunities made available to him in accordance

with his native ability, it can be done only through a concentration of resources and our best teaching skills in nursery schools, kindergarten and the first three grades.

. . . In keeping with the general tendency to downgrade the importance of the early years of school-ing, summer trained inexperienced teachers have been assigned in many instances to the primary grades, on the fallacious assumption that the least experience and training is needed at this age. The consequences in terms of failure to overcome early learning disabilities are inestimable.

But even when elementary school standards have been placed on a professional basis, . . . another major obstacle will remain. With classes of the size to be found in most of our schools today, it is impossible for a teacher to establish the kind of individual relationship with the pupil which makes for good teaching. With 35 or more pupils, the best that the teacher can be is little more than an educational policeman.

. . . We can never have a truly democratic educa-tional system until we raise the standards of teachers in some way–through the reduction of class sizes, pro-vision of auxiliary teachers or otherwise–make it possible for the establishment of a closer personal relationship between teacher and pupil, particularly in the primary grades.

. . . Undoubtedly some of this frustration arises from the regimentation of a graded school system, which chops the learning process into artifical sections that have no real meaning. . . . [The ungraded school provides] movement without the straitjacket and the regimentation. . . .

. . . Extra dollars spent on the child in the early school years may well mean the saving, or the making, of many more dollars throughout the full lifetime of the child (June 9, 1966: 4481-82).

In June 1968, Mr. Pitman ([NDP], June 4, 1968: 3905) in talking about the need to motivate students in their early years, urged that the province needs to recognize its responsibility "to give grants to special classes, pre-school classes for those who are culturally deprived" and he further recommended that a "head start programme" be instituted, as in the United States. These suggestions are similar to some of our own recommendations.

Losers and Winners

In addition to socially- and culturally-based structural in-equalities, some legislative debate centred on age discrimination. For example, it was brought to the attention of the legislature in 1962 that the Ontario College of Education had at that time stipulated that applicants must not be over age 45; and the Apprenticeship Act disallowed anyone over the age of 21 from becoming an apprentice (Mr. B. Newman [NDP], Feb. 22, 1962: 558). Again in May 1969, the question of age discrimination was raised. Mr. Reid (Liberal) questioned why qualified persons who were over 30 years old were not gaining admission to university. In response, the Hon. W. Davis (Conservative), Minister of Education, said that the information he had from the universities was that age was not a factor "in the main", and exceptional people over 30 years old might be admitted (May 20, 1969: 4543).

Another important issue that was frequently discussed dur-ing the 1960s was gender discrimination. In criticizing the government's student aid program it was pointed out that the "programme still allows those that have the least to go furthest into debt. It is still a negative feature for women . . ." (Mr. Pitman [NDP], June 10, 1968: 4185-86). In essence, it was noted that the student assistance program did not address the special situation of women and there was a need to look into this matter. It was not until the 1970s, however, that debate on this issue brought gender discrimination into more prominence than ever before. The thrust of this debate is reported in the section "Dimensions on Accessibility."

The government position throughout the 1960s and into the 1970s has been one of attempting to ensure equality of oppor-tunity through the expansion of facilities and the provision of financial aid to remove financial barriers to post-secondary education. The rapid expansion of Ontario universities in the 1960s and the creation of the system of Colleges of Applied Arts and Technology (CAATs) in the late 1960s and their expansion in the 1970s reflected the government's view that provision of such facilities was perhaps the major plank in policy regarding acces-sibility. In a presentation by the Hon. W. Davis (Conservative) on financial estimates for the Department of University Affairs, it was claimed that the province had provided access to university and, consequently, there was a great increase in students entering post-secondary institutions. But, Mr. Davis noted that at that time there was less money available for educational pro-grams. He suggested that the department had to be conscious of spending, while weighing the costs and benefits to be gained from post-secondary education (June 10, 1977: 3845-46).

Probably the most heavily debated issues concerning government policy revolved around policies concerned with financial barriers to post-secondary education: the Ontario Student Assistance Plan and tuition fees as barriers to post-secondary enrolment. A glimpse of the government's position and opposition criticism of it is given in the following exchange over the matter of tuition fees.

> Mr. Bryden (NDP): I would like to put to the Minister-to-be of the department which is to be created shortly (DUA), that a basic objective should be to reverse this trend and to ensure that sufficient funds are made available so that fees can be reduced and ultimately eliminated, so that students of merit will be able to attend university regardless of their financial means.

> Hon. Mr. Davis: . . . I feel quite frankly that there are very few students . . . with merit—who are prejudiced from obtaining a university education because of the fact that they cannot afford to pay the fees. The bursary system is . . . quite generous (May 5, 1964: 2831).

The passive equality-of-opportunity position taken by the government, in which the student is required to have the appropriate motivation (as opposed to a more active equality-of-results perspective), is evident from an exchange between Mr. Cooke (NDP) and the Hon. Mr. Parrott (Conservative), Minister of the Department of Colleges and Universities, over the provision of equal educational opportunity.

> Hon. Mr. Parrott (Conservative): I guess it gets down simply to this, we can't be all things to all people, much as we might like to be. We just can't evolve a system that will allow everyone to have equal opportunity. That's a great concept and I don't fight it in principle. But when you get down to the specifics of doing it, it's next to impossible.

> Mr. Cooke (NDP): That's a pretty significant statement, saying we can't develop a system to provide equal opportunity.

> Hon. Mr. Parrott (Conservative): No, I said there is access there now, and excellent access. If you are hoping that everyone will have equal access, I think you are hoping for something that can't be delivered.
> First of all, not every one has equal ability. We rule those out.

> Mr. Cooke (NDP): I realize that. I'm not talking about that at all.

> Hon. Mr. Parrott (Conservative): So many of those people have decided to go other ways earlier in their

career. It doesn't mean they haven't a great opportunity. They have access to many programs, but it
means that they don't show up as a statistic in university enrolments. It doesn't mean they are necessarily disadvantaged. I guess we perhaps have put too
much emphasis on the fact that unless you have had an
opportunity in the university you somehow come out
second class. . . (May 29, 1978: S-698).

As early as 1970, however, the government recognized that
financial intervention strategies in the form of student aid were
not the complete answer to equalizing education opportunities:

As we move into the 70's, our major goal remains that
of providing equality of educational opportunities to our
citizens. . . . An important factor in seeking true
equality of educational opportunity is the need to ensure that economic requirements do not create barriers
to the legitimate educational goals of individuals. . . .
Student aid, in itself, is not the complete answer or,
necessarily, the most important factor in providing
equal opportunity. A good number of talented
people . . . still reach the levels of education where
current student aid programmes apply. [We intend to]
make a concerted effort to examine these issues and to
consider approaches in the use of public funds that may
help us to overcome such problems effectively (Hon. W.
Davis [Conservative], June 10, 1970: 3847).[4]

By 1979, however, opposition members criticized the government for failure to develop a policy that dealt with more than
providing financial aid at the point of post-secondary entrance.

Mr. Sweeney (Liberal): I simply want to say, Madam
Minister, that I think we need to see a strategy
developed in this province. Rather than the Premier
simply saying, "we're committed to equal accessibility
for students from all classes," I want to see something
concrete, I think there should be a plan come out of
the social policy field either enunciated by yourself or
by your colleague, the Provincial Secretary for Social
Development (Mrs. Birch), which will represent
government policy. . . . Hence: I would suggest,
Madam Minister, that a strategy for accessibility should
include some of the following things: First, a study
that I talked about; second, expansion of day-care programs whether we are talking about full-day kindergarten or other programs at elementary level, to give
children who don't have the same opportunities to come
in at a lower level than the head start they need.

In talking about accessibility to post-secondary education you can't avoid talking about smaller class sizes at the primary level because I think the start the children get in school is very important as to how they will succeed all through the system (Dec. 4, 1979: S-1506).

REPORTS OF ADVISORY BODIES AND GOVERNMENT COMMISSIONS

In this section we summarize the major findings and conclusions of a number of influential advisory bodies and government commissions regarding equality of access to post-secondary institutions in Ontario.[5] Importantly, these reports often have a narrow set of references, or a mandate to examine specific issues. Thus, taken individually, they may not present as broad a view of factors associated with unequal opportunity as we would like, and their recommendations may be likewise narrowly focused. Nevertheless, they have had an impact on the body of ideas presented in the legislature and in the wider public arena. Our aim here is to point out the highlights of the various reports. Discussion of these reports in relation to specific dimensions of structural inequality (social class, ethnicity, gender, and region) is combined with discussion of parliamentary debates in the next section.

Economic Council of Canada (ECC)

The ECC is a research and policy advisory agency created by act of Parliament in 1963. The council attempts to improve public understanding of important economic issues and offer sound advice to governments, Parliament, and the country as a whole. In its report Design for Decision Making: An Application to Human Resources Policies (1971), the ECC outlined the various ways in which "equitability of access" has been defined. For example, one definition given is "a situation in which equal access to and equal participation rates in non-compulsory education for individuals of equivalent ability and all socio-economic groups in society" (p. 199). The report specified that in Canada the major efforts that governments have made to achieve equity of access have been towards reducing financial barriers and removing institutional differences. The report suggests that these efforts have not been totally successful:

. . . there are some indications that access to the educational system (and hence its benefits) is not as equitable as one might wish. For example, children from low income families still have problems financing

30

their post-secondary education. More important, the effects of family background and community values on the motivations and aspirations of children produce the observed inter-generational links between the educational levels of parents and children, and these links tend to perpetuate certain barriers to mobility between socio-economic classes. Also, the individual's access to education appears to differ considerably among regions in ways that appear to have no relationship to ability (p. 213).

In its more recent report, A Time for Reason (1978), the ECC took a more positive view of equality of opportunity in Canada, stating that "Canada has proportionately more of its young people in post-secondary educational institutions than does any OECD country except the United States" (p. 107). This is facilitated by the fact that a greater proportion of education costs comes out of general revenue rather than through student fees. Therefore, "post-secondary education in Canada is probably more accessible to students from lower income families than it is in most other countries" (p. 107). However, the council suggested that secondary education for recent immigrants still needs substantial improvement.

Ontario Council on University Affairs (OCUA)

OCUA was officially appointed on September 24, 1974 as "Ontario's independent advisory body with respect to universities and certain other post-secondary educational institutions" (First Annual Report, p. 4). The council is also involved with the decision-making processes of the government pertaining to post-secondary education. Members include individuals appointed by the Lieutenant-Governor-in-Council from the Ontario Universities and the public at large.

The council's 1975 report paid attention to the changing demographic profile of Ontario's student population. In its demographic analysis, the report focused on the 18-24 age group which, it suggested, "has traditionally accounted for some four-fifths of full-time university students" (p. 7). It predicted that in the short run, there will be a continuous flow of students into the age group, "fueled by the tail end of the 18-24 population bulge" (p. 8), a prediction at odds with the decline in post-secondary student population foreseen by others. This in turn will negatively influence "open accessibility policies, social preferences for additional higher education as a path toward equality of opportunity, and greater demand for highly qualified manpower", all events presumed to be associated with smaller numbers of university-age persons (pp. 7-8).

Losers and Winners

With these considerations in mind, several important questions concerning universities were raised. How can accessibility be sustained in the short run when enrolment projections for later years caution against the acquisition of additional long-run commitments to personnel and plant resources? To what extent can the severity of potential trade-offs be mitigated by deliberate attempts to ensure that the capacity of the university system is fully utilized in each and every institution? Given the likely spatial distribution of candidates for university admission, what measures might be contemplated to make it easier for students to attend university away from home? (pp. 8-13). The council took the position that:

> questions such as these deserve a place of primacy in the dialogue between Government and the university system. It of course bears repetition that the future of the university system will be conditioned by changes in participation rates and not simply demography. Indeed, this future will also be shaped by the manner in which universities exercise their own responsibilities in devising new patterns of higher education (p. 13).

The Third Annual Report (1977) of the council addressed the question of the capacity of the university system to accommodate students. The report states: "In Ontario, the phrase 'accessibility for all qualified applicants' has been anything but an empty slogan. It has captured the essence of a major policy commitment by Government" (p. 7). The report mentioned that the seriousness with which the government attempts to maintain this commitment is reflected by the fact that fourteen of the fifteen universities are publicly assisted and have facilities designed to accommodate large numbers of students. However:

> The active pursuit of Government of "accessibility for all qualified applicants" must be understood in the context of two specified points. First, what constitutes a "qualified" applicant has been left for each university to determine in the context of each of its programs. Second, it has always been understood that no applicant is entitled to a place in the program or institution of his or her choice. What is envisaged is that a qualified applicant will be able to find a place in some program at some institution in the province (p. 7).

The consequence of this is that over a period of time, admission to some programs at universities has become highly selective-e.g., dentistry, law, and medicine. Also, these institutions have become full to capacity; thus accessibility for all qualified applicants is limited.

The report suggested that it is necessary for universities to indicate to the government where their changes in standards are a result of an excess number of students who take advantage of the opportunities. "Only thus can government gauge the extent to which its accessibility policy is in jeopardy" (p. 14).

The council recognized that education in Ontario is accessible to individuals who meet university admission requirements, but that some individuals do not attend. If their inability to attend is attributable to their socio-economic backgrounds, then this can be regarded as a denial of accessibility, and it is a problem that should be addressed at the primary and secondary school levels. However, as long as financial assistance is available to university students regardless of socio-economic background, it was felt that the decision to attend must clearly "be a matter of individual choice" (p. 25).

In addressing the current issue of tuition fees and how fee increases influence accessibility, the council, in its Sixth Annual Report (1980), stated that the government must consider the goal of accessibility in formulating tuition fee policy and should maintain its accessibility policy. The "Council believes that tuition fees should not become more of an obstacle than they are perceived to be at present and that a student aid program should be an integral part of any tuition fee policy" (p. 61).

The OCUA reports reflected a satisfaction with the government's attempt to provide equal access to post-secondary education to all Ontarians. Government provision of substantial financial support for post-secondary institutions, and financial assistance to eligible students, was seen to indicate a genuine effort on the part of the government to provide access to post-secondary education. While there was some "denial of accessibility" for persons of different socio-economic background, the main sentiment was that there was equal access to post-secondary education for all "qualified" applicants (qualification being based on the universities' criteria) as far as is economically and politically feasible. Little mention was made of social and cultural factors early in life affecting one's motivation to pursue post-secondary education.

Ontario Economic Council (OEC)

The OEC studies problems in the area of natural resources, human resources, government and provincial economic development. In a special report, Issues and Alternatives: 1976, Education, the OEC examined the problems of accessibility and cost distribution—the latter being an investigation of whether the taxpayer or the university student should pay more of the cost of post-secondary education.

The council suggested that the objectives of the education system should encompass greater equality of opportunity, efficient allocation of resources, freedom of academic choice, and promotion of the cultural and intellectual development of students (p. 5). The council felt that education played an important role in the social and economic advancement of the individual; thus, equality of educational opportunity for all citizens was a desirable goal.

The council wrote that "individuals generally have access to education according to their intellectual, environmental, and financial resources and those are certainly not equally distributed" (p. 5). Thus, in providing equality of opportunity for individuals, it must be recognized that "the unequal distribution of innate talents and intelligence is beyond the purview of educational policy" as well as "to a slightly lesser degree, the advantages or disadvantages of home or other environmental factors" (p. 5). To the extent that policies can affect equality of access to education, the council stated:

> It is also taken as a given that an objective of education per se is not to achieve equality of opportunity by reducing, in any sense, the environmental and/or financial circumstances of the most advantaged: the objective, in the view of the council, is to improve the opportunities of the least advanced (p. 5).

The government's responsibility, then, is to provide these opportunities through aid.

The Commission on Post-secondary Education in Ontario (COPSEO)

The commission was established by the government in 1969 to investigate all aspects of post-secondary education. It was also mandated "to consider . . . the patterns necessary to ensure the further effective development of post-secondary education in the Province during the period to 1980" (p. iii). Included on the commission were representatives from government, academics, and the public at large. The commission's final report, The Learning Society, was published in 1972.

The commission took a very strong position on equality of opportunity in calling for universal accessibility.

> We must have a continual broadening of skills and knowledge to enable us to live in a world where the problem of providing sufficient goods, the social strains of living closely together, and the ecological dangers of ruining our environment all threaten survival itself. When faced with the imperative need of education for survival, universal access should seem, not a benevolent dream, but a categorical necessity. (p. 33)

The commission also stated that

> "all facets of the post-secondary educational system should be oriented towards serving the individual student, . . . the whole spectrum of educational services must be available to each individual, not just a degree program, a certification process, or what the institution thinks may benefit him. If the individual is at the center, he must have the opportunity and the responsibility as an adult to decide on the educational experience that is best suited for him (p. 35).

The commission argued that for the individual to succeed, he must have access to appropriate educational services throughout his life and not just after high school.

It was suggested that there should be a more open and flexible relationship between post-secondary education and employment possibilities. This is necessary since accessibility to post-secondary education and its linkage to careers, particularly professional careers, is an important aspect in the decision-making process of students who plan to pursue post-secondary education. Furthermore, accessibility by design must counteract discrimination and regional disparities.

DIMENSIONS ON ACCESSIBILITY

The social-stratification perspective outlined in Chapter 1 argues that there are several analytically different dimensions of social inequality relevant to education. In this section we examine the discussion in Hansard and in the reports of various organizations along each of the dimensions of social class, ethnicity, gender, and region, noting key developments in the period and positions taken by different persons or groups.

Social Class

Legislators discussed the role of social class throughout the decades. But unlike the discussions in earlier years, during the 1960s legislators became quite explicit in analysing how the "class structure" in society was responsible for inequalities in educational opportunity. Quoting academic research findings and position papers put out by government and non-governmental bodies, legislators reiterated the point of socio-economic inequality inherent in our social system. Since little empirical social science research in Canada was published in the early 1960s,[6] more references to social class were made during and after the late 1960s. The following three statements made in 1966, 1969, and

1978 typify the statements of opposition legislators during the past two decades.

> Ironically, all our emphasis on higher educational op-portunities, while necessary because development of our educational system was neglected for years, has tended to freeze our class-structured society. These broader educational opportunities are for the select few, the one-fifth who survive to the latter stage of the educational system (Mr. MacDonald [NDP], June 9, 1966: 4480).

> Today we do not question the proposition that every Canadian in Ontario should have equal access to the benefits of society including the benefits of education. But there is a strong feeling among the young that the university, despite its "objective" criteria of scholar-ship, is really geared to maintaining the status quo in terms of the class system (Mr. Reid [Liberal], Nov. 25, 1969: 8861).

> Statistics show that students who have a professional parent or high-income earners as parents are vastly over represented in universities, especially in pro-fessional schools, and students who have parents with low incomes are over represented as a percentage of part-time students and community college students. It is clear from this that finances play a large role in who attends institutions and whether they can afford to go full time or part time (Mr. Cooke [NDP], May 23, 1978: 644).

Government reactions to such claims have been generally consistent during the 1960s and 1970s. A recent statement by the Minister of Education typifies the government view:

> If we look at the number of students coming from the income groups about which we have fairly accurate information, it would appear that income is not neces-sarily a barrier to the decision taken to attend uni-versities (Hon. Ms. Stephenson [Conservative], May 21, 1980: S-431).

In the 1970s the government's cutback of funding to institu-tions and to students was cited as a major reason for lack of adequate post-secondary facilities and programs and for the overrepresentation of students from high-income families in post-secondary institutions. Legislators contend that low-income students, whether from minority groups or not, suffer the same fate - that is, low participation in post-secondary education due to lack of funds. These arguments are detailed in the section "Removing Financial Barriers".

Losers and Winners

As mentioned previously, opposition MPPs have periodically
indicated that motivational factors acquired early in life through
socialization within particular social or ethnic cultures are important factors influencing subsequent post-secondary education.
The Ontario Federation of Students (OFS), an organization
supported by university and college students across the province
and independent of the government, continually voices its doubts
concerning the realization of universal accessibility. Its position
is emphatic: social, cultural, and economic factors significantly
influence accessibility. Specifically, "at some stages in the educational selection process social and cultural barriers are more at
work than economic barriers, at other stages the process is
reversed." Thus, government and researchers who have primarily investigated the economic barriers "which manifest
themselves at a relatively late stage in a student's educational
career" have overlooked other important barriers to accessibility
(OFS, 1979: 2).

In a paper entitled "The Unequal Pursuit of the Golden
Fleece" (May 1979), the OFS claimed that high tuition fees, inadequate student aid, and the rapidly rising cost of personal and
living expenses constitute three of the most visible barriers to
the realization of universal accessibility. The financial barrier is
but one aspect of the social and cultural factors which limit
accessibility. Citing references, the OFS notes that universities
are more accessible to males than to females; to urban than to
rural residents; to Anglophones than to Francophones; and,
above all, to those from middle-class rather than lower-class
backgrounds. The federation states that the bulk of empirical
research suggests that, after all these years, social class still
remains the prime determinant of who will go to university in
Ontario.

Ethnicity

In the legislature, concern for diverse ethnic groups has been
varied; it has included "the children of immigrants of non-English
origin, the native people, the Franco-Ontarians" who "are educationally disadvantaged by our system" (Mr. Dukszta [NDP], Nov.
18, 1974: 5413). But, as will be made clear later, more effort
was placed on discussing the opportunities provided to Francophones.

> Hon. P. M. McGibbon (Lt.-Gov.) (Speech from the
> Throne): The fundamental rights of Franco-Ontarians
> to education in the French language has long been
> recognized in Ontario. . . . We will continue to build
> upon the strong foundation already laid in the field of
> education to ensure that French language programs are
> available at all levels, where practicable, to French
> speaking Ontarians (Feb. 21, 1978: 8).

37

Losers and Winners

In most of the legislative sessions, it was also pointed out that Native Indians and Inuit had not received equal access to education and that this problem resulted at least in part from the unresolved issues of jurisdiction over education for Indians. That is, the federal and provincial governments still had not worked out how they were going to share the responsibility of providing education for Indians (see statement by Mr. Renwick [NDP], April 17, 1969: 3231-34). However, since, constitutionally, education is a provincial matter, legislators recognized that they had a responsibility to Indians and saw education as "the most important aspect of the whole Indian problem if we are going to integrate these people successfully into our population" (Mr. Wren [Liberal], March 1975: 960). Later, it was proposed that "some sort of post-secondary school which emphasized the special needs of Indians and their culture be developed" (Mr. Nixon [Liberal], Oct. 19, 1970: 5223).

The situation of the Native Indians continued to be seen as a limitation in the Canadian education system to the extent that the Organization for Economic Co-operation and Development (OECD)[7] reported that:

> While continuing disparity of opportunity across income groups is the broadest problem, there are pressing questions of effective policies in ensuring special resource needs for handicapped children and for the education of native people (1976: 124).

In addition to identifying the special needs of ethnic minority and immigrant groups during the late 1960s, opposition members went as far as suggesting strategies that would co-opt minorities into the educational system. For instance, Mr. Reid (Liberal) suggested that quotas for ethnic minority students be introduced (Nov. 25, 1969: 8863-64). While admitting that implementing a quota system "for students of poor or culturally deprived backgrounds" would be difficult, Mr. Reid pointed out that a similar scheme in Chicago was successful; thus Ontario would do well to examine "their role in relation to the oppressed groups" in the society.

While passing reference was made to other minority and immigrant students, very little was done regarding these students. The legislators' preoccupation with Franco-Ontarians, especially during the later part of the decade, was not without a tactical basis. It was during this time that the discussion of Canadian unity, triggered by the Quebec referendum, gained prominence. The issue was aptly brought up for discussion:

> Mr. Sweeney (Liberal): Given the results of last night's vote in Quebec, it is appropriate that we spend a little time on French-language instruction in our universities. I am sure you are aware that recently

38

Maxwell Yalden, federal commissioner of official languages, made the observation in his report to Parliament
that the French fact in our universities is the weakest
link. Of course, he was referring to a Canada-wide
phenomenon. (May 21, 1980:S-435).[8]

Gender

The educational process was also examined in terms of the extent
to which females were discriminated against in gaining access to
post-secondary education. Here, members of the legislature
referred to studies and reports[9] which showed that financial
barriers as well as sex-stereotyping were responsible for the low
participation rate of women. According to Mr. Laughren (NDP):
"Thirty-five percent of the full-time undergraduate students in
University were women; in 1970 at the graduate level there was
twenty-one percent; and in 1968, at the postgraduate level, there
were nine percent." Mr. Laughren attributed this low participation rate to "earlier conditioning", suggesting that it may be
necessary to offer women special assistance to encourage them to
continue education so as to counter the "problem of sex discrimination in our universities" (April 5, 1973: 576). Furthermore, vocational guidance should be provided for girls in order to
stimulate and broaden their career and educational choices.

In some ways, the legislators placed on the universities some
responsibility of compensating for inequalities due to gender.
With reference to a 1975 paper entitled "Women in Universities",
one legislator suggested that to address the problem of women not
entering traditional male fields, "universities should do more to
assist women by offering degree programs in courses in places
more accessible to them" (Mr. Warner [NDP], May 27, 1976:
2678). Legislators in the 1970s were generally aware of findings
of various research reports concerning gender inequality in
education. Reports like the Ontario Status of Women Council's
(OSWC) 1975 annual report, Gail McIntyre's Women and Ontario
Universities (1975) funded by the Ministry of Colleges and Universities, and others, documented the underrepresentation of
women in universities despite increasing enrolments proportional
to men. Also discussed was the tendency for women to be enrolled in part-time studies and to be tracked into traditionally-
accepted women's career courses. Of particular interest, the
McIntyre report stated that in order to increase equality of
educational opportunity for women, attitudinal and structural
barriers needed to be eliminated. This must be accomplished
through recruitment, career counselling, women's studies, and
research. In addition, the problem of child care needs to be
addressed, since it has sometimes acted as a barrier to women
seeking to continue their education.

Losers and Winners

Concerned about the impact of sex-role stereotyping by guidance counsellors and its effect on differences between males and females in career interests and anticipated occupational levels to be attained, the Ontario Ministry of Education contracted a study with J. R. B. Cassie and others. Their report entitled Sex-Role Stereotyping: Incidence and Implications for Guidance and Counselling of Students (1980) argued that while parents were central in the decision-making process of secondary school students, guidance counsellors also played a prominent role since they "provide students with assistance in their personal, social, educational, and career planning" (pp. 3-4). Thus, "guidance and counselling provides an excellent opportunity for raising of student consciousness about the limitations of sex-role sterotyping" (p. 4). Furthermore, compared with teachers, guidance counsellors have the time and special training to counsel students in educational and career decision making.

Guidance counsellors, however, would be fighting an uphill battle. Parents, friends, and teachers were perceived to encourage females to enter communication subjects (i.e., business and secretarial courses), and males to enter science, mathematics, and technical courses. A female required a high level of independence to make a non-traditional subject selection in the face of such negative support. Cassie et al. (1980) wrote:

> The serious implication of this sex bias in subject selection is that neither males nor females have opportunities to engage in the full range of vocations once they have limited their educational choices. Clearly, one can pick up courses at a later date. However, most students grow into career patterns as a natural extension of at least some of their subject selections. This fact means that sex differences in subject selection, based more on sex-role stereotyping than reason, must be looked at as a serious barrier to males breaking through non-traditional career options (p. 16).

> Furthermore, misconceptions of the sexes probably contribute immeasurably to students' attitudes about what educational and vocational options are open to males and females. Unfortunately, the changing of such attitudes requires the combined efforts of parents, educators, community leaders, and the media. Until there is a raising of consciousness among these agents, coupled with a sincere desire to change the proverbial status quo, only modest changes in attitudes should be expected to be in the years ahead. In the meantime, students continue to be immersed in subtle influence that appears to shape their minds in the direction of sex-role stereotypes (p. 19).

Despite increasing attention given by the government to increasing the quantity and type of women's educational attainment, some limitations have been noted by others. For example, according to OECD (1979), programs that are designed to assist women to gain equal access to educational opportunities are unlikely to be successful since only those women who are "already endowed by wealth and earlier educational attainment seem to be the primary beneficiaries" (p. 52). Furthermore, it was claimed that the task of improving opportunity for women is almost impossible since it first has to be established whether their vocational position is beginning to change and what public policy initiative is being considered to ensure greater equality (p. 52).

Region

Politicians in Ontario have long recognized regional disparities in the provision of educational facilities. For example, in 1959 the Hon. W. J. Dunlop (Conservative) stated that "we must give our boys and girls in Northwestern Ontario an equal opportunity with the rest of the province to receive the best in educational facilities" (1959: 344). It was necessary, then, to expand educational facilities. Typical of the government concern in this area was the statement of Mr. Yakabuski (Conservative) in 1966:

> Equal opportunity does not yet exist across our province. The educational achievements of the people in North Eastern Ontario do not compare with the province average because the right to education has been denied them by these reasons of finance and distance. Across the province 6.2% of the people have some university training or a degree; in North Eastern Ontario only 3.9% are in this group. At the post-secondary school level North Eastern Ontario was void of opportunity until a few years ago when Laurentian university was established. . . . Community colleges are sorely needed in North Eastern Ontario if equality of opportunity is to be available (Feb. 22, 1966: 756).

Further discussion on regional disparities dealt with the fact that "constituents from certain geographic areas pay more for university costs for their children because of the distance they live from universities" (Mr. Sargent [Liberal] April 21, 1968: 1552). In light of this, the budget for 1966 gave special financial consideration to students from rural areas. In his budget address, the Hon. J. W. Allan, (Conservative) Provincial Treasurer, mentioned:

> New attention is being given to the provision of adequate opportunities for education in thinly populated areas. Nearly 1000 students in northern and north-

Western Ontario are now assisted financially in meeting transportation costs to university and technical institute centres (Feb. 9, 1966: 346).

Towards the end of the decade, however, levels of post-secondary enrolment in Northern Ontario remained low relative to the rest of the province and one legislator was moved to suggest that opening teacher colleges in the part of the province should take precedence over expanding the University of Toronto (Mr. Martell [NDP], Nov. 25, 1969: 8893-94).

In a recent study entitled The Northern Dilemma, carried out by the Ontario Economic Council between 1975 and 1977, the author, D. M. Cameron, states that "there could be no doubt that additional costs are involved in assuring Northern Ontarians access to post-secondary education similar to that available in the south" (p. 140). Still, accessibility could be ensured either by building institutions or expanding programs, or by students moving or travelling south for their education. These kinds of costs, he argued, must be accepted to ensure equality. The fact remains, however, that not everyone can or is willing to travel; "first generation students" may not consider post-secondary education if no institutions exist nearby. Thus, if equality of access to post-secondary education is to be pursued in a mean-ingful way, "that pursuit cannot be limited to the young, mobile and already motivated members of society" (p. 141).

COLLEGES OF APPLIED ARTS AND TECHNOLOGY (CAATs): AN ALTERNATIVE STRATEGY OF ACCESSIBILITY

In an attempt to provide post-secondary educational opportunity to students who had such aspirations, and to accommodate the increasing number of students vying for post-secondary educa-tion, the community college system was introduced. This system was seen by government as an answer to a number of barriers to equal opportunity. Colleges of Applied Arts and Technology provided alternatives to universities; their new facilities and programs were expected to increase opportunities for rural and lower-class students. The colleges were built in communities that previously had no facilities and in relatively less-populated com-munities, thus making them accessible to rural students. For the government, this alternative to university, and the increase in post-secondary facilities were seen as their attempt to provide equality of education opportunity to all sectors of the poulation.

In introducing the bill enabling the establishment and operation of Colleges of Applied Arts and Technology (CAATs), the Hon. W. Davis (Conservative) said that the bill

Losers and Winners

goes far towards making a reality of the promise . . .
to provide through education and training not only an
equality of opportunity to all sectors of our population,
but the fullest possible development of each individual
to the limit of his ability. . . .

. . . this expansion of our school system is
imperative to meet the need of individual citizens as
well as those of society as a whole. . . .

The university doors should always be open to
capable and ambitious young men and women. . . .
Students who have completed successfully an appropriate program at one of our colleges of Applied Arts
and Technology and who have demonstrated they are
prepared to undertake university work, may be
admitted to university.

. . . We simply must provide opportunities for the
higher education of this segment of our population as
well as the university-bound group. (February 17,
1965:pp. 3186-92)

However, although the establishment of community colleges
was a welcomed alternative to university, some politicians argued
that:

It is not enough to say piously that no student with
ability will be denied an opportunity to continue.
There has to be a clear pathway, whereby these
students can take a course that will lead them to placement in university. If these institutions are going to
be established, . . . there are many people who would
otherwise be denied . . . the opportunity for post-
secondary education. We are going to be dealing with
what has been called first generation students. . . .
These people are going to be forced . . . into the
community college system, through the fact that it is
closer to home and it would obviously be cheaper to go
there. They will lose the opportunity for higher
academic work. (Mr. R. Nixon [Liberal], May 31,
1965:p. 3473)

Furthermore,

If community colleges are going to be sharply oriented
to technology, without a core of liberal arts, and with
ill-defined and limited opportunities for transfer to
university for the brighter students, they will cement
the fate of the disadvantaged child. Even if he does
overcome earlier handicaps sufficiently to reach high
school and complete years in the non-university stream,

43

there is little prospect that he can go beyond the community college. (Mr. MacDonald [NDP], June 9, 1966:p. 4483)

Essentially, the opposition critics were concerned with the fact that the increase in the number of post-secondary education facilities "did not create the kind of social mix and did not end the social stratification that we had expected" (Mr. Pitman [NDP] June 10, 1968: p. 4186.) Also, the issue of transferability from college to university was of tremendous concern, especially to opposition members of the legislature who suggested that there should be some policy established which would assure students of opportunities in continuing education after college. But Mr. W. Davis (Conservative), the minister responsible for colleges, reasserted that in a way community colleges prepared students for university and was also an alternative to university. Moreover, he maintained that there was transferability in some course areas between the two institutions (Oct. 19, 1970: p. 5208).

REMOVING FINANCIAL BARRIERS

It is important to note that the discussion of dimensions of structural inequality in Ontario is closely tied in with a discussion of financial barriers to education in both Hansard and in the reports of the various advisory bodies and government commissions. This stems largely from the government view that structured inequalities are best attacked through removing financial barriers to education for all disadvantaged groups. This section examines the public debate over the two key components of government financial aid - direct student aid and tuition fees.

Direct Student Aid

The Ontario Student Awards Programme, [is] the means by which we attempt to ensure that students of this province are not denied post-secondary education because of lack of financial resources:
- The Ontario Student Awards Programme is intended to supplement rather than replace family and/or student resources. . . .
- We are attempting to the best of our ability to combine the inherent equity which basic rules provide, with the degree of flexibility required to deal with individual situations (Hon. W. Davis [Conservative], Nov. 25, 1969: 8857).

The OSAP[10] is the current means by which the government attempts to ensure that accessibility, particularly, for students

44

from lower-income groups, will be maintained. Over the years since its inception, members of the opposition parties and external reports have heavily criticized it. One report, <u>Towards</u> <u>2000</u>, published in 1971 by the Subcommittee on Research and Planning of the Committee of Presidents of the Universities of Ontario (CPUO), was especially critical of the loan as opposed to grant orientation of OSAP. It was argued that this would be to the disadvantage of students from low-income families, since they inevitably would get into debt.

> There is a very real cost to being in debt, and it is difficult to see how the principle of equity is served by requiring some to incur debts and others not. Equity is neither served nor denied by conferring a benefit on an individual that he did not previously enjoy. Equity must be determined by examining a person's position relative to others. When the benefit conferred imposes a penalty . . . which is not required of others who enjoy the same benefit . . . this is scarcely equitable (p. 148).

The committee argued for a progressive development from the present loan/grant arrangement to a greater proportional reliance on grants subject to a means test (p. 169).

The Ontario Federation of Students claims that the debts which students are required to incur in order to obtain a post-secondary education act as a social-psychological deterrent to many contemplating higher education:

> . . . numerous studies, . . . have shown that the prospect of indebtedness is a very real barrier to any working class student entertaining the prospect of a university education, almost as great a barrier as the existence of no aid at all (OFS, 1979: 25).

Of particular significance is the small number of students from low-income families who are willing to undertake the cost of schooling.

Recent changes in rules allowing grants for only the first four post-secondary years have drawn criticism. The "eligibility period", as it is referred to, was called the "most negative part of the program" and as such was "a barrier which discouraged students from middle- and low-income families from taking advantage of the aid program" (Mr. Cook [NDP], May 23, 1978: 644) The program would especially discriminate against students supporting themselves in graduate and professional schools.

Another criticism was that parents would not be able to make the expected financial contribution to their children's education during their first four years of post-secondary education, because they would not be able to afford it. This was especially important in the context of the sluggish economy of the 1970s. In this regard, the following exchange took place in the legislature recently.

> <u>Mr. S. Smith</u> (Liberal): . . . Is she (Ms. Stephenson) sure that there has not been a shift towards the higher socio-economic groups in terms of those who are now seeking post-secondary education? . . . Is it not very important to clarify that there hasn't been some financial barrier suddenly set up in these difficult economic times? Shouldn't we have that clearly in our minds before we make any further changes in what might be an impediment to post-secondary education?

> <u>Hon. Ms. Stephenson</u> (Conservative): I am not absolutely certain, because the total information is not as yet available. . . . It is my impression, from speaking to faculty members, to deans and to university students - including some members of the OFS - that there is an increasing number of students from the lower socio-economic strata attending university than perhaps was general in years gone by, but I don't have that as factual information. It's a strong impression. . . (May 21, 1980:4284).

Apart from the legislators, other groups pointed out the discriminatory nature of the assistance program. For example, in its brief to the Federal/Provincial Task Force on Student Assistance, the OFS noted:

> In fact in Ontario, OSAP has systematically become more regressive, by demanding unrealistic parental contributions, underestimating a student's needs and costs and re-directing more grants into loans. In fact, while participation from low income groups has been declining, the Ministry of Colleges and Universities introduced limits to grant eligibility periods, which cut off all grant assistance to graduate and professional students. This is perhaps the single most repressive example of the Ontario Government's response to declining participation rates among low income groups. Close to 3,000 graduate students and over 7,000 professional school students . . . were cut off the next fall (1978) . . . As a result, it is in those programs where students from low income families are most under-represented-graduate and professional programs-that OSGP [Ontario Study Grant Plan] functions in the most retrograde fashion (OFS, 1980a:4).

Commenting on this limitation of the number of years students can receive assistance, Dr. Harry Parrott, then Minister of Colleges and Universities, stated: "We have to conserve public funds by encouraging students to complete their studies as quickly as possible" (August 17, 1977 news release). However, the Ontario Council on University Affairs (OCUA) in its 1980 report made this comment on the grant eligibility period:

> These may not be the years when the student is most in need of assistance. There is much to sustain the validity of this criticism and it should be considered in any serious reassessment of the Ontario Student Assistance Program (p. 61).

From an equality-of-results perspective, a study entitled Who Benefits from the Ontario University System by O. Mehment (1978) is interesting in that it employed a group-level analysis. Comparing taxes paid and benefits received among different income groups, Mehmet wrote that there is

> strong evidence that the Ontario university system as presently financed and supplied is quite regressive. Although at the lowest income level it appears to be progressive, the number of graduates is too small to be significant. The principal net gainers from the university system are the middle-and-upper-income groups at the extense of the lower-income groups. In this sense the university system is a large public expenditure program in which the relatively poor groups tend to subsidize the relatively rich (p. 46).

Mehmet further stated that "if the elitist tendencies [of the university system] are socially or politically unacceptable," then policies have to be changed. He cited the example where students participating in law, dentistry, and medicine tend to be those "from well-to-do families," particularly in cases where their parents have similar professions. He suggested a point system with extra points for low-income-group students. Alternatively, aid should be given only to low-income students. Mehmet also argued that "the present system appears to favour students who do not work during the summer and who tend to repeat borrowing public funds to finance their studies" (p. 42).

A report entitled Accessibility and Student Aid (1971), carried out by a subcommittee of the Council of Ontario Universities, acknowledged that the effectiveness of a student aid program is reflected by the extent to which it is able to make post-secondary education accessible to all those with the necessary qualifications (p. 2). Furthermore, it stated:

> We believe the effectiveness of a student aid program is the degree to which the socio-economic mix of the post-secondary enrolment approximates that of the society as a whole (p. 3).

The report admitted that student aid cannot compensate for social and cultural biases in our society, but it is not unreasonable for one to expect that student aid programs would overcome the relative reluctance of students from lower socio-economic groups to undertake debt in financing their post-secondary education (p. 3).

How effective have student aid programs been? Many argue that student assistance programs have not succeeded in increasing the accessibility of lower SES groups in Canadian society. In John Porter's words:

> Perhaps the most widely debated aspect of the relation-ship between education and equality is the question of how it is paid for, particularly at the higher levels. We have seen extraordinary ingenuity in the attempts to measure and partition the costs and benefits between individuals and society. The debates have led to a variety of patchwork student aid programs, their promoters suggesting equality is being served. But the conclusion which is extremely important in the present context is that the less well-off contribute substantially in relation to their resources for educational services which they do not use or do not see as useful to them (Porter, 1979: 259).

In the ongoing debate on student aid, arguments developed against current student aid programs have focused on the key issues of loans, high tuition fees, students' ability to contribute, and expected parental contributions. It is claimed that these factors still act as hindrances to post-secondary education, most notably for individuals from low-income families (OFS, 1979).

Tuition Fees

A discussion of the role of financial factors in determining participation in post-secondary education would not be complete without some mention of the role of tuition fees. After all, tuition fees are the major visible expense first encountered by students once they enrol in post-secondary institutions. According to one MPP:

> Tuition represents another financial barrier to many students. Even though a grants and loan program is available, the fact remains that low-income children learn at a very young age that university or college education is very costly and therefore it is eliminated as a goal in their life.

> While I realise that tuition fees represent only a portion of the actual cost to the student and that living

costs represent a larger portion, it is none the less true that tuition fees are the most visible cost and if lowered and gradually eliminated the results would be, I am sure, increased participation by children of low-income families (Mr. Cooke [NDP], May 23, 1978: S-644).

A study conducted by Peter Leslie, and released by the Association of Universities and Colleges of Canada examined "the role of tuition fees in university financing" (p. iii). Leslie discussed the impact of fee reduction as it pertains to access to post-secondary education. He started with the premise that:

the usual rationale for a policy of reducing fees is the supposition that there remains significant financial barriers to attending university, and that student loans and grants cannot overcome those barriers as effectively as fee reductions. An implication is that if fees are kept down as much as possible, access will be improved and participation rates will raise. This may be judged important for its contribution for achieving equality of opportunity and to serving public purposes such as economic growth and cultural development (p. 340).

Leslie examined the argument of private versus social benefits of university education and concluded that this type of analysis would point towards an increase in fees, given that the intrinsic and extrinsic rewards of learning result in greater benefit to individuals. The social benefits of equal access for all did not seem relevant, since "the class composition of university students by no means matches the class composition of the 18 to 24 age group as a whole" (p. 341), because non-financial factors and high school attribution serve to eliminate students from aspiring to post-secondary education at a very early stage.

If we take into consideration program costs and the private versus social benefits argument, the issue of setting fees for different programs becomes significant.

For as Stefan Dupré has noted, Art students in Ontario during the years 1970/71 to 1977/78 paid something like 25 to 33 per cent of programs costs (depending on the year), whereas medical students paid seven to nine per cent. . . . those programs which can be expected to have the highest long-term financial payoff are precisely the programs which the student contributes the lowest percentage of the costs. . . . "There is no question that tuition fee determination in Ontario has totally ignored the issue of equity among students that is posed by the principle of benefits received" (Leslie, 1980: 342).

49

Losers and Winners

Thus, the suggestion of the Ontario Commission on Post-secondary Education that students pay one-third to one-half of the instructional costs would drastically increase tuition fees out of the range of some students, for in some professional programs students would be required to pay six times the fees of undergraduate arts students.

On the alternative of shifting costs to students so that students would bear a higher proportion of university operating costs than presently occurs, Leslie commented that "it involves also increasing the availability of student assistance to counteract the presumably adverse impact on access and participation rates" (p. 343). The earlier arguments that loans would assist in paying higher fees is considered especially unattractive by students from low-income families.

However, despite the arguments that tuition fees are barriers to access to post-secondary education, the government feels that this is a weak argument. The Minister of Education, the Hon. Ms. Stephenson (Conservative), stated it this way:

> There are a very large number of students in this province for whom the tuition fee is not a matter of concern when seriously considering post-secondary education. The tuition fee is really relatively small factor in the decision-making process. There are many other factors involved, and we are attempting to delineate those factors and to find ways in which they can be modified for the benefit of those students who would achieve benefit from a university education for themselves and for our society as a whole (March 25, 1980: 191).

Whether or not tuition fees are a large percentage of the total cost for students, tuition does affect the ability of the students to participate in post-secondary education. And as we suggested previously, the visibility and prominence of tuition fees interact with social, cultural, and regional factors and importantly influence the perceived ability of adolescents to finance their future post-secondary studies.

A great deal of the debate concerning equality of post-secondary educational opportunity has centred on financial barriers. Their reduction through the provision of student aid (OSAP) and policies regarding tuition fees (along with the provision of facilities) have been the basis of government policy concerning accessibility.

CONCLUSIONS

In this chapter we have examined the nature of the public debate over post-secondary accessibility in Ontario through an analysis of Hansard and reports of various influential governmental and non-governmental organizations. Over the past two decades or so, legislators and researchers have indicated a number of barriers to accessibility, including social, cultural, ethnic, regional, financial, gender, age, and physical barriers. These have tended to proliferate with increasing awareness of social inequality stemming from the social unrest of the 1960s and social science research which has documented the existence of such inequalities.

Throughout the decade, some groups, such as Native People, those of lowest social class, and rural residents, were consistently mentioned as being disadvantaged. Other groups, such as Francophones and women, were the topic of public debate as wider political events and changes made these groups more visable and important. Thus, our general view that the nature of the public debate over post-secondary education reflects changes in the broader society became even more plausible as our analysis proceeded. However, legislators were not only guided by national issues; they were also equally concerned with issues in their respective constituencies. Thus, it was possible to find representatives from Northern Ontario, or political parties whose major support was from a particular region in the province, making a case for better educational facilities for that area.

While a number of legislators (usually opposition members) have noted inequality at the post-secondary level, government policy has centred around the provision of physical facilities (an important concern in the 1960s) and the provision of student aid as cure-all solutions to documented structured inequality. Even in the late 1970s when the government acknowledged that the barriers to post-secondary education were not just financial, politicians continued to place emphasis on student aid. In this, they received support from reports which lauded the apparent commitment of the government to public financing of post-secondary institutions and students and which subscribed to a passive equality-of-opportunity orientation.

The government's insistence that the student assistance programs provide assistance to a "vast majority" of students from low-income families suggests that financial problems are seen to underlie all other factors. Would this be the reason why the government continues to focus on providing financial assistance when, by its own admittance, finance might not necessarily be the most important factor? At any rate, one can question why policy makers, having identified the importance of factors other than money, did not develop educational strategies to reduce social, cultural, and geographic barriers to accessibility. In the absence of more comprehensive policies, one wonders about the depth of commitment and priority assigned to equality of opportunity by the government.

That no simple solution exists to the problem of equity in educational opportunity is clear. Education necessarily involves all aspects of an individual's social life, not just the period immediately following high school. This is borne out by the Minister of Education's avowal, with the support of all legislators, that a "stratification study" be implemented.

This examination of the public debate alerts us to the fact that equality of educational opportunity continues to be a difficult debate issue. Although it has been noted that the solution to the accessibility problem is not only financial, since cultural and gender factors also play a role, recommended solutions have largely operated within a financial framework. For example, in the debates on the low representation of minorites, low-income students, and women, in post-secondary institutions, we see an emphasis on providing more grants or financial assistance to these students. We need to recognize that in addition to providing direct financial assistance, there should be a corresponding emphasis on overcoming those social, cultural, and geographical barriers which direct financial assistance cannot resolve. The next chapter reviews major empirical accessibility studies in Canada, and further documents, from a social science standpoint, the influence of stratification factors (e.g., class, ethnicity) in developing inequalities in educational opportunity.

Notes

1. In examining legislative debates we went back to 1956. This is an appropriate cut-off date since it was the start of the period (1956-59) of the last legislature before the 1960s. Also, coincidentally, it was the year John Porter accumulated data for his seminal work The Vertical Mosaic. Therefore, it was a period of significant activities which would lead us into the 1960s.

2. In these debates we assume that the degree to which existing social, cultural and economic issues get discussed is a consequence of various constituencies' needs and priorities. In addition, debates reflect party policies and a party's role in the legislature. But we recognize that government's approach to the issue of equality of opportunity will differ from that of the opposition parties. During the entire period (1956-1980), the Progressive Conservative party has been in power in Ontario, though at times it has formed a minority government. The chief opposition parties are the Liberals and the New Democratic Party. Unlike government-appointed policy committees, legislators have a responsibility

to their constituencies and thus will usually respond to local pressures and interest groups.

3. Mr. Wintermeyer (Liberal), Feb. 25, 1956. He specifically argued that student population from rural areas was decreasing due to the high cost of living (p. 60).

4. This argument continued into the 1980s. For instance, the following exchange took place on May 20 and 21, 1980. The exchange was during a Standing Committee meeting on "Estimates, Ministry of Colleges and Universities." The Committee was made up of legislators from all three political parties.

> Mr. Sweeney (Liberal): . . . This government is on record for a long time as saying that post-secondary education is open to all on an equal basis: it is the government's belief that this is happening. I want . . . to indicate, in fact, it is not happening; that there are studies to indicate clearly that there is a wide discrepancy in terms of availability of post-secondary education to many segments of our society; that there is research suggesting strong evidence that only a rather limited segment of society is able to take advantage of post-secondary education. . . .
>
> I recognize that post-secondary education is not for everyone and in terms of accessibility I am not a proponent who would say that everyone ought to go to university or college. For many it is not appropriate because of their particular desires. . . .
>
> But for those who have the ability, for those who have the desire, . . . there must be tremendous encouragement and support, more so perhaps than what we have given at the ages before we reach university or college. . . .
>
> Hon. Miss Stephenson (Conservative): . . . I do not disagree with Mr. Sweeney at all. The universities should deal with the brightest people, and I think in most instances they do. There is some concern within the university community that they may not be having the opportunity to deal with all the brightest people, as a result of increased persistence on the part of parents and others that some young people attend university when they might be more appropriately employed in some other area. . . .
>
> We are attempting to remove at least one barrier which may be present, as signified—not too clearly, mind you—by the Anisef study. That is that the prospect of the cost may dissuade a young person from considering a university education. We are moving to increase the distribution of information which will very shortly be available to senior students in the elementary

system in some appropriate form. They just need to be aware . . . that cost need not be a significant problem for young people who may have some difficulties in attending university. . . .

Mr. Sweeney (Liberal): I want to identify what I mean by an equal opportunity. . . . I accept the premise that there is indeed an equal opportunity to get to university and in, literally, any program, if one can meet the admission standards.

But accessibility and equal opportunity surely mean more that that. It means that the predisposition that is often required receives an assist and some incentive. It also means that we have to take a look at some of the things that may be inhibiting students from coming into university, and we have discussed a number of these. Money and concern over current economic conditions are surely factors, and parental and family attitude is another. Surely another factor is the kind of counselling and guidance that a student either does or does not get at the secondary school or in the upper grades of the elementary school.

When I talk about accessibility and equal opportunity I am referring to that broad range. I am not speaking just to the fact that the building is there, the programs are there and if you have the money and the ability you have the opportunity to get in. . . .

Hon. Miss Stephenson (Conservative): . . . There are, . . . a number of items which I believe have some bearing upon the decision making process involving young people in terms of selecting or rejecting university. . . .

Nonetheless, the parental attitude towards post-secondary education I think is of great significance in the choice made by the student. . . . The peer pressure which develops as a result of a number of different circumstances is yet another. So is the guidance process. . . . It has been said that our guidance has been directed in the past primarily by those who have a post-secondary education rather than anything else and therefore they could be directing more young people into post-secondary education rather than in other areas.

Mr. Sweeney (Liberal): . . . I also wonder whether we have guidance people in the schools who are sufficiently aware of the kinds of counterpressures on students. . . .

Mr. Cooke (NDP): . . . Does the minister agree that there is a problem with accessibility?

Hon. Miss Stephenson (Conservative): Within some communities, and certainly within some groups in our society. . . . accessibility is not necessarily related to financial matters as far as university is concerned. . . .

Mr. Cooke (NDP): You would agree that is one of the factors.

Hon. Miss Stephenson (Conservative): Yes, but I am not sure I would call it a problem of mental attitude related to the usefulness and desirability of a university education. . . .

Mr. Cooke (NDP): The problem is there is no equal opportunity for all people in our society. . . . (May 20, 21, 1980:pp. 388-89; 425-32)

5. The following is a listing of the organizations, commissions, and committees (and their acronyms) referred to this chapter:

AUCC - Association of Universities and Colleges of Canada

CAATs - Colleges of Applied Arts and Technology

COPSEO - Commission on Post-secondary Education in Ontario

CORSAP - Contingency Repayment Student Assistance Program

COU - Council of Ontario Universities

CPUO - Committee of Presidents of the Universities of Ontario

CSLP - Canadian Student Loan Program

ECC - Economic Council of Canada

EOB - Educational Opportunity Bank

OCUA - Ontario Council on University Affairs

OEC - Ontario Economic Council

OECD - Organization for Economic Co-operation and Development

OFS - Ontario Federation of Students

OLANG - Optional Loan and Need-Tested Grant Program

OSAP - Ontario Student Assistance Program

OSBP - Ontario Special Bursary Plan

OSGP - Ontario Study Grant Plan

OSWC - Ontario Status of Women Council

6. The major empirical works in the early 1960s included Porter's The Vertical Mosaic (1965) and Hall and McFarlane's Transition from School to Work (1962). See the review of major works in chapter 3.

7. OECD was originally founded in 1948; at that time it was named Organization for European Economic Co-operation. OECD consists of twenty-four member countries, including Canada, and attempts to promote economic and social welfare among its member countries. In 1976, the Education Committee of OECD published its Review of National Policies in Canada. It reported that during the 1960s Canada saw great progress in education. Student enrolments increased, and there were improvements in student-staff ratios and educa-

tion funding between 1960 and 1976. Access to post-secondary education also broadened in areas of vocational and
technical schools and community colleges, and the number of
part-time and mature students also rose. However, with all
these improvements, OECD reported that there were still
problems in the provision of equal educational opportunities
for all in Canada.

8. The following debate further reflects the concerns of the
legislators:

> Hon. Miss Stephenson (Conservative): Seminars have
> been held with the Guidance Counsellors' Association in
> order to inform them fully of the student assistance
> program. So not only do they have the information in
> printed form at hand, they are also told verbally about
> the need to give students this information.
> You are right. The materials are sent out. They
> are sent out widely as a matter of fact, in order to
> ensure that at least all the secondary school students
> are aware this kind of assistance is available.
> In spite of the best efforts to do this, there are
> still some students who obviously are not aware, and
> there are some who do not read what is made available
> to them.
> Mr. Cooke (NDP): What about the liaison officer you
> used to have? There was an OSAP liaison officer–
> Hon. Miss Stephenson (Conservative): We have been
> concentrating, as I am sure you are aware, on the
> French-language students because of–
> Mr. Cooke (NDP): I read in one of your publications
> that you have just hired someone.
> Hon. Miss Stephenson (Conservative): Yes, because of
> the relatively low application numbers from that com-
> munity within the university system. But we have been
> relying on our contacts with the guidance counsellors,
> with the publication material and with the information
> which is distributed through the guidance system to the
> students, to get that information out to the high
> schools. . . .
> Mr. Cooke (NDP): So you obviously think it is a good
> idea. Is there any thought of re-establishing an English
> officer to go around and do the same type of thing?
> Hon. Miss Stephenson (Conservative): At this point
> we will certainly look at it, but I am not sure that is
> the most appropriate way to inform young people. . . .
> Mr. Cooke (NDP): What about establishing liaison
> officers in some of the other languages to get more
> people from different ethnic backgrounds involved in
> our university system?
> Hon. Miss Stephenson (Conservative): The liaison
> officer has functioned with students rather than with

parents and one would assume that students who are graduating from secondary schools and are able to go to university would understand English or French.

Mr. Cooke (NDP): But one of the things we have to do is get to the parents, as I think you agree, at least by your opening statement and your response to Mr. Sweeney and myself.

Hon. Miss Stephenson (Conservative): The liaision officer's function in the past was not related to parents at all. I think there are other methods that we could consider in attempting to reach parents at an earlier age. Utilizing the elementary and secondary school systems would probably be more effective than attempting to establish a liaison officer who, in many instances, would have to visit relatively small groups in scattered parts of the province and might not be very effective.

Mr. Cooke (NDP): Do you have Ontario Student Assistance Program brochures and information on OSAP in various languages?

Hon. Miss Stephenson (Conservative): Just in English and French.

Mr. Cooke (NDP): It might be a good idea to put those in some other languages and distribute them at the elementary level as well.

Hon. Miss Stephenson (Conservative): For parental purposes, a booklet regarding OSAP, rather than a brief information brochure, in other languages might be interesting.

9. Commission on Post-secondary Education in Ontario (1972); Organization for Economic Co-operation and Development (1975); Anisef et al. (1980).

10. The current Ontario Student Assistance Program (OSAP) administered by the province provides assistance to Ontario university and college students through the Ontario Study Grant Plan, the federally-financed Canada Student Loans Plan, the Ontario Student Loans Plan, and the Ontario Special Bursary Plan. More precisely, assistance is provided through any one, or combination of the above-mentioned plans. For instance, the Ontario Study Grant Plan (OSGP) is particularly geared to undergraduate students from less affluent families. The Canada Student Loans Plan (CSLP) provides need-tested loan assistance to students up to the doctoral level of study at recognized post-secondary institutions throughout the world. The Ontario Student Loans Plan (OSLP) makes loan assistance available to students whose needs are not fully met by CSLP. In 1978-79 OSLP was extended to assist part-time (students enrolled in fewer than three courses), and full-time students. The Ontario Special Bursary Plan (OSBP) is particularly geared to needy part-

time students and special students like single parents and welfare recipients, and is applicable only to students who study in Ontario. Single parents compose a fair percentage of OSBP recipients.

Other essential features of the current Ontario Student Assistance Program (OSAP) are:

1) Any person who is enrolled, either full- or part-time (except for CSL), in a post-secondary institution and taking a program of study approved by the Ministry of Colleges and Universities, is eligible for assistance. All Canadian universities and all Ontario Colleges (including Quebec's CEGEPs), other Ontario public post-secondary institutions, and some registered private vocational (including hairstyling) schools are recognized for this purpose.

2) As of 1978, under the Ontario Study Grant Plan of OSAP, students are able to receive nonrepayable grants from the province as their first form of assistance during their first four years of post-secondary study. Prior to this time, students had to take on a $1,000 Canada Student Loan each year before they became eligible to receive a grant.

3) Under the Ontario Study Grant Plan, students have eight non-renewable eligibility periods, each varying from 10-19 weeks. In practice, students who qualify for grant assistance are only eligible to receive these grants for eight semesters or four years. Grant eligibility periods not used by the student cannot be credited to that student for future academic work.

4) In determining the students' eligibility for OSG, the calculation of costs includes allowances for tuition fees, books, equipment, instruments, living and travel costs and in some cases medical insurance premiums. Resources include summer and part-time jobs income, income from capital assets, percentage of parents' or spouse's income or assets investments and other income. The grant assistance amount is based on the difference between costs and resources.

5) Full-time students are expected to contribute to their schooling from their summer earnings, in this case actual earnings are taken into account. This revision of 1978, differs from earlier procedures under which students were expected to make a fixed contribution regardless of actual earnings.

6) Part-time students are expected to make a contribution to their schooling in proportion to the time they have available for employment. These students are more likely to qualify for OSLP than OSG.

7) To obtain grant assistance without any parental contribution as resources, the student must fit the OSAP definition of "independence". Present regulations stipulate that the student must be married or must have worked full-time for three years (including being a homemaker). This only pertains to getting OSG.

8) Since May 1977, students enrolled in two full-time summer-term courses are eligible for financial assistance. This excludes courses which students are repeating. Previously, students were required to take a minimum of three full-time courses.

9) Because of the four-year limit during which students can qualify for OSG, graduate students are ineligible for grants. However, they can qualify for loan assistance under the CSLP, and OSLP, and for scholarship under Ontario Graduate Scholarship Program on a merit basis.

10) Under the assistance programs students can qualify for "away" allowance. This means that they would be eligible to obtain assistance for board, lodging, and travel costs. Students who attend school while they continue to live "at home" have these costs built into the parental contribution table.

11) All loans received by students during their years of schooling are interest free (the governments pay the interest). Students are expected to repay their loans starting six months after they have ceased being a full-time student. Part-time students have their interest-free status reviewed periodically.

CHAPTER 3

Accessibility Studies: A Brief Review

Unfortunately, universal accessibility is but one of many areas where stated government policy is at loggerheads with actual fact. Universities in Ontario are quite simply not universally accessible. They are less accessible to females than to males; they are less accessible to those from the country than those from the city; they are less accessible to Franco-Canadians than to Anglo-Ontarians; but above all else, they are less accessible to those from lower-class backgrounds than to those from middle- and upper-class backgrounds - and in such dimensions that could prove a rude awakening to anyone who still believes in Horatio Alger stories of honesty, diligence, and perseverance being the sole ingredients necessary for success (Ontario Federation of Students, 1979:ii).

This quote and the analysis of equality of educational opportunity provided in Chapter 1 illustrate the desirability of evaluating accessibility of higher education in non-monetary terms. More precisely, the success of any society in providing universal accessibility must include a consideration of a number of social factors, including social class or socio-economic status, gender, ethnicity, and urban-rural location. In this chapter we briefly review a number of empirical accessibility-related studies.[1] These studies, whether national or provincial in scope, provide information on the impact of social factors on accessibility for Ontario for the period 1956-79 and empirically confirm the relevance of employing the social-stratification model, outlined in Chapter 1, in understanding accessibility.

Included in this review are the following works: (1) John Porter, The Vertical Mosaic: An Analysis of Social Class and Power in Canada, 1965; (2) Robert Rabinovitch, An Analysis of the Canadian Student Population, 1964; (3) Raymond Breton, Social and Academic Factors in the Career Decisions of Canadian Youth, 1972; (4) E. Clark, D. Cook, G. Fallis and M. Kent, Student Aid and Access to Higher Education in Ontario, 1969; (5) M. R. Porter, J. Porter, and B. R. Blishen, Does Money Matter? Prospects for Higher Education in Ontario, 1979; and (6) P. Anisef, J. G. Paasche, A. H. Turrittin, Is the Die Cast?

Losers and Winners

Educational Achievements and Work Destinations of Ontario Youth, 1980. For each work reviewed we will provide a brief description of the target population surveyed; the methods employed in gathering information; how key variables were defined; and a concise listing of the major findings as they relate to social class or socio-economic status, gender, ethnicity, and urban-rural location.

The studies listed above were selected for review in that they (1) represent major empirical and descriptive works that implicitly or explicity employ social-stratification assumptions; (2) provide information specifically relevant to Canada and/or Ontario; and (3) cover a span of approximately 25 years.[2]

Although detailed trends cannot be established on the basis of the studies reviewed here, broad patterns with respect to each social factor may be discerned. For example, if in 1965 and in 1980, significantly fewer economically disadvantaged adolescents enrolled in post-secondary institutions than middle-class adolescents, then the pattern of post-secondary enrolments by socio-economic status remains essentially similar over this time period. A measurement of subtle or exact change, however, is not feasible with the data at hand.[3]

1.   John Porter, **THE VERTICAL MOSAIC: AN ANALYSIS OF SOCIAL CLASS AND POWER IN CANADA, 1965**

Description of Study: Population, Methods, Variables

In The Vertical Mosaic, now a landmark work in Canadian sociology, Porter analysed the power and stratification systems of Canadian society. He argued that in industrial societies school attainment becomes an increasingly important resource for both the individual and society. The forces of industrialization result in demand for technically qualified manpower, and pressure is developed to transform the educational system. Democratic ideals require that an individual's occupational choice be based on abilities and interests; in fact, the Canadian class structure militates against equality of educational opportunities for individuals possessing certain social qualities.

Porter assembled a vast array of empirical data from different sources in analysing class and power in Canada. One part of this total effort was the analysis of the social-class origin of some 8000 university students, drawn from all provinces in Canada, who were attending universities in 1956-57. This survey was conducted by the Dominion Bureau of Statistics (DBS).

61

Losers and Winners

Porter classified the occupations of the university students' fathers, using the Blishen socio-economic index. This was a scale in which occupations were classified on the basis of the average annual income and average years of schooling of members of the occupation. Porter divided it into seven classes. Thus, class 1 included the higher professions; classes 2 and 3 consisted primarily of white-collar and some higher blue-collar occupations; class 4 contained some high-level blue-collar jobs and lower-level white-collar jobs; class 5 was the category of skilled trades; and classes 6 and 7 consisted mainly of semi-skilled and unskilled occupations. Porter also included a later survey of 11,858 Canadian university students conducted, as well, by DBS in 1961-62.

Major Findings

- About one-half of those university students surveyed in 1956-57 reported parental incomes of less than $5000; in 1956, 70 per cent of Canadian families had incomes of less than this amount.

- Children with fathers in class 1 constituted 11 per cent of the total sample of university students (1956-57), but only 1.4 per cent of all Canadian children at home in families with the male head in the work force.

- Children whose fathers were in classes 6 and 7 constituted 11.1 per cent of the university sample, but no less than 31 per cent of all fathers were engaged in class 6 and 7 occupations in Canada.

- Women students, on the average, came from higher income groups than did men.

- While 20.6 per cent of the students in Arts and Sciences had fathers who had completed university degrees, less than 4.6 per cent of all family heads between 35 and 65 had comparable educational achievements.

- The 1961-62 DBS survey essentially confirmed the results of the 1956-57 study.

2.   Robert Rabinovitch, **AN ANALYSIS OF THE CANADIAN STUDENT POPULATION**, 1966

Description of Study: Population, Methods, Variables

In 1965 the Canadian Union of Students conducted a detailed

survey of income and expenditures of Canadian university and college undergraduate students.

Data was collected for 1887 students in Ontario; the grand total for all of Canada (excluding three universities in Quebec) was 7611, yielding a 74.4 per cent response rate for the sample. The objective of this study was to collect social and economic background information on students currently studying at Canadian universities and colleges.

Socio-economic status (SES) was measured by using father's and mother's occupation, parents' income, and parents' education. However, these separate measures were not combined into a composite scale comparable to the Blishen socio-economic index used by Porter in analysing the 1956-57 DBS survey of Canadian university students.

Major Findings

- Analysis revealed that 19 per cent of students came from families with incomes in the $3000-$4999 range, while over 32 per cent of the Canadian family population fell within this range.

- While fully 48 per cent of the students' fathers were classified as either in professional, managerial, or proprietary positions, only 23.3 per cent of the Canadian population were comparably employed.

- At the other end of the occupational spectrum, 64.1 per cent of employed Canadians, but only 35 per cent of Canadian post-secondary students, came from families where the fathers were classified as holding "blue collar" or "working class" jobs.

- National figures demonstrated that only 5 per cent of Canadian male household heads graduated from university, while this survey indicated that fully 25 per cent of the student population had fathers who held university degrees.

- Gender was not directly discussed in relation to accessibility to higher education; however, in a breakdown of the student sample, the male/female ratio in all provinces was shown to be approximately two to one.

- There was a similarity between the percentage of Canadians residing on farms according to the 1961 census and the percentage of the Canadian university population whose home residence was a farm (approximately 11.4 per cent in both cases). For Ontario, however, only 7 per cent of undergraduate students claimed they lived on a farm.

- Small centres of population were grossly underrepresented in the post-secondary student population: whereas 19 per cent of the Canadian population resided in population centres of less than 1000 persons, only 3 per cent of the Ontario student population claimed a similar home residence.

3. Raymond Breton, **SOCIAL AND ACADEMIC FACTORS IN THE CAREER DECISIONS OF CANADIAN YOUTH, 1972**

Description of Study: Population, Methods, Variables

In a national study, conducted in 1965, of 145,817 Canadian secondary school students and 7884 teachers in 373 schools, Breton analysed the impact of psychological and sociological factors on career expectations and plans. Included were schools in each of the ten provinces, small and large, rural and urban, and schools of different types (e.g., academic, technical, commercial, etc.). The major premise underlying this study was that an adolescent's career development or his/her career intentions and decisions depended on a set of interrelated factors: social origin, present experience, attitudes (expectations, sense of efficacy), and preparedness (information, competence) with respect to dealing with the future.

Questionnaires were filled out by all students in secondary schools in the sample. Questions covered a range of areas including: school and program of study, educational plans, access to counselling, ideas and attitudes to work and the future, and background information on the respondent and his/her family. A mental ability test accompanied the questionnaire; principals and teachers were responsible for the administration of both. All teachers and guidance counsellors were asked to complete a separate questionnaire. A second series of briefer questionnaires was also completed by students and principals in the spring of 1966.

Socio-economic origin in this study was measured by the occupational status of the father. The 1961 DBS Occupational Classification Manual was employed to classify respondents' answers. The high SES category included managerial, professional and technical, clerical, and sales occupations; the middle SES category included craftsmen, foremen, and operatives; the low SES category included service workers, labourers, and farm workers.

The size of community (i.e., urban-rural location) was determined on the basis of the 1961 census. In the case of urban communities, the coding was done using metropolitan area rather than municipality data.

Losers and Winners

Students in "all-French schools" were classified as French speaking while students in "all-English schools" were classified as English speaking. This classification was initially derived from the principal's request for either an English or a French questionnaire.

Though Breton's study concentrated on vocational decision making among secondary school students, the results are clearly relevant to post-secondary accessibility since, in many cases, occupational plans entail educational plans and ambitions.

Major Findings

- The higher the father's occupational status, the lower was the likelihood of vocational indecision. But the relationship was weak, as indicated by the fact that the individual's SES had less importance for the vocational decision making than his own occupational expectations.

- The educational background of parents was unrelated to vocational indecision.

- Francophone students were more likely to be without a career goal than their Anglophone counterparts. This remained so when SES and mental ability were controlled.

- Fourteen per cent more high SES students compared with low SES students planned on completing secondary school; 12 per cent more of this high SES group planned to pursue a post-secondary education.

- The effect of community size (urban-rural location) in terms of completing secondary school was slightly weaker for girls than for boys. Thus, for example, 85 per cent of boys and 87 per cent of girls who lived in large urban areas, and 69 per cent of boys and 75 per cent of girls living in rural areas, planned on finishing high school.

- At comparable levels of mental ability, boys from urban areas were more likely to plan to finish high school and attend post-secondary institutions than boys from rural areas. For girls of high mental ability, there was virtually no relation between community size and plans for further education.

- Approximately the same proportion of Francophone and Anglophone boys were definite about finishing high school. The situation differed for girls with 83 per cent of Anglophone girls and only 74 per cent of Francophone girls planning on finishing high school.

- Francophone students (both boys and girls) displayed higher post-secondary aspirations than their Anglophone counterparts. These differences were especially evident in the lower-SES and lower-mental-ability groups.[4]

- SES was found to be positively related to a student's subjective evaluation of his intelligence, sense of control over events, and confidence concerning finding a job.

4. E. Clark, D. Cook, G. Fallis and M. Kent, **STUDENT AID AND ACCESS TO HIGHER EDUCATION IN ONTARIO, 1969**

Description of Study: Population, Methods, Variables

The first three social-stratification studies of the university student population reviewed in this chapter were conducted at the national level. Perhaps the first exhaustive study of accessibility in Ontario was conducted by E. Clark et al., who were then graduate students at the Institute for the Quantitative Analysis of Social and Economic Policy of the University of Toronto. This study was undertaken at the request of the Ontario government and was primarily designed to test the influence of financial and economic variables on accessibility to higher education. Data derived from questionnaires administered to 8700 male and female students enrolled in Grades 9 to 13 in twenty-five schools across Ontario in April 1969. A stratified sample was selected to ensure that it was representative of the secondary school student population in Ontario.

Socio-economic status was defined on the basis of the responses to fifteen income-related questions, including such variables as father's and mother's occupation, subjective and quantitative estimates of family income, and family consumption habits. Thus class 1 contained those students whose annual family income before taxes was less than $5000; class 2 contained those between $5000 and $8000; class 3 between $8000 and $10,000 and class 4 over $10,000.

Students were sampled from large urban centres with populations over 100,000, as well as medium (10,000-100,000) and small (under 10,000) centres. The authors then divided the student population into rural and urban sectors. The rural sector was further divided into rural I (family income below $8000) and rural II (family income above $8000). The urban sector was divided into four classes, by family income, as previously indicated (e.g., class 1 - less than $5000, etc.). Ethnicity was not evaluated in this study and, although gender information was obtained, its influence on aspirations and expectations was not given much consideration.

Losers and Winners

Major Findings

- Students at all SES levels agreed equally with the statement that a post-secondary education offers other than financial rewards.

- Only 38 per cent of urban class 1 and fully 69 per cent of urban class 4 Grade 9 students were found to <u>desire</u> a university education. With respect to <u>expecting</u> a university education, the percentages were 26 and 63 respectively.

- By Grade 12 the desirability of university education increased for all urban classes, ranging from 75 per cent for class 1 to 86 per cent for class 4.

- Only 25 per cent of class 1 students in Grade 9, compared with 65 per cent of class 4 students, responded that their parents encouraged them to achieve a university education.

- Students from class 4 almost exclusively entered five-year programs; only 13 per cent entered four-year programs. In contrast, 41 per cent of class 1, 35 per cent of class 2, and 26 per cent of class 3 selected four-year programs.

- Only 26 per cent of class 1 students reached Grade 13, compared with 36 per cent of class 2, 42 per cent of class 3, and 58 per cent of class 4 students.

- In Grade 9, 37 per cent of class 1 and 58 per cent of class 4 students had IQ scores exceeding 110.[5]

- Once in school, higher-income students, even with ability held constant, remain in school longer than low-income students.

- In Grade 9, 21 per cent of rural I and 31 per cent of rural II students were found to have the <u>desire</u> to enrol in university; 17 per cent of rural I and 22 per cent of rural II actually expected to enrol in university.

5. M. R. Porter, J. Porter, and B. R. Blishen, **DOES MONEY MATTER? PROSPECTS FOR HIGHER EDUCATION IN ONTARIO, 1979**

Description of Study: Population, Methods, Variables

In <u>Does Money Matter?</u> Porter et al. contribute to the ongoing debate concerning the effect of student aid on educational aspirations and attainment. The authors gathered questionnaire data in

1971 from 8548 Ontario students in Grades 8, 10, and 12 and also interviewed a number of parents.

The Survey Research Centre at York University pre-tested and carried out the field work of the Survey of Student Aspirations (SOSA) study. Schools throughout the province were stratified on a number of bases, including degree of urbanization, whether students attended English, French, or bilingual schools, and the type of programs offered by these schools. The response rate to questionnaires administered within 405 classes in 355 schools was generally excellent, ranging from 94 per cent for Grade 8 to 84 per cent for Grade 12.

Socio-economic status was measured through the use of the Blishen occupational index and based on the 1961 census; a detailed description of this index was given on page 48. Only six classes are employed in the SOSA study, compared with seven classes employed in the analysis reported in The Vertical Mosaic. In many instances, the SOSA study collapses the six classes into high (classes 1 and 2), medium (classes 3 and 4), and low (classes 5 and 6).

The urban-rural factor was derived within two subdomains (Anglophone and Francophone schools) and resulted in four strata based on size of jurisdiction of the board of education and degree of urbanization in the jurisdictions.

Students in French-speaking schools were oversampled, given the relatively low number of such students in the Ontario population. Even so, the sample sizes of Francophone students in Grades 8, 10, and 12 were only 346, 249, and 162 respectively. This, however, permitted some general comparison of Anglophones and Francophones in the SOSA study.

Major Findings

- The short answer to the question "Does money matter?" (i.e., does student aid affect educational plans and attainment?) is yes, especially for women and all but the very brightest in school.

- Sixty per cent of Grade 12 students in class 1 and only 24 per cent in class 6 expected to enrol in university.

- Twice as many high-mental-ability students (based on the application of a Culture Fair Ability test) from low socio-economic families expected to go to work after high school, compared with comparably bright students from families with high SES endowments.

Losers and Winners

- Among Grade 12 students of high IQ and high SES, 69 per cent aspired to enter university and 68 per cent expected to get there; 49 per cent of medium-status, high IQ students aspired to enter university and 46 per cent expected to enrol; among low-status, high IQ students only 38 per cent aspired to enter university and 35 percent expected to enrol.

- Seventy-three per cent of students with low mental ability from high SES backgrounds planned on finishing Grade 13; this was in contrast with 59 per cent of students with high mental ability from low SES backgrounds.

- Forty-two per cent of Grade 12 students from metropolitan areas aspired to enrol in university, compared with 27 per cent from rural areas. Comparable differences, of a lesser magnitude, characterized Grades 8 and 10.

- Social class was a more significant factor than rural-urban residence, since differences were greater among social classes when place of residence was controlled than among those of the same social class living in more or less urbanized areas.

- The most deprived group in Ontario in terms of educational opportunity were lower-social-class girls, particularly those with high mental ability.

- Girls were more disadvantaged than boys, because they were unlikely to be hired for the best paying summer jobs. In 1972, male students earned $1295 at summer jobs, and female students only $780.

- In classes 1 and 2 the male-female difference in the expectation to enrol in university was minimal; however, at the lower socio-economic level (classes 5 and 6), 30 per cent of males and only 18 per cent of females expected to attend university.

- Francophone students tended to come from larger families than Anglophones, and family size was causally related to the former group's lower educational aspirations.

- Proportionately more Francophone students were characterized by lower SES levels than were Anglophones.

- The parental level of aspirations was essentially similar for both Francophones and Anglophones; 53 per cent of the former and 48 per cent of the latter wanted their children to go on to university.

-        In terms of expectations, 39 per cent of Francophone and 49
         per cent of Anglophone mothers actually expected their
         children to pursue a university education. Consistent with
         this finding was the fact that proportionately more Anglo-
         phone parents (36 per cent) than Francophone (26 per cent)
         had made plans for financing their children's higher educa-
         tion.

6.   P. Anisef, J. G. Paasche, and A. H. Turrittin, IS
       THE DIE CAST? EDUCATIONAL ACHIEVEMENTS AND WORK
       DESTINATIONS OF ONTARIO YOUTH, 1980

Description of Study: Population, Methods, Variables

        This study examined the link between education and work in
Ontario as well as the accessibility to post-secondary education of
various social groups. Excluded from the accessibility analysis,
however, was a consideration of ethnicity. The study was based
on the fourth phase of a panel survey conducted in 1979. The
study began in 1973 with a survey of 2555 Ontario Grade 12
students and the objective of establishing their educational and
vocational plans. The most recent follow-up study in 1979
utilized a mailed questionnaire, and a shortened version of the
same questionnaire was administered by telephone to persons not
responding to the mailing; 1522 responded in all, yielding a 59.6
per cent tracing of the original cohort from the 1973 survey.

        Socio-economic status (SES) was based on five items in-
cluding: mother's and father's formal level of education; parents'
total income; mother's and father's occupations. An SES scale
was constructed with the use of these items, through factor
analysis. Urban-rural origin of respondents formed the basis for
the original selection of high schools employed in the panel survey; schools were drawn randomly from four strata. These strata
ranged from the most urban (i.e., Toronto) to the most rural
regions of Ontario (e.g., Blind River, South Porcupine).

Major Findings

-        High school program selection was strongly related to SES
         and urban-rural origin. Proportionately more respondents
         who selected academic programs came from higher SES back-
         grounds and the more urban areas.

-        Two in ten college (CAAT) enrollees, compared with almost
         half of university enrollees were from the highest SES level.
         College enrollees were spread fairly evenly across the class
         structure, while university enrollees were drawn heavily
         from the higher SES levels.

Losers and Winners

- SES was related to the importance of different sources of financing post-secondary education, with the Ontario Student Assistance and Canadian Student Loan programs as the second most important source (after summer earnings) for the two lowest SES levels.

- The proportion of young people with post-secondary educational experience varied strongly within the province: it was 74 per cent in Toronto, 67 per cent in other large and small cities, and 52 per cent in towns and smaller rural areas.

- Approximately 67 per cent of young persons who lived in rural areas, and even in the smaller cities, expected to leave home in order to pursue post-secondary education. The lower SES characteristics of such areas and their distance from post-secondary institutions posed a double hardship to their residents in terms of access to higher education.

- Summer earnings were a more important financial source for urban-origin post-secondary students than for those of rural origin; this suggested fewer good-paying summer jobs in small towns and rural areas than in urban centres.

- Gender and the selection of one's program of study were strongly related in both colleges and universities, indicating a kind of internal tracking based on sex.

- In financing their post-secondary education, men relied more heavily than women on summer earnings, while women were more dependent on parental support.

- Women fared more poorly than men in terms of enrolment in post-secondary education and enrolment in professionally-oriented courses within post-secondary institutions.

- While SES was moderately related to early job prestige, gender and educational achievement exerted stronger influences.

- The segregation of the labour market on the basis of sex appeared strongly to affect the kinds of jobs obtained by men and women. The majors and programs selected in university and CAATs seemed to feed into, and reinforce, the sex segregation of occupations.

- Women were found most in white-collar fields, irrespective of educational achievement; at the highest levels of educational attainment, men obtained higher-prestige, upper-level white-collar jobs more easily than women. At lower educational levels, women did better in terms of prestige (but not pay) than men, essentially shunning blue-collar jobs in favour of clerical and sales jobs.

A Concluding Note

The six accessibility-related studies reviewed in this chapter offer rich material that documents the social stratification effects on access to higher education. The findings across all six studies reveal that lower socio-economic status constrained, and continues to constrain, university-level aspirations of young persons in Ontario. Less influential perhaps, but still significant in its influence, has been the limit placed on the development of educational aspirations and expectations by one's place of birth. The post-secondary horizons of urban youth have been, and continue to be, wider in scope than those of rural youth. Although women's current participation in post-secondary education is dramatically higher than in 1956, there are a number of factors (including program choice and occupational attainments) that support the observation that women today still fare more poorly than men with respect to equality of educational opportunity. The information provided by the studies reviewed regarding cultural groups is far more sketchy; further empirical work is required before commenting in depth.

One important concluding note may be drawn as a result of reviewing these studies. With respect to the measurement of socio-economic status or social class (perhaps the most important feature of social stratification), the studies vary tremendously in the operational definitions provided. Rabinovitch employed disaggregated measures of occupation, income, and education; Clark et al. essentially employed an "income-related" measure, related, that is, to fifteen questions concerning occupations and income; Breton merely collapsed the census classification of occupations to derive an SES measure; Porter in The Vertical Mosaic employed the Blishen Socio-economic index with 7 categories , while Porter et al. in Does Money Matter? broke the Blishen index down into 6 classes or collapsed it into three major socio-economic classes; Anisef et al. derived a measure of SES by employing factor analysis on five separate indicators of SES. Suffice it to say that systematic comparison of these major accessibility-related studies with respect to socio-economic status is virtually impossible, given the different operational definitions of the concept. Naturally, variations in sample design and study methodology contribute to this difficulty.

Canadian trend studies relating to accessibility and Canadians in perspective are reviewed in Chapter 5. More importantly, a strategy for monitoring accessibility which also resolves many of the methodological problems discussed above is presented. This strategy is applied to 1971 and 1976 census data, and changes with respect to equality of results are analysed in the context of our social-stratification perspective.

Notes

1. These studies represent the major research studies on social factors affecting accessibility to higher education. Omitted are works like Pike (1970) which, although providing an incisive analysis of the concept and a summary of studies in the related area, does not offer original survey findings.

2. The reader should note that no attempt is made in this review to discuss <u>trend</u> changes with respect to various social factors (e.g. gender, social class, etc.). Several methodological problems inhibit this type of comparison: (a) the target populations sampled in each of the six studies vary; (b) sampling and weighting procedures employed also vary; (c) the measurement of variables (e.g., educational aspirations, plans, attainments) are different. Some of these problems might be overcome through a reanalysis of data sets, employing standardized operational definitions of variables. This could be a valuable exercise insofar as trend data would then become available, permitting an examination of change over a relatively long time span.

3. This is a major rationale for exploring the census in Chapter 5 as a basis for generating trend data as a means of monitoring accessibility.

4. The reader may wish to consult our discussion of ethnicity in the following chapter for insights into Francophone/Anglophone socialization differences. Additional articles pertaining to these cultural groups may be located in our annotated bibliography in Appendix C.

5. Although some may claim that middle-class adolescents are smarter at birth than their working class counterparts, most social scientists agree that there is a middle-class bias built into most IQ tests.

CHAPTER 4
Sources of Structural Inequality

INTRODUCTION

The review of major accessibility studies provided in the previous chapter clearly documents the impact that social-stratification factors (e.g., social class) have on the educational decisions made by young persons. In the next chapter we will provide empirical evidence that social-class disparities in educational attainment have remained constant in the 1970s, while cultural group and gender disparities decreased. With the remarkable educational expansion evident in the 1960s and the strong pledge by government to reduce inequalities in educational opportunity through grants, loans, scholarships, and special bursaries, one may well question the resistance of social class to various strategies of democratization.

As we argued in Chapter 1, efforts to aid persons financially at the point of entry to post-secondary education, sincere as they may be, primarily serve to remove external financial barriers to equal participation. By this late date, however, many economically disadvantaged persons have chosen vocational routes that do not require post-secondary education.

Our objective in this chapter is to discuss in some depth the sources of structural inequality in Canadian society in relation to social class, gender, and cultural origin or ethnicity. As we argued earlier, people selectively perceive opportunities. These perceptions are learned early in life and frequently create internal barriers, affecting school performance levels and post-secondary aspirations. What this implies is that any significant reduction in structural inequalities requires an initial understanding of the sources of these inequalities.

Insofar as the sources of structural inequality are aspects of learned behaviour we will employ the concept of socialization in explaining how families informally educate their children. After briefly treating the concept of socialization, we will present a literature review organized around socialization differences associated with: (1) social class, (2) ethnicity, and (3) gender.

Our review of literature regarding socialization processes and outcomes in the family will be highly selective. The research literature is huge (although mostly non-Canadian) and cannot adequately be dealt with in one brief chapter. For this reason an annotated bibliography is provided in Appendix C of this book. The major objective in presenting this selective review is to illustrate the relevance of early events in a person's life for later educational opportunities. In addition, a documentation of structural inequalities (e.g., social class, cultural, gender) per se provides little insight into the social dynamics or processes producing and maintaining such inequalities. By gaining an understanding of how families transmit beliefs and socialize their children to assume positions within society, more effective strategies for achieving equality in educational opportunity may yet be devised.

THE CONCEPT OF SOCIALIZATION

"Socialization" is a term social scientists employ in describing "the process by which individuals acquire the knowledge, skills, and dispositions that enable them to participate as more or less effective members of groups and the society" (Brim, 1966: 3). Insofar as socialization prepares individuals to take their place in society, it provides a major means by which social origin and educational and occupational destinations can be interrelated. In essence, an understanding of socialization processes is crucial for a meaningful interpretation of social stratification and social mobility. Infants do not choose their cultural or social origins. They are, in their early years, captive subjects and specifically exposed to the value orientations and expectations of parents. Moreover, the family plays a crucial role in the development of cognitive abilities, language facility, and self-concept of ability. How all these tasks are accomplished will vary and reflect, in large part, the social and cultural backgrounds of families.

In this discussion we do not wish to overemphasize the significance of early family experiences; to do so would suggest that the child moves out of his family into the larger society with firmly embedded values and a fully developed self-image. This is not the case. What we are suggesting, is that what is learned and how learning occurs early in life will strongly influence adolescent decision making at several critical junctures. One illustration might be the choice among different academic programs in high school. Although, in a democratic society, many early choices are reversible or alterable, they tend to structure future choices. Moreover, family differences in child-rearing practices mean that children entering schools are not only different but "unequal" relative to the middle-class yardsticks of performance, the yardsticks normally employed by public schools. How schools

75

take account of these differences and adapt to them as socialization agencies is yet another important area of inquiry in understanding the sources of structural inequality.

Socio-economic origin plays a crucial role in what is learned (e.g., values, beliefs, motivations) and how this learning takes place. Social-class differences importantly influence the nature and type of parental expectations for children, as well as the encouragement offered children in planning for the future. Recent studies also emphasize that acquisition of language skills is strongly influenced by social origin. Finally, the social development of the child with reference to clarity and security of self-image and self-concept of ability is influenced by socio-cultural beginnings.

In examining Canadian society we must not forget its multi-cultural nature. Families of different ethnic background emphasize varying cultural values in raising children; these variations imply different socialization outcomes relative to goal-striving, achievement motivation, and achievement values. Part of our literature review will focus on the interrelationship of cultural values and socialization processes among different ethnic groups.

Any parent casting a first glance at her or his newborn infant is immediately affected by one overriding fact, that is, the gender of the baby. This single piece of information has far-reaching consequences in terms of child-rearing practices and sex-role socialization processes. The latter, in turn, also contain important implications for equality of educational opportunity. Thus, the differences between boys and girls with reference to the early acquisition of values and motivations in the family of origin constitute another relevant area of inquiry in analysing sources of structural inequality.

LITERATURE REVIEW

Social Class

Values and Child-rearing Practices

Melvin Kohn published Class and Conformity in 1969 and argued the following thesis, nicely summarized in the second edition:

> The higher a person's social-class position, the greater is the likelihood that he will value self-direction, both for his children and for himself, and that his orientational system will be predicated on the belief that self-direction is both possible and efficacious. The

76

lower a person's social-class position, the greater the likelihood that he will value conformity to external authority and that he will believe in following the dictates of authority as the wisest, perhaps the only feasible, course of action (Kohn, 1977: xxvi).

The self-direction referred to by Kohn means "thinking for oneself", as contrasted with following the dictates of authority. One very important measure of social class is occupation, and naturally, across and even within all occupations there are wide-ranging opportunities for exercising personal discretion and being reflective. In evaluating his original thesis eight years later and the research studies it generated, Kohn essentially concludes that a "consistent and meaningful relationship between people's social class positions and their values and orientation" continues to be maintained (1977: xxv). Bronfenbrenner (1958), in studying the child-rearing practices of middle- and working-class mothers indicates that, since World War II, working-class mothers have tended to be more demanding of conformity and obedience from their children, while middle-class mothers are consistently reported as more acceptant and equalitarian. Insofar as working-class or blue-collar jobs typically involve routinized physical work which is strictly supervised and requires few interpersonal relationships, this emphasis in the family on obedience to rules is quite consistent with the assumption of later adult statuses (Kerckhoff, 1972: 44).

In seeking to explain why lower-class children, in comparison with higher-class children, tend to be less successful with school work, perform more poorly on exams, and develop lower educational and occupational aspirations, sociologists have explored the role of "achievement motivation" in addition to early socialization practices. They posit, for example, that: "there might exist different degrees of ambition or 'achievement motivations' between children of different social - and, incidentally, ethnic - backgrounds which are, in turn, linked to a complex body of values more supportive or less supportive of high educational and occupational attainment" (Pike and Zureik, 1978: 5-6). Some researchers concentrate on the cognitive and linguistic development among children of various strata (see section [b] following, while others focus attention on the content of socialization, that is, values relevant to academic performance and success (e.g., achievement, autonomy, independence). Hyman, for instance, used American data to demonstrate that working-class in contrast to middle-class parents tended to place less value on formal education, were less anxious for their children to remain in school, and less likely to express ambition for themselves and their children (Hyman, 1979). The basic thesis embodied in Hyman's and other empirical studies is that middle-class parents communicate a set of values and ideological perspectives on life which stresses educational and occupational success, which in turn produces higher actual achievement in school.

Losers and Winners

Bernard Rosen (1959) characterizes the typical middle-class family value system and child-rearing pattern as an "achievement syndrome". The internal impetus to excel in situations involving standards of excellence combine with cultural components or values emphasizing the implementation of achievement-motivated behaviour.

Social Class, Linguistic and Cognitive Development

Children not only learn values in their family but also acquire language skills. The level of such skill would appear to depend on family socialization. It has been explicitly observed that poor family backgrounds handicap children in terms of their acquisition of language acceptable in school (Ishwaran, 1979: 23). Since language is a threshold skill for virtually all school work (especially academic performance tests), children who are equipped with the sort of language used by teachers and text-books will enjoy a distinct advantage in most classrooms.

Recent research by sociologists specializing in socio-linguistics supports the notion that these advantages are primarily accrued by those children reared in middle- and upper-middle-class homes (Boocock, 1980:49). Basil Bernstein, an English sociologist, has been most influential (and controversial) in this area. He argues that social-class structures promote different linguistic systems. Thus, "the middle class, relative to the working class, place a greater emphasis upon the use of language in dealing with the person area. The working class, relative to middle class, place a greater emphasis upon the use of language in the transmission of various skills" (Bernstein and Henderson, 1974:283). Middle-class children learn an "elaborated" linguistic code, based on abstract general principles applying to any social situation, while working-class children acquire more of a "restricted" code, reflecting the more limited life situation of the working class. Bernstein also posits a relationship between language use and self-concept, with more positive self-concepts developing when language use is strongly oriented to persons (middle-class) rather than skills (working-class) (p. 286-87). Insofar as schools require middle-class language skills and attempt to develop interpersonal skills that are important in assuming adult statuses, the working-class student lacking these particular linguistic skills is ill-equipped to compete at school or, later, at work.

Hess and Shipman (1965) summarize the state of knowledge with respect to language use, parent-child relationships, and cognitive development, especially as it applies to lower-class children. They write:

> The picture that is beginning to emerge is that the meaning of deprivation is a deprivation of meaning - a cognitive environment in which behavior is controlled by

status roles rather than by attention to the individual characteristics of a specific situation and one in which behavior is not mediated by verbal cue or by teaching that relates events to one another and the present to the future. This environment produces a child who relates to authority rather than to rationale, who, although often compliant, is not reflective in his be- havior, and for whom the consequences of an act are largely considered in terms of immediate punishment or reward rather than future effects and long-range goals (p. 886).

Self-image

One very important consequence of the socialization process is the development of a self-image. A child not only learns who or what he is, but also acquires attitudes and feelings about himself that help distinguish the "self" from "significant others". The development of the social self is a process involving linguistic development, value acquisition, and the socialization influences of family, peers, and schools. Self-image is a view of oneself in relation to one's environment, and this environment includes the perception of an opportunity structure. Access to rewards in one's perception of an opportunity structure relate, in part, to the clarity and potency of self-image (Kerckhoff, 1972: 56). In families where the stress on achievement motivation and values is strong, the likelihood of developing a clearer, more competent self-concept is high (Clausen et al., 1968). Middle-class child-rearing practices provide more information and greater motivation for developing a clearer self-image. This fits nicely with our earlier discussion of the achievement syndrome. Lower-class parents relate to their children in such a way as to inculcate lower levels of achievement motivation and less of a desire to establish long-range goals. These children enter achievement-oriented schools and perform relatively poorly in exams, thereby reinforcing the development of an inadequate and less focused self-image.

Raymond Breton (1972), in a national study of Canadian adolescents, discovered that the intention to complete high school and attend a post-secondary institution was related to positive self-attitudes, including self-knowledge, self-acceptance, and a favourable subjective rating of mental ability (p. 129). Breton notes that:

> the adolescent's formulation of an educational plan and career-goal is based on his views of the future and of himself in relation to it. For some, self-knowledge may be the pivotal variable; for others it simply may be the self-concept of ability or the sense of control over the course of events; or it may be a combination of these attitudes (p. 382).

Losers and Winners

Coopersmith (1967), in a major study of pre-adolescents, demonstrated the consequences for young children of differences in self-esteem. He found that persons with high, medium, and low self-esteem live in a markedly different world. High-esteem children, for example, had more friends and found it easier to make friends; in groups they tended more to play leadership roles. Low-esteem children were more conformist, tended to be listeners, were more sensitive to criticism and rebuke. Those children high on self-esteem also had higher academic achievement and were perceived by others as being both academically and socially more successful.[1]

Research findings regarding self-image are by no means consistent or conclusive, given the diverse measurements of the concept and lack of standardization of research methodologies. But the importance of one's self-image in the socialization process and its consequences for educational and career decisions should not be underestimated. For educators and policy makers concerned with increasing equality of educational opportunity, programs directed at increasing the clarity, stability, and knowledge components of pre-adolescents' and adolescents' social selves offer a fertile area for future investigation.

Parental Aspirations, Expectations and Encouragement

Sewell and Hauser (1980), in reviewing their longitudinal research in the area of educational and occupational aspirations and attainments, have this to say:

> We were particularly interested in the effects of parents on the development and maintenance of their children's aspirations. Parents serve as models to be emulated, and they are constantly revealing their overt and covert evaluations and expectations through interactions with their child. We believe that it is the child's perception of the parents' intent to encourage or discourage his/her educational aspirations that is crucial to the development and maintenance of those aspirations (pp. 65-66).

Mackinnon and Anisef (1979), in examining the status-attainment process among young males in Ontario, found that socio-economic status continued to affect family encouragement towards higher education for secondary school students even when several other variables were held constant. In turn, family encouragement had an even more powerful effect on the educational expectations of these students. They found, in fact, that the influence of family was more than twice that of peers.[2]

It is clear that achievement-oriented children with strong ambitions to succeed come from families in which parents set comparably high standards. The likelihood is also high that parental expectation will vary with the families' socio-economic level. A classic study by Kahl (1953) of Boston high school boys pinpoints an important aspect of this process. Kahl's objective was to explain the educational goals of boys with different levels of IQ and social class. He found it easy to predict the educational goals of boys with high IQ and from high SES families. Similarly, predicting educational futures for low IQ boys from low SES families offered few problems. But what of high IQ boys from low-status families? Kahl conducted intensive interviews with boys subjected to these "cross-pressures". Half the boys were planning on going to college and half were not. His conclusion was that parents accounted for the difference in the boys' plans. Those boys planning on continuing their education had parents who were unsatisfied with their own position and thus applied steady pressure on their sons to do better. Kahl's study demonstrated the <u>independent</u> force of parental aspirations on children's educational aspirations and expectations. More recent research in both the United States and Great Britain lends support to Kahl's original research (Boocock, 1980: 72).

In an attempt to explore the relevance of Kahl's findings for Ontario, Anisef, Paasche, and Turrittin (1980) reanalysed panel survey data on 1522 persons who were Grade 12 students in Ontario secondary schools in 1973. Most of these persons have had ample time to fulfil original educational aspirations. Unlike Kahl, the researchers were unable to gather information concerning IQ, and thus grades achieved in Grade 11 were employed as a substitute measure for academic potential (or performance). The respondents were asked retrospectively to indicate the highest level (e.g., high school graduation, community college, bachelor's degree, etc.) of formal education their parents expected them to attain. The results are reported in Table 4.1. Table 4.1 strongly suggests that family expectations play a significant role in influencing the educational attainments of Ontario adolescents. At all academic performance levels in school and/or the family's socio-economic level, parents' expectations exert a clear and significant effect on their children's educational attainments. For example, low socio-economic status males with high marks in high school, and who were exposed to parents with high educational expectations, were 28 per cent more likely to enrol in higher education than peers whose parents had low educational expectations. This also holds for low SES women, but to a lesser extent. Parental encouragement makes a much stronger difference for high SES women with good grades. Even where the child's socio-economic background is relatively disadvantaged and his/her marks are low, a specific stress by parents to pursue higher education makes an emphatic difference in terms of educational outcomes. This result holds whether we consider males or females.

It should also be noted that low SES parents have less steering effect on their children than high SES parents. This

Table 4.1 Effects of Parental Educational Expectations on Children's Attainments, Controlling on Socio-economic Status and Academic Performance Levels

LOW SOCIO-ECONOMIC STATUS

	High Grades				Low Grades			
	(Males)		(Females)		(Males)		(Females)	
	Parental Expectations				Parental Expectations			
Educational Attainment	Low %	High %	Low %	High %	Low %	High %	Low %	High %
Post-secondary	60.0	88.0	70.8	85.4	7.8	58.6	41.4	66.2
No post-secondary	40.	12.	29.2	14.6	92.2	41.4	58.6	33.8
Sample size	20	67	48	82	77	87	58	80

HIGH SOCIO-ECONOMIC STATUS

	High Grades				Low Grades			
	(Males)		(Females)		(Males)		(Females)	
	Parental Expectations				Parental Expectations			
Educational Attainment	Low %	High %	Low %	High %	Low %	High %	Low %	High %
Post-secondary	36.4	96.0	31.8	95.7	25.0	87.5	31.3	83.5
No Post-secondary	63.6	4.0	68.2	4.3	75.0	12.5	68.7	16.5
Sample size	11	100	22	139	36	96	32	91

becomes apparent once the reader examines the upper and lower panels of Table 4.1. In most instances, the percentage gap in post-secondary attainments with respect to differences in parental expectations is significantly greater among high SES families. Although this is so, parents of economically disadvantaged children do have a significant impact on the educational decisions of their children.

Peer Groups

Of the socialization agencies outside the family, schools and peer groups have the most significant impact upon the development of children. In Canadian society, the importance placed on establishing one's independence and gradually assuming adult roles means that peer groups become increasingly significant as individuals move from pre-adolescence to adolescence.

In 1961 James Coleman's The Adolescent Society was published and presented the thesis that there exists, within schools, strong student peer cultures that subscribe to values and goals frequently at variance with those found in adult society. Peer culture, maintained Coleman, emerges as a consequence of a highly technological society where youth attend school and need not work, and acts as a main source of emotional support and solidarity - a function traditionally served by the family unit. Although the various peer subcultures (e.g., academic, athletic, popularity) within a school may tend to be controlled by students of well-off, middle-class families, the effect is mediated by the socio-economic composition of the school itself. Coleman writes:

> The leading crowd of a school, and thus the norms which the crowd sets, is more than merely the reflection of the student body, with extra middle-class students thrown in. The leading crowd tends to accentuate those very background characteristics already dominant, whether they be upper- or lower-class. A boy or girl in such a system, then, finds it governed by an elite whose backgrounds exemplify, in the extreme, those of the dominant population group. In particular, a working-class boy or girl will be most left out in an upper-middle-class school, least so in a school with few middle-class students (as quoted in Boocock, 1980: 219).

Research in Ontario high schools supports the presence of distinct peer cultures. Anisef et al., (1980) indicate:

> Academic performance is a significant value; over 3 in 10 respondents wanted to be remembered as a "brilliant student." Over one-quarter chose "leader in activities," nearly one-quarter chose "outstanding athlete," and fewer than 2 in 10 wanted to be remembered as "most popular" (p. 62).

Losers and Winners

Data gathered by Campbell and Alexander on American high school seniors in thirty high schools showed the effect of peers on academic aspirations. There was a clear consistency between the educational plans of individual respondents and the plans of the students they named as their best friends (Boocock, 1980: 224). The exact nature of the relationship between peer cultures and educational aspirations appears complex. Gender, region, and in some instances, socio-economic status need to be considered. For example, James (1980) writes:

> But when parental influence is taken into consideration social class background makes the interaction different between peers and students, and parents and students. In other words, while there will be positive relations between peer group aspiration and parental aspiration for students of higher social class background; the relationship will be different for the lower-class student (p. 62).

Although research concerning the nature of the impact of peer groups, both outside and inside schools, on an adolescent's academic aspirations is not yet conclusive their influence cannot be underestimated. If the distance between family and peers does increase as we climb down the class ladder, this lack congruency may well affect strategies for alleviating inequalities in educational opportunity. In addition, family instability, as illustrated by the increase of single-parent families, may signal, for a larger number of adolescents, the increased importance of peers in making crucial educational and career decisions. Clearly, this is an increasingly important area for further investigation.

Ethnicity

Ethnic groups "consist of those who conceive of themselves as being alike by virtue of their common ancestry, real or fictitious, and are so regarded by others" (Shibutani and Kwan, 1965: 47). In Canada this common ancestry has generally been defined, for statistical reasons, in terms of the individual's male ancestry. In its everyday use, however, the concept may include citizenship, national or cultural origins, race, religion, or some combination of all these traits.

Although the two major charter groups have persisted as major entities in terms of numerical strength, four distinct phases of immigration have made Canada an ethnically diverse country (Ramu and Johnson, 1976: 216). Large differences in value systems, life styles, and life goals accompany such diversity and frequently present problems of adaptation, both for recently arrived immigrants and the host society. The latter is under constant pressure to develop new strategies for accommodating and assimilating its new arrivals.

Losers and Winners

Within recent decades, Canada's public policy statements indicate an ideological bent in favour of "pluralism" or "multi-culturalism". Essentially, such policies favour the maintenance of distinctive linguistic and cultural identities rather than employing the "melting pot" accommodation model of the United States (Carlton et al., 1977: 120-21). Rather than infusing diverse ethnic groups into the larger, dominant culture, through a process of Anglo-conformity or assimilation, in Canada ethnic groups may sustain their own institutions and therefore their cultural uniqueness. Driedger and Church in a study of Winnipeg found, for example, that both French and Jewish Canadians maintain a considerable degree of "institutional com-pleteness" (Ramu and Johnson, 1976: 221). This policy of multi-culturalism may, however, promote certain inequalities among minority or ethnic group members insofar as the schools with persons from such backgrounds may produce students unable to cope with the social and economic requirements of the larger system. Vallee and Shulman (1969) suggest that:

> the more a minority group turns in upon itself and concentrates on making its position strong, the more it costs the members in terms of their chances to make their ways as individuals in the larger system. . . .

> Among ethnic minority groups which strive to maintain language and other distinctions, motivation to aspire to high-ranking social and economic positions in the larger system will be weak, unless, of course, it is characteristic of the ethnic groups to put a special stress on educational and vocational achievement (p. 95).

If parents of minority or ethnic-group children socialize their young in a manner that diverges sharply, in terms of values and goal orientations, from techniques generally employed by majority-group parents, certain educational and work options may be curtailed when pre-adolescents mature. Children, unschooled in middle-class success values and the appropriate child-rearing practices that contribute to high-status attainment, may find that they are, indeed, unequal at the "starting gate", namely, elementary school. For instance, Bernard C. Rosen compared Greeks, Jews, Italians, and French Canadians in terms of the relative strength of the "achievement ethic" held by members of these ethnic groups. Italians and French Canadians were found to be significantly less achievement-oriented and less likely to pursue a higher education than the other ethnic groups (Pike, 1970: 77). This difference holds true even if we control for social class. Thus, A. J. C. King has also shown that grade retention rates were highest among Jewish children and lowest among French-speaking children (Pike, 1970: 77). On the other hand, Danziger, in analysing patterns of socialization among predominantly lower socio-economic status Italian immigrant boys in Toronto, challenges the notion that a strong commitment to a family-oriented ideology and a suspicion of intellectual matters acts to block upward mobility. He concludes:

> For the immigrant boy, on the other hand, the family is clearly an important source of motivational influence, and the stronger his family solidarity the more effective this influence is likely to be. His aspirations are not simply individual goals but represent the goals of his primary group and his concern to be worthy of them. The immigrant child's family is much more likely to be a source of motivational strength than of weakness. This fact will often counter balance the inability of foreign-born parents to provide the child with all the cognitive skills needed in the new society (Pike and Zureik, 1978: 156).

This "culturalist" view of the positive effects of family solidarity on producing motivational strength among Italian adolescents is at odds with traditional analyses of Francophones and Franco-Ontarians. Léon Gévin, in attempting to explain the lower educational levels of French Canadians in relation to British-born Canadians in the late nineteenth century, turned to family socialization differences for an explanation (Curtis and Scott, 1979: 243-44). According to Gévin, Anglophone families helped develop initiative, craftsmanship, respect for knowledge, a love of work, and competitive individualism. For French Canadians, solidarity and a sense of belonging were of paramount importance, and personal ambition or competitiveness could be sacrificed to sustain these values. Ann Denis points out that although Quebec's "Quiet Revolution" has decreased the salience of these goals, attitudes, and values, cultural differences in Quebec between Francophones and Anglophones remain. She states:

> Where it has entailed sacrifices in personal life, achievement in a competitive work situation has not been highly valued by French Canadians. They have tended to prefer jobs which did not make great demands in terms of overtime, resulting in neglect of their homelife, and also jobs in smaller firms where relationships were on more of a particularistic basis (Pike and Zureik, 1978: 228).

The situation for French Canadians outside of Quebec is also seen to be quite distinct. An Ontario study indicated that lower levels of educational attainments of Francophones related closely to the perceived threat of public school to themselves and their culture (Curtis and Scott, 1979: 245). In fact, no other ethnic group in Ontario finds itself in a situation as conflicting as French Canadians. As Guy Rocher comments, "For the latter, the public school is in open contradiction with both their national identity and their fundamental values" (Curtis and Scott, 1979: 245).

Johnstone (1969) investigated young people's perceptions of the Canadian opportunity structure and found that Anglophones were more likely than Francophones to think a university education important for getting ahead. Francophones felt that bilingualism would help more than academic achievement in overcoming inequalities in condition. However, Breton in a national study of Canadian adolescents discovered that French students of low SES were more likely than English students of comparable status to aspire to white-collar jobs, regardless of mental ability (Tepperman, 1975: 130).

In Canada, we have just begun to scratch the surface in revealing the unique attributes of our diverse cultural groups and how the constellation of values, beliefs, and family practices that characterize such groups interact with the major ideological structures of Canadian society. Essentially, we should question the implications of fully implementing multicultural policies for sustaining an open society where contest forms of mobility are the predominant avenue to upward social mobility. Do all ethnic groups want to participate? Should they or must they? To succeed in Canadian society and to adhere to widely accepted standards may require relinquishing some valued practices. Then, again, as Danziger indicates, seemingly contradictory elements may, in fact, produce positive effects. Stodolsky and Lesser (1967), in studying the relative influence of social and ethnic groups on mental ability patterns, concluded that certain cultural groups may nurture special attributes and skills, and thus the pursuit of equality in educational opportunity may not be bolstered by imposing uniform standards of learning on all children. These questions, and the somewhat sketchy research literature relating to socialization processes (e.g., family, peer groups, school) typically found among first-, second-, and third-generation members of diverse cultural or ethnic groups, mean that specific predictions and policies relating to the effects of ethnicity on equal opportunity must await additional research.

Sex-role Socialization

. . . I believe that the Women's Movement has a long, hard struggle before being able to proclaim a major victory. Whether we consider accessibility, equality of opportunity within post-secondary institutions, or the consequences of acquiring a higher education, women fare more poorly than men. Proportionately more women, in spite of generally superior academic performances, are tracked into vocationally-oriented CAAT's where they primarily train in female dominated programs for placement in sex-segregated occupations.

> The situation of women in universities is no different. Sex stereotypes occur and women are still attracted to programs such as household sciences, nursing, fine, applied, and performing arts, psychology, sociology, etc. Insofar as these programs are hardest hit in times of economic recession, women are most likely to suffer the brunt of unemployment crises (Anisef, 1980:12).

Whatever measure of equality of condition is employed in contrasting the social and economic positions of men and women in Western society, there can be little doubt concerning the relative success of men. Some scientists have maintained that differences in status and achievements between the sexes are best explained by innate (biological or genetic) differences (Boocock, 1980: 85). Maccoby and Jaklin, in reviewing well over one thousand studies on sex differences regarding intellectual abilities, motivation, self-concept, and social behaviour, concluded that for only four traits is there any convincing evidence for differences not attributable to culture or education. While girls appear to have greater verbal ability than boys, boys' visual-spatial and mathematical abilities exceed those of girls. Finally, boys do appear to be more aggressive than girls in both physical and verbal terms (Boocock, 1980: 88-89).

Although the nature-nurture controversy continues, gender-role socialization, or the processes through which individuals learn to become masculine or feminine according to expectations current in their particular society, is an important starting point in grasping the aspiration differences (Ishwaran, 1979: 137). Mackie has this to say concerning sex-role differences in Canadian society:

> . . .the organization of the pivotal family and work institutions indicates that men are expected to work outside the home, marry, and support their families, while women are expected to marry, carry the major responsibility for child-rearing, and rely on men for financial support and social status. For women, attracting a suitable mate takes priority over serious occupational commitment. These future adult activities require cultivation of appropriate skills, attitudes, and comportment in children (Ishwaran, 1979: 137).

This passage and others (Carlton et al., 1977: 299) indicate that attitudes in Western society in the 1970s regarding the appropriate educational position of women, although altering on an absolute basis, have not changed drastically, relative to men. To understand this lack of substantive change we must grasp the role of parents, peers, and schools in sustaining sex-role differences.

Losers and Winners

Lambert's study of sex-role images documented the relationship of parents' education and social-class position relative to the
parents' perception of roles (Ishwaran, 1979: 148). Generally, the
less their education and the lower their socio-economic position,
the more traditional were parents' views. Porter et al. (1979:
104) indicate that parents usually support and show greater
interest in their sons' education and training. Low social-class
standing exacerbates inequalities for girls inasmuch as far fewer
lower-class girls than boys aspire to a university education. To
a large extent, lower-class parents are less willing to support
their daughters financially than they are their sons. Since
summer jobs are harder to come by and pay less for girls than
for boys, females' aspirations are dampened. Breton, in his
study of Canadian adolescents, showed that girls are more likely
than boys to be without a career goal. However, this male-female
difference cannot be explained completely in terms of parental
aspirations: gender differences remain when parental aspirations
are statistically controlled (Tepperman, 1975: 169). Thus, although childhood socialization produces marked gender differences
from birth, a simple model that attributes exclusive importance to
the family avoids the complexity of the process (Ishwaran, 1979:
141). A recent analysis by Turrittin et al. (1980) indicates this
complexity as follows:

> Clearly, then, in addition to the greater encouragement
> to continue education given by higher SES families,
> there is a gender bias in encouragement. Girls receive
> less overall encouragement than boys, and support
> seems not to be related to academic achievement but
> rather contingent on having entered an academic pro-
> gram in high school, with such family support having a
> greater ultimate impact on girls than on boys with
> respect to ultimate educational attainment (p. 15).

For some time, social scientists argued that sex differences
in achievement orientation was to be explained by the greater
"task orientation" of males and greater "person orientation" of
females (Boocock, 1980: 91). Recent work tends to discredit this
claim; if anything, males are more subject to "peer effects" than
females. Further, research evidence does not indicate less
achievement orientation for females than for males. However,
although girls' motivations may equal those of boys, girls may be
exposed to a "double bind" situation that affects their ultimate
achievements. Although wanting to succeed in school, their
realistic appraisal of life chances and a fear that high achievement
may bring social rejection, not approval, present a dilemma not
easily resolved.

At the early stages of schooling, girls primarily encounter
sympathetic female teachers. These teachers are more supportive
of girls than they are of the more aggressive and active boys.
Elementary school is seen mostly, then, as a "feminine" environ-

ment by elementary children (Carlton et al., 1979: 299). Pyke also documents the presence of texts, in early grades, that downplay female creativity: males outnumber females as protagonists, are pictured in traditional (superior) roles, and are presented as aggressive rather than passive (Carlton et al., 1979: 430). Pyke summarizes many of the disparate findings relative to school socialization:

> . . . it is not unreasonable to conclude that male students capture more of the teacher's attention than female students. This is true for both male and female teachers and particularly the case with high-achieving boys in post-elementary grades. This differential attention seems to encompass not only the delivery of positive and negative effect but also more instructional contacts. Over-responsiveness to boys may reflect a positive bias toward boys and/or be generated by the more assertive behavior of male students. From a socialization standpoint, teachers seem to be rewarding male students by providing attention (positive, negative and instructional). On the other hand, they seem to be reinforcing passivity and dependence in girls by ignoring them or attending to them only if they are under the teacher's nose (Carlton et al., 1979: 433).

Richer (1977), through observational studies of Canadian kindergarten children, provides good examples of how schools reinforce sex differences. He found that lining up to move from one activity to the next was usually done by sex, or teachers assigned a "boys' leader" or "girls' leader". To motivate participation or completion of tasks, teachers might ask, "Who can clean up the fastest, the boys or the girls?"

Our discussion of sex-role socialization should not be taken as a glorification of the male role in today's society. Boys who are exposed to an early feminine school environment that emphasizes conformity and obedience must cope with inflexibility and rigidity. At later grades, where male teachers begin to predominate, boys are encouraged to be competitive. At the same time, for girls, intellectual interests and potentialities are increasingly repressed as they move from elementary to secondary schools. The pressure on boys to excel or achieve and the parallel pressure on girls to avoid unfeminine competition cannot, and should not, be invidiously compared. Both groups suffer inequalities in opportunity as a consequence of sex-role expectations, although females are more subject to pressures that would result in disadvantaged conditions.

This brief review of sex-roles socialization is designed to illustrate the relevance of gender in addressing the issue of inequalities in educational opportunity. Our concluding suggestion is nicely expressed elsewhere:

Our analysis suggests that a concern with equal opportunity and its relationship to quality of life be expanded to not only include but emphasize gender. The marked differences among men and women displayed in our study reflect basic differences in the society-at-large and in our schools. Since schools are provided with a mandate to inculcate core social values, a more complete understanding of how they go about transmitting (or perpetuating) these values to girls and boys calls for in-depth analysis of this process. Hopefully, this increased understanding will suggest strategies for increasing the equality of result among men and women (Anisef, 1980: 12).

CONCLUSION

This review of various sources of structural inequality (e.g., socioeconomic status, ethnicity, gender) illustrates that financial accessibility is only one of many potential obstacles experienced by adolescents in planning their educational and occupational future. Social scientists continue to document the important effects upon school performance and academic potential of social class, cultural origin, and sex-role socialization. Thus, lower-class children are less likely than middle-class ones to entertain the idea of a university education. The fact that future tuition fees act as an unsurmountable psychic barrier is not the only reason for this decision. Rather, a whole chain of subtle and not so subtle socialization effects create, within the mind of the lower-class adolescent, images of appropriate future social positions he/she should and could occupy. Parents, peers, and school agents frequently transmit consistent messages and social values that help form "realistic" expectations which exclude the decision to enrol in post-secondary institutions after high school. The adolescent is exposed to the cultural values commonly associated with particular ethnic groups or gender, and these, too, can act as a motivational barrier in the formulation of post-secondary aspirations. As we indicated in Chapter 2, the provision of grants, loans, and scholarships to disadvantaged groups of students rapidly became the short-run, apparently easy solution for ameliorating inequalities in educational opportunity. Reducing the underlying sources of such inequalities is a more complex and difficult task, as this review should indicate.

Notes

1. One can, of course, question the direction of the relationship between academic and social success and self-concept. For example, do people like confident persons, or does being liked give more self-esteem? It is likely that such relationships work in both directions.

91

2. Other research (e.g., Picou and Carter, 1976) indicates that how one measures "influence" is important in assessing the relative strengths of peer and family encouragement regarding higher education. When verbal measures of influence are employed (as in Mackinnon and Anisef's study), family encouragement is more important, but when role modelling is employed (i.e., when friends plan or actually attend post-secondary institutions), peers have about the same influence as parents.

CHAPTER 5

Monitoring Trends in Accessibility: A Census Strategy

The social-stratification perspective employed in this book draws attention to structured inequality and the way in which such structured inequality is maintained - and thus, perhaps, the way in which it can be reduced. Our general argument is that differences in socialization processes occurring relatively early in life affect an individual's likelihood of attaining post-secondary education, and that those socialization processes are related to dimensions of stratification like social class, ethnicity, and sex. In this view, policies aimed at decreasing structured inequality which intervene relatively late in the educational process - those aimed at reducing financial barriers through student aid or altering tuition fees and the like - are doomed to relative ineffectiveness. In this chapter, our goal is to provide recent documentation of the effect of structural inequalities on post-secondary educational attainment in Ontario. To what extent do social class and ethnic background affect university and college involvement? Has this altered over the five-year period from 1971 to 1976? Do part-time students differ from full-time students in family background? On which dimensions of stratification has progress been made, and on which has there been little improvement?

Our strategy for monitoring such changes in Ontario involves use of special computer runs of the 1971 and 1976 censuses by Statistics Canada. In spite of the fact that, as our earlier review of literature has shown, a large number of empirical studies in Canada have reviewed the socio-economic, cultural, demographic, and other background characteristics of persons enrolled in post-secondary education, few have actually shown temporal trends in accessibility. With our census strategy, it was possible to compare university and post-secondary non-university (PSNU) participation rates of groups differing in parental education, mother tongue, and gender. Specifically, we examine, for males and females separately:

- the university and PSNU attainment rates for those of different levels of parental education.

- the university and PSNU attainment rates of different mother tongue groups.

- the parental education and mother-tongue composition of part-time university and PSNU students, full-time university and PSNU students, and the general population aged 18 to 21.

The rationale and methodology for the monitoring of temporal changes in structural inequalities in post-secondary educational enrolments is described in detail in the Technical Report available separately from the Ontario Ministry of Education/Ministry of Colleges and Universities.

To summarize, it was our judgment that special runs from the full census were required to form an accurate picture of trends in accessibility in Ontario. This involves identifying those variables asked identically in 1971 and 1976 and having Statistics Canada process the census data similarly, for the entire population which filled out the long form of the census. In our view, a similar strategy can be employed for monitoring accessibility patterns by using census data in the future.

For the reader not desiring to follow some of the details of the discussion, summaries appear at the end of each section of analysis . Longer notes, or notes of a technical nature regarding this chapter are found in Appendix B.

AN EQUALITY-OF-RESULTS ORIENTATION

Throughout this chapter, an equality-of-results orientation, as outlined in Chapter 1, is taken. Equal opportunity is assessed by measuring equality of student outcomes - in this case, the rate of enrolment or attainment of post-secondary education among different social-class or mother-tongue categories.[1] The unit of analysis is the group. Equal participation rates among different subgroups in the population is the implied ideal. Equal subgroup participation rates, of course, do not mean that equality of opportunity within groups or among individuals has been obtained. Within larger groups such as males and females, there might still be differences between smaller subcategories such as females with English mother tongue versus females with French mother tongue. However, it was not possible to obtain subcategory participation rates because of limitations associated with sample size and the costs of such special runs.[2] In most of the analysis in the chapter, differences are examined for only one variable at a time, for males and females separately.

Assessment of the relative sizes of the participation rates of subgroups in Ontario needs to be supplemented with consideration of the absolute size as well. Relatively equal participation rates may be low, moderate, or high in absolute size. Should our

94

post-secondary educational system attempt to cater to a large number of persons (mass accessibility), or should we be concerned, simply, that any person has the same chance at a small number of post-secondary positions (elitism)? Regardless of our views, we would probably agree that those persons selected, whether few or many, ought to be chosen on the basis of individual achieved merit (e.g., grades), rather than ascribed criteria like sex, ethnicity, or social class.

While our data are meant to measure trends in the operation of such ascribed criteria in post-secondary participation, we have not, of course, been able to control for differences in intelligence. This does not mean that we accept the nature side of the nature-nurture controversy. If we did, we would have to indicate which subgroups were smarter than others, and adjust our expectations regarding participation rates, given the ideal of meritocratic selection based on intelligence. In general, we do expect that social-class and mother-tongue groups are approximately equal in innate intelligence, though it would be hard to show this since the literature (e.g. Jencks, 1972: 64-77) indicates it is hard to distinguish nature from nurture effects. Thus equal group participation rates would signify equality of opportunity only if we assume a general equitable distribution of intelligence among social and ethnic groups.

Persons not subscribing to an equality-of-results orientation may argue that subgroup differences in post-secondary participation rates reflect voluntary choices and decisions, not a dearth of opportunity. A person can choose not to avail him/herself of an opportunity for personal reasons, or because of general cultural attitudes or alternatives perceived as better elsewhere, as seen in our earlier discussion. However, as we pointed out in Chapter 4, a large body of literature suggests that early socialization experiences tend to determine subsequent educational motivation and attainment long before an individual reaches the point where a specific decision to go to university or community college is made.

Finally, it is important to note that the focus on educational attainment or participation rates implicitly suggests that this is an important end in itself. If equal group participation rates indicate equality of opportunity, the question arises, Opportunity for what? Unfortunately one cannot assume that, if participation rates appear to be relatively equal among subgroups in the population, subsequent occupational outcomes will also be equal. However, as Chapter 2 indicated, equality of educational opportunity in itself has been an overriding educational goal for Ontario.

In taking an equality-of-results orientation, we recognize that many questions regarding equality of educational opportunity are left unanswered. Importantly, however, we are explicitly presenting some of the assumptions made in subscribing to the equality-of-results orientation.

DATA AND METHODS

As our earlier review of literature in Chapter 3 has shown, a large number of empirical studies in Canada have reviewed the socio-economic, cultural, and other background characteristics of persons enrolled in post-secondary education. For the most part, these studies have been one-time affairs, measuring the background characteristics with whatever metric was deemed suitable for the occasion. Few replications have been done. While valuable cross-sectional data have been obtained, one-time surveys do not generally lend themselves to monitoring trends in the accessibility to post-secondary education over time, one of the major goals of this chapter. The few trend studies that have been done in Canada are reviewed in note 1 of Appendix B, with a particular emphasis on the method employed for analysing patterns over time. In general, this research has been relatively unsophisticated and has led to very tentative statements about changing patterns of post-secondary participation among different social and cultural elements of Ontario society. Importantly, the Harvey (1977), Von Zur-Muehlen (1978), and Pike (1970) studies do not provide feasible methodologies for ongoing examination of temporal trends in accessibility.

For our own analysis, specially designed computer runs of data from the long-form census questionnaires given to one-third of the population were obtained from Statistics Canada. These special runs were employed to assess recent Ontario trends in the socio-economic and cultural background of post-secondary students. A careful assessment of the 1971 and 1976 census information yielded two variables which were considered comparable enough for valid time trend analysis. These were parental educational attainment, a proxy for social class, and mother tongue, an indicator of ethnic origin. Both of these variables are discussed in greater detail later in this chapter.

In order to focus on post-secondary educational accessibility, we selected the 18 to 21 age group for analysis. It is true that some persons younger and older than this range attend post-secondary educational institutions, but because our concern is with major trends in accessibility, the 18 to 21 age group was considered most appropriate. Others have examined a wider age range (e.g., 18- to 24-year-olds by Leslie, 1980), but by focusing on the younger cohort, a greater proportion are classed as children in the census and thus information on parental background is available. Clearly, however, few persons aged 18 to 21 will have completed university, and the data will be of little help

Losers and Winners

in assessing accessibility to graduate and professional programs at university. All in all, the 18 to 21 age group provides us with a key group for whom post-secondary non-university, and under-graduate university education are relevant.[3]

Analysis of the Public Use Sample Tapes (PUST) data (Table 5.1) shows that the 1971 population aged 18 to 21 was very similar to the 1976 cohort in terms of sex, marital status, mother tongue, and age composition. Age is not shown in Table 5.1, since each individual year of age contributed equally (within one per cent usually) to the sample. The 1976 cohort is larger in absolute size, reflecting the impact of the baby boom on the absolute numbers in the post-secondary educational age bracket in this period.

The sex ratio is, as expected, nearly unity. About four in five (in either census) indicated that English was the mother tongue. The other major mother tongues were French (6 to 7 per cent) and Italian (3 or 4 per cent). It is important to note the decrease in the proportion of persons claiming non-English mother tongues over the five-year period, a point that is explored in more detail later in this chapter.

Most persons aged 18 to 21 were single (never married) in 1971 and 1976, though this is clearly truer for men than women, reflecting the later average age of marriage of men. There was a trend towards later marriage from 1971 to 1976 for both sexes.

The statistics on post-secondary participation rates among different subgroups presented in this chapter are based on self-reports of school attendance during the year prior to the census. How do census-based statistics on participation rates differ from other commonly used sources, specifically, institutional statistics? Note 2 of Appendix B examines this question in some depth. Taking into account the varying definitions of and strategies for arriving at a participation rate, the evidence indicates that em-ploying census statistics yields systematically lower rates of post-secondary school attendance, but since this is consistent over time, time series or trend patterns are accurately reflected. Indeed, comparing 1971 to 1976 overall enrolment trends based on census data with institutional enrolment statistics as reported to Statistics Canada for the same years yielded approximately similar patterns, thus providing support for our use of census statistics for trend analysis.

TABLE 5.1: PERCENTAGE BREAKDOWN OF 18 TO 21 AGE COHORT BY BACKGROUND VARIABLES, 1971 AND 1976, FROM THE PUST DATA

BACKGROUND VARIABLE	ALL		MALES		FEMALES	
	1971	1976	1971	1976	1971	1976
Sex						
Percent male	49.5	50.4	--	--	--	--
Marital status						
Percent single	78.9	81.6	88.7	89.7	69.2	73.3
Percent married	19.8	17.4	10.4	9.6	29.1	25.2
Mother tongue						
Percent English	79.9	82.9	79.9	83.3	79.8	82.5
Percent French	6.7	5.6	6.3	5.2	7.1	5.9
Percent German	1.6	1.0	1.7	1.1	1.6	0.9
Percent Italian	4.4	2.8	4.6	2.7	4.2	2.8
Percent Netherlandic	1.0	0.3	0.9	0.2	1.1	0.3
Percent Other	6.4	7.4	6.6	7.5	6.2	7.6
Sample size	5216	6166	2583	3107	2633	3059

TRENDS IN THE EDUCATIONAL ATTAINMENT, 18 - 21-YEAR OLD BY PARENTAL EDUCATION

Methodological Notes

For 18- to 21-year-olds classed as children living at home, infor-mation on parental education was computed for us by Statistics Canada. This data provides us with a picture of accessibility for about two-thirds of this cohort. Actually, since males tend to marry later than females, it provides us with a slightly more representative picture of male accessibility than female accessi-bility. Though the data provide us with an accurate view (be-cause of sample size) of accessibility among this subgroup, caution should be exercised in extrapolating to the entire 18 to 21 age group. Finally, the reader should note that throughout this section, rates are based on educational attainment or highest level of education received, not current attendance at school.

For the reader interested in examining the type of raw data which form the empirical basis of this chapter, note 3 of Appendix B presents a detailed description of one particular table showing the relationship between the educational attainment of Ontario males 18 to 21 years old and the highest parental educa-tional attainment. Summaries of detailed tables are located in note 4 of Appendix B. For the general reader, information on rates of post-secondary educational attainment for each level of parental education in both 1971 and 1976 is presented in graph form in subsequent sections. However, two observations not discernible from graphs are important (see note 3, Appendix B). First, the absolute size of the 18 to 21 cohort living at home has increased, reflecting part of the baby boom reaching post-secondary age. Secondly, overall levels of parental education increased from 1971 to 1976. The ramifications of these findings are discussed later in this chapter.

Three measures of parental education were employed in the special runs analysis: father's, mother's, and the higher of the two. Do the results depend on which is used?[4] The short answer to this question is that it does make a small difference which measure of parental education is used. Note 5 of Appendix B elaborates why.

Because the impact of parental education depends somewhat on how parental education is measured, we will only discuss general patterns in this section. To clarify matters further, university and post-secondary non-university attainment rates are analysed separately. Finally, before proceeding with the analysis, one should note that male and female university attain-ment rates should not be compared directly if one wishes to extrapolate to all 18- to 21-year-olds. The reason is that pro-portionally fewer females are still single and living at home, and they are thus less representative of all females aged 18 to 21 than are the males of all males in that age group.

Male and Female University Attainment, By Parental Education

Figure 5.2 shows the rate of attainment of male students with at least some university education and living at home, measured against their fathers' education. The latter was selected for presentation because it is probably the most commonly used measure of parental education. The other two parental education indicators (mother's and highest parental education) show similar results. The most striking observation from the 1971 and 1976 data is that the amount of education received by the father has a very strong effect on a son's subsequent educational attainment. Less than 10 per cent of those with fathers with no schooling attained university, compared with well over 40 per cent of those whose fathers had a university degree. Social-class back-ground is thus shown to be extremely important in determining male university attainment, even in 1976.

From 1971 to 1976 there was a small absolute increase in university attainment rates at all levels of the fathers' education. The increase was generally less than 2 per cent. Insofar as the increase was practically uniform across all categories of the fathers' education, little narrowing or convergence of social-class differentials in university attainment among males occurred. Neither, however, has any further widening occurred. The structural inequalities associated with social class have essentially remained unaltered. The reader is reminded here that about two-fifths of the population are in the lowest three parental educational categories (Grade 10 or lower), so that increasing the attainment rate of this group requires more students, in absolute numbers, being enrolled than is required to raise the attainment rate of a smaller group.

Lumping together all males aged 18 to 21 and living at home, there was an overall increase from 1971 to 1976 of about 2.5 per cent (to 21.5 per cent) in those attaining at least some university education (from Table B3 in note 4 of Appendix B). Yet Figure 5.2 shows that within parental educational categories the rise in student participation was almost always under 2 per cent. How can we explain this? The answer is that the overall increase over the five-year period is the result of two components: the in-crease in the attainment rates within each level of parental educa-tion, and the change in the proportion of the population between categories of parental education (see Kitagawa, 1955). Note 6 of Appendix B explains this in more detail and provides a method for decomposing overall participation rates into the two com-

FIGURE 5.2: PERCENTAGE OF 18 TO 21-YEAR OLD MALES AT HOME WITH AT
LEAST SOME UNIVERSITY, BY FATHER'S EDUCATIONAL
ATTAINMENT.

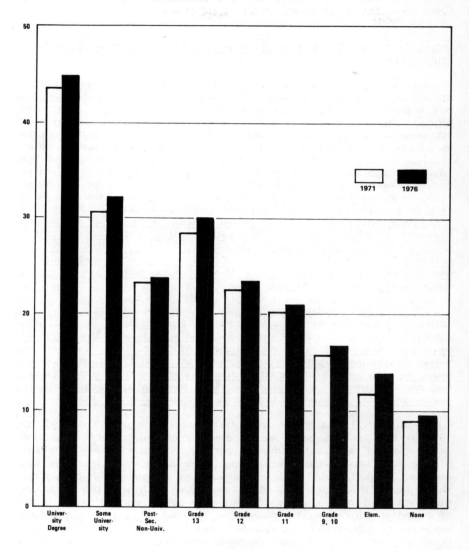

FATHER'S EDUCATIONAL ATTAINMENT

ponents.   The results indicate that about half of the overall increase of 2.5 per cent in the proportion of males attaining university can be attributed to the increase in the proportion of
the population with higher levels of parental education.   This can
be likened to a "forced" or structural mobility, resulting not
from changes in participation rates within categories but from
changes in the distribution of persons into categories where they
are more likely to go to university.

The fact that a substantial part of the overall increase in
university attainment among males from 1971 to 1976 is "forced"
has important ramifications for equality of opportunity.   Since the
higher social classes generally have high rates of university
attainment, an increase in their number requires a rapid increase
in places at university for them just to keep participation rates
stable.   In the period from 1971 to 1976, the absolute size of the
18 to 21 age group also increased.   Thus, given the baby boom
and increasing levels of parental education, expansion of post-
secondary institutions was necessary just to maintain the same
rate of university attainment at all levels of education, neglecting
any rate increase.   In the decade ahead, a period of shrinking
numbers of college-and university-age youths, encouragement of
groups with low university participation rates may help utilize
existing facilities at full capacity and provide another rationale for
implementing strategies of equalization of opportunity such as
those suggested in this report.

Figure 5.3 illustrates the relationship between fathers' education and the university attainment of females aged 18 to 21 and
living at home, for 1971 and 1976.   As with males, the effect of
parental education is striking.   For example, in 1976, a woman
whose father had a university degree was about five times as
likely to attain some university education as a woman whose father
had no schooling.   Social-class barriers to equal university attainments are thus at least as important for women as for men.

Figure 5.3 also shows that the absolute increase from 1971 to
1976 in the percentage of each category of the fathers' education
who attained at least some university education was generally
higher for females than for males.   The percentage increase was
in the 2 to 6 per cent area, and was generally consistent
throughout the parental education scale.   Since the absolute
percentage increases were roughly the same, regardless of level
of parental education, no noticeable narrowing of accessibility by
social class appears to have taken place.   The possible exception
is for those whose parents themselves had university education,
where the percentage increase was slightly smaller than elsewhere
(especially when the mothers' education is considered).   This
suggests that a ceiling effect may be operating.   It may be
difficult to increase the proportion of any subgroup attaining
university much beyond 50 per cent, since as well as requiring
appropriate motivation and qualifications, more and more persons

FIGURE 5.3: PERCENTAGE OF 18 TO 21-YEAR OLD FEMALES AT HOME WITH
AT LEAST SOME UNIVERSITY, BY FATHER'S EDUCATIONAL
ATTAINMENT.

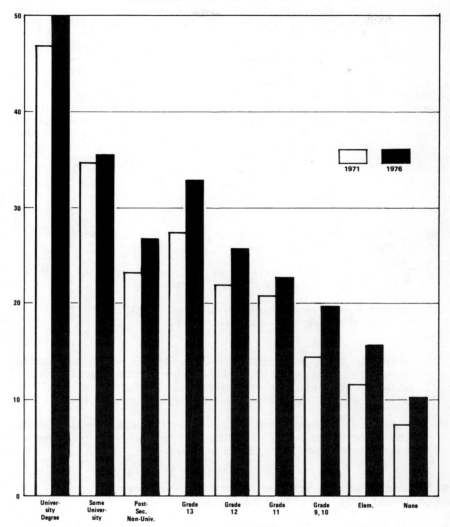

FATHER'S EDUCATIONAL ATTAINMENT

with lower grades would have to be admitted. To the extent that entry to Ontario universities is based on academic performance, an upper limit on the proportion of a subgroup that might feasibly attend university exists. Clearly, however, this ceiling has not been approached by those in lower-social-class categories.

The overall increase in the percentage of women living at home who attained at least some university education was about 5.4 per cent, over twice the increase for males. Breaking this down, between 26 and 29 per cent of the overall increase could be attributed to increases in the proportion with higher parental levels of education. The rest (about three-quarters of the 5.4 per cent increase) represented a "real" gain in university accessibility among women living at home. Thus, it appears that the early and mid-1970s were a period of substantial gains in accessibility to university by women relative to men, a phenomenon probably influenced by the women's movement and other social concerns of the time.

Summary

The important findings regarding parental education and university attainment are as follows:

-   Parental education had a very strong effect on sons' or daughters' university attainment probability.

-   Females had greater gains in university attainment from 1971 to 1976 than males and thus closed the gap between the sexes.

-   Since for both males and females, increases in university attainment rates were roughly uniform across parental education categories, no narrowing or widening of the gap between advantaged and disadvantaged groups took place.

-   A substantial proportion of the overall increase in university attainment rates is due to "forced" mobility or increases in parental education over the five years.

Male and Female Post-secondary Non-university Attainment, By Parental Education

Figures 5.4 and 5.5 summarize rates of attainment of post-secondary non-university (PSNU) education in 1971 and 1976 for males and females. (The reader interested in detailed tables is referred to Tables B4 in note 4 of Appendix B.)

The general pattern for male PSNU attainment in 1971 was that between 8 and 9 per cent of those living with their parents, who had obtained an education ranging from elementary school to

FIGURES 5.4 AND 5.5: PERCENTAGE OF MALE AND FEMALE 18 TO 21-YEAR-OLDS AT HOME WITH POST-SECONDARY NON-UNIVERSITY EDUCATION, BY FATHER'S EDUCATION.

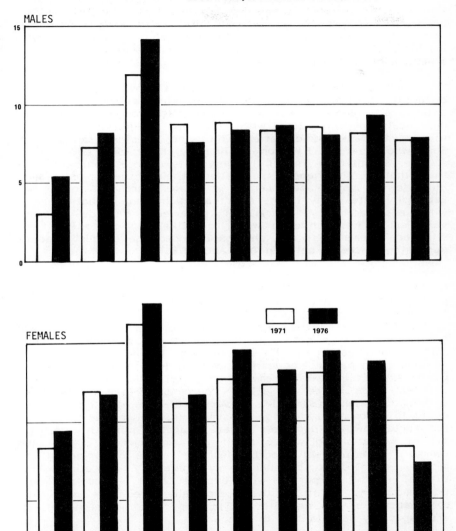

MALES

FEMALES

1971   1976

FATHER'S EDUCATIONAL ATTAINMENT

University Degree   Some University   Post-Sec. Non-Univ.   Grade 13   Grade 12   Grade 11   Grade 9, 10   Elem.   None

Grade 13, attained PSNU education. By 1976, this percentage had not altered significantly, with most changes being under one per cent in either direction. Thus, in the middle parental education (or social-class) categories, the percentage attaining PSNU education did not change for males in the five-year period, although the absolute size of the 18 to 21 cohort increased. PSNU institutions draw students of middle parental educational levels at a remarkably uniform rate.

At high levels of parental education, the pattern was slightly different. Relatively few males who had at least one parent with a university degree chose a non-university post-secondary level of education. This fits in with the strong likelihood that persons with such backgrounds attend university, as we saw earlier. Sons whose parents had some university chose PSNU education to a lesser extent than that of the university-degree group and more than that of the general population, though there was a small increase (1 to 2 per cent) in PSNU enrolment generally. Especially noteworthy is the effect of having one or both parents with post-secondary educational experience outside of universities. These children were more likely to go to PSNU institutions themselves, and also experienced the biggest absolute percentage increase between 1971 and 1976.

At the other extreme, slightly fewer males with parents having no education attained PSNU education, and their proportion did not change over the five years.

Among women, the overall pattern of PSNU attainment was similar to the male pattern, with some exceptions. The general rate of participation in 1971 was between 11 and 13 per cent for all those with parental education between elementary schooling and Grade 13, but instead of remaining more or less stable as was the case for males, there was a 1 to 2 percent increase in 1976. For those whose parent(s) had a university degree, the likelihood of going to a community college or similar institution was lower than for persons whose parents had less education, but this gap was not as large among women as it was among men. It is more common (and probably acceptable) for female offspring of the highly educated to pursue a non-university education. For women, having a parent with experience at a non-university post-secondary institution was especially predictive of similar experience for the daughter. Thus, parental modelling effects are especially important in this regard.

Summary

-   Post-secondary, non-university institutions seem to recruit students fairly evenly from across a broad spectrum of parental education, as others have noted (see review by Okihiro, 1981, and Anisef et al., 1980). Social class barriers are not of major significance. PSNU institutions also tend to recruit more women than men, though our sample does not allow definitive comparisons since more males than females are represented.

- The proportion of persons of different parental education with PSNU attainment remained approximately stable for men, whereas women have made greater strides in their PSNU attainment.

- The pattern of more or less egalitarian attainment across parental education levels (except at the extremes) remained constant over the five years.

- Because there are no dramatic differences in the rates of PSNU attainment by parental educational categories, the gradual increase in the proportion of persons with higher parental education has virtually no effect on the overall rates of PSNU attainment for either males or females. Thus, there was no point in breaking down the PSNU rate change into forced and unforced components.

TRENDS IN ACCESSIBILITY, GROUPS WITH DIFFERENT MOTHER TONGUE

Methodological Notes

The only variable associated with cultural or ethnic origin common to the 1971 and 1976 censuses is mother tongue.[5] This refers to the language first learned and still understood. As a measure of ethnicity, mother tongue has a number of advantages. The mother tongue item has been employed very consistently across censuses, and is asked of all respondents. In a country in which language is an important dimension of stratification, mother tongue reflects current language capability. Those who still understand a foreign language are likely to have closer ties with ethnic traditions than those who have been assimilated to the point where they do not understand the language of their ancestors. Thus, the use of a mother tongue will put ethnic differences in post-secondary educational attainment into sharper relief than other indicators of ethnicity used in some censuses such as the ethnic origin variable.

Using mother tongue as a measure of ethnic background does have some limitations. About four-fifths of Ontario's population claimed English as their mother tongue (a fact which should not be confused with British ethnic background). Moreover, more recent cohorts are less likely to cite a non-English mother tongue (see note 7, Appendix B). In addition, most of the mother-tongue groups classified by the census are European in origin and have, for the most part, ceased immigration. On the other hand, the more important recent groups (e.g., East and West Indians) are categorized in the "other" or "English" group. Ethnic groups also vary widely in the proportion claiming a mother tongue corresponding to their ethnic background.

All in all, mother tongue data provide a highly consistent if restricted measure of ethnicity. Because of the limitations noted above, however, only major trends indicated by the data are discussed in the following section.

Three measures of ethnic background using mother-tongue data were available - respondent's, mother's, and father's. As with parental education, mother-tongue data are available for parents only if the person is classed as a child living at home. However, one advantage of using parental mother tongue is that more persons in the parent generation have a non-English mother tongue. In 1971, for example, 81 per cent of males aged 18 to 21 claimed English as their mother tongue, but the percentage of males at home whose father claimed English as their mother tongue was only 72 per cent. It was 73 per cent for those whose mothers claimed English as their mother tongue. Thus, parental mother tongue may give us a broader range of people of non-Anglophone background.

Our presentation of results regarding the post-secondary educational attainments of different mother-tongue groups derives from analysis of the three mother-tongue measures. Generally, using parental mother tongue (father's or mother's) instead of the respondent's results in higher post-secondary attainment rates (see note 8, Appendix B) because this group of respondents includes offspring who have been in Canada for some period of time, have assimilated, and may not themselves have a non-English mother tongue. Because of the variation across measures of mother tongue, only general trends in accessibility indicated by all measures of mother tongue are reported here. The reader wanting a detailed analysis can refer to Tables B5 and B6 in Appendix B. For most readers, the graphs depicting respondent's mother tongue and educational attainment provide sufficient information for discerning major patterns and trends.

Male and Female University Attainment

Figure 5.6 shows the percentage of 18- to 21-year-old males of different mother-tongue groups attaining at least some university education. From a social-stratification viewpoint, some of the results are surprising. By 1971, most mother-tongue groups had rates of university attainment approaching the English group, and the Polish and Ukrainian groups had surpassed the English

FIGURE 5.6:   PERCENTAGE OF 18 TO 21-YEAR OLD MALES WITH AT LEAST SOME
UNIVERSITY, BY MOTHER TONGUE

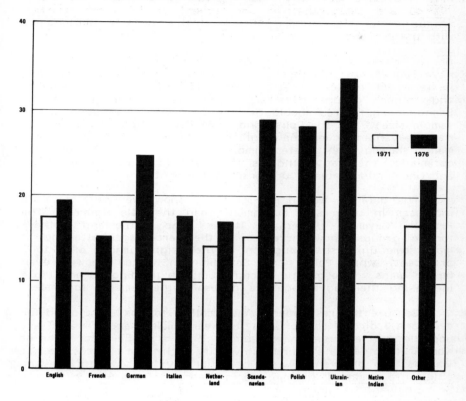

MOTHER TONGUE

mother-tongue group. Those conspicuously below were the French, Italian, and notably the Native Indian groups. From 1971 to 1976, taking the large, heterogeneous English mother-tongue group as a standard, it appears that every ethnic group, with the exception of Native Indians, has experienced a greater absolute percentage increase in those attaining university education. The French, Italian, and Netherland mother-tongue groups have reduced the gap between themselves and the English group in terms of university attainment. The German, Scandinavian, and "other" groups have surpassed the English (though the Scandinavian figures should be looked at with reservation due to sample size), and the Polish and Ukrainian groups have increased their advantage over the English. German, Italian, and Polish males showed the greatest improvement. Lest we become too optimistic, the Native Indians continued to show extremely low and unchanging rates of university attainment.

The data for women in Figure 5.7 show even more dramatic increases in university attainment than the male figures. The French, German, Ukrainian, Italian, and Netherland mother-tongue groups show increases in the percentages attaining at least some university education in the neighbourhood of 5 to 9 per cent, while Polish and Scandinavian women showed even larger gains. The groups catching up with the English and those increasing their advantage are generally the same as for males.

Because the respondent's own mother tongue is reported for everyone, direct comparisons between males and females are possible. In every ethnic group in 1971, a smaller proportion of women than men attained university. In some cases (e.g., Italians) the difference was substantial. By 1976, women in every ethnic group closed the gap and in the case of the French, Scandinavian, Ukrainian, and Native Indian groups, proportionally more women than men attained at least some university education.

Mother-tongue patterns are surprising for those who feel that offspring of immigrants are usually at a social disadvantage in education. However, other studies have suggested that ethnicity is not a major barrier for many ethnic groups. In reviewing literature, Pike (1970:77) discussed A. J. C. King's study of Ontario students in the 1950s in which children from homes where the language spoken was Ukrainian, Greek, Polish, Slovak, Hungarian, Italian, and Dutch were shown to maintain high school retention rates similar to those of the English-speaking subgroup. Francophones had lower retention rates. Porter's (1965) analysis of school attendance of males aged 15 to 24 in 1951 and 1961 essentially points out similar patterns (p. 89).

Also of related interest is the fact that there have been changes in the urban-rural location of people of different ethnic

FIGURE 5.7: PERCENTAGE OF 18 TO 21-YEAR OLD FEMALES WITH AT LEAST SOME UNIVERSITY, BY MOTHER TONGUE

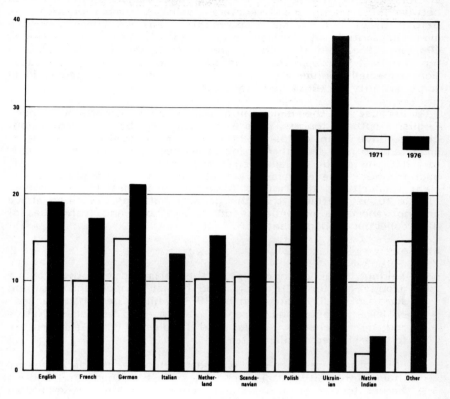

MOTHER TONGUE

background. For example, the Ukrainians, Russians and Germans all increased strikingly in the percentage located in urban areas between 1951 and 1961 (Porter, 1965:75) compared with the British group. In terms of occupation, Eastern Europeans were overrepresented in primary-sector and unskilled occupations (Porter, 1965), so that the pattern which seems to be depicted for the East European group in particular is that higher education, especially university, is seen as a means of intergenerational social mobility for unskilled labour in urban areas.[6]

Because of the diminishing numbers of persons with non-English mother tongue, there is some doubt that equivalent groups have been compared between the censuses. Also, it is important to note that trends indicated here cannot be generalized to what the public usually regards as persons of a given ethnic background.[7] Nevertheless, we feel that there has been sufficient similarity in the figures from the three measures of mother tongue to be confident that the general patterns described above are not anomalies or artifacts of the methods and techniques of data collection and presentation.

Summary

- Taking the English group as the norm, some mother-tongue groups (eastern European) had higher proportions attaining some university education by 1971, while others had markedly lower proportions (French, Italian, and especially Native Indian). Generally, males and females of the same mother tongue showed similar rates.

- For both sexes, non-English mother-tongue groups increased their university attainment rates faster than the English mother-tongue group. The exception was the Native Indian group.

- Females of various mother tongues have increased their university attainments more so than the respective male groups.

Male And Female Post-secondary Non-University Attainment

Figures 5.8 and 5.9 show the proportion of 18- to 21-year-olds who attain post-secondary non-university (PSNU) education by mother tongue. For males, the French, Italian, and Scandinavian mother-tongue groups had about the same rate of PSNU attainment as the English in 1971, the Native Indians were substantially underrepresented, and the remaining groups had higher attainment rates.

FIGURE 5.8: PERCENTAGE OF 18 TO 21-YEAR-OLD MALES WITH POST-SECONDARY
NON-UNIVERSITY EDUCATION, BY MOTHER TONGUE

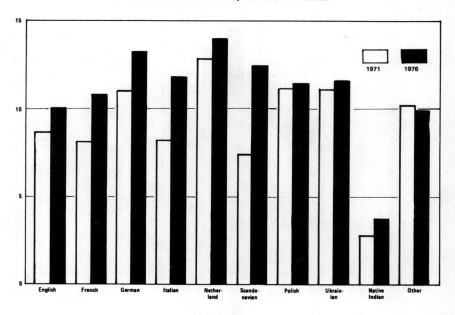

MOTHER TONGUE

FIGURE 5.9: PERCENTAGE OF 18 TO 21-YEAR-OLD FEMALES WITH POST-SECONDARY
NON-UNIVERSITY EDUCATION, BY MOTHER TONGUE

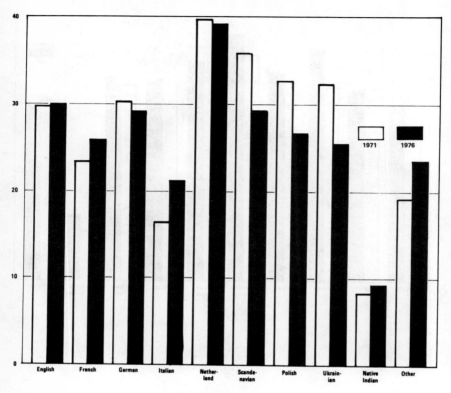

MOTHER TONGUE

Losers and Winners

From 1971 to 1976 it appears that the French, German, Italian, and Netherland groups gained more in PSNU education than the English mother-tongue group, with the Polish remaining stable and the Ukrainian and Indian groups (the extremes in terms of university attainment) increasing less. The increases were all, in general, very moderate. By 1976, there was a rough equivalence among mother-tongue groups in the proportion of males attaining PSNU education, with the exception of male Native Indians.

In 1971 the rates of PSNU attainment among women were much more varied than the male rates. They also tended to be higher, indicating that more women attended such institutions than men. Among mother-tongue groups that were well below the dominant English mother-tongue group in PSNU attainment, there was a catching-up from 1971 to 1976 as these groups (French, Italian, Native Indian, and Other) showed larger percentage increases over the five years.

For those with 1971 levels above the English group, there was a stablilizing or decrease in the proportion attaining PSNU education. These groups (primarily Nordic and Eastern European) showed the greatest increments in university enrolment among women. One might interpret their decreasing enrolments in other post-secondary institutions as the result of competition between types of institutions. In this view, Nordic and Eastern European women who might have previously gone to PSNU institutions decided in the early and mid-1970s to attend university, thereby decreasing enrolments in PSNU establishments and increasing enrolments in universities.

The net result of the catching up of mother-tongue groups that were below the English group and the decreasing or stable participation by those above was a general equalizing of PSNU attainment rates among all groups. However, the 1976 female rates are not as uniform across mother-tongue categories as are the male rates. The Native Indian group is again the only one that is well below the others in PSNU attainment.

Summary

-   Among males, the French, German, Italian and Netherland mother-tongue groups showed greater increases (1971-1976) in PSNU education than the English mother-tongue groups; increases for the Ukrainian and Native Indian groups were significantly less.

-   By 1976, there was a rough equivalence among all mother-tongue groups (Native Indians excepted) in the proportion of males choosing PSNU education.

- Among females the patterns were more varied. The increases in PSNU attainment for some non-English mother-tongue groups (e.g., French, Italian) were significantly larger than for the English-speaking group. However, there were some sharp decreases for other groups over the five-year period.

FULL-TIME AND PART-TIME ENROLMENT

In this last section, our attention turns to trends in full-time and part-time enrolment in post-secondary institutions. The special runs from Statistics Canada enabled us to explore two areas of concern: to compare full-time and part-time enrollees on the basis of parental education and mother tongue, and to discern changes in patterns of such enrolment from 1971 to 1976.

Methodological Notes

Before discussing the analysis, there are several remarks about the nature of the census data used which should be noted. First, the data employed for the analysis is flow (attendance) data, enquiring about educational experiences in the census year. The rates of enrolment reported or participation rates will be markedly lower than the stock (level of educational attainment) data presented up to this point in this chapter. In addition, the type of institution attended (university or PSNU) is inferred from level-of-education data. It is possible for a small number of persons, for example, to have actually been enrolled in a high school at the time of the census but to have attended a university sometime in the past: such persons would be classed as university enrollees in the present section.

Of particular importance to the full-time and part-time comparison is the fact that our data is restricted to 18 to 21-year-olds. Part-time students are considerably older - eight years older than their full-time counterparts in the same fields of study (Secretary of State, 1976:27) - so our part-time sample is very biased. Thus, the results of this analysis should not be generalized to all part-time post-secondary students.

Parental Educational Background

Table 5.10 shows the highest parental education composition of part-time and full-time university and PSNU male students and the base population of males aged 18 to 21 living at home.

TABLE 5.10: PROFILE OF FULL- AND PART-TIME UNIVERSITY AND POST-SECONDARY NON-UNIVERSITY STUDENTS AND POPULATION 18-21 AT HOME, BY HIGHEST PARENTAL EDUCATION, MALES, 1971 AND 1976

HIGHEST PARENTAL EDUCATION (Ratio of Representativeness)	1 9 7 1				Population 18-21 At Home
	Post-secondary Non-university		University		
	Full-time	Part-time	Full-time	Part-time	
University Degree	4.86 (0.60)	3.81 (0.47)	18.92 (2.23)	13.75 (1.67)	8.14
Some University	6.02 (0.93)	5.40 (0.84)	9.95 (1.54)	9.62 (1.49)	6.46
Post-secondary Non-university	20.28 (1.39)	24.13 (1.65)	17.33 (1.18)	20.62 (1.41)	14.64
Grade 13	7.74 (1.18)	3.81 (0.58)	9.09 (1.39)	7.56 (1.16)	6.54
Grade 12	13.45 (1.14)	12.70 (1.08)	12.14 (1.03)	10.31 (0.88)	11.76
Grade 11	9.21 (1.02)	8.57 (0.95)	7.44 (0.82)	7.90 (0.87)	9.04
Grades 9, 10	18.41 (0.92)	19.37 (0.97)	13.00 (0.65)	14.43 (0.72)	20.02
Elementary	19.52 (0.86)	21.27 (0.93)	11.91 (0.52)	14.78 (0.65)	22.81
No schooling	0.46 (0.77)	0.63 (1.05)	0.27 (0.45)	0.34 (0.57)	0.60
Total percent	100%	100%	100%	100%	100%
Number	9,885	1,575	30,155	1,455	176,245

TABLE 5.10: PROFILE OF FULL- AND PART-TIME UNIVERSITY AND POST-
(contd.)   SECONDARY NON-UNIVERSITY STUDENTS AND POPULATION
             18-21 AT HOME, BY HIGHEST PARENTAL EDUCATION, MALES,
             1971 AND 1976

| HIGHEST PARENTAL EDUCATION (Ratio of Representativeness) | 1 9 7 6 | | | | Population 18-21 At Home |
| | Post-secondary Non-University | | University | | |
	Full-time	Part-time	Full-time	Part-time	
University Degree	7.02 (0.73)	5.30 (0.55)	21.14 (2.20)	11.76 (1.23)	9.60
Some University	10.66 (1.03)	10.82 (1.04)	14.91 (1.43)	17.09 (1.64)	10.40
Post-secondary Non-university	27.58 (1.56)	28.92 (1.64)	19.12 (1.08)	21.57 (1.22)	17.63
Grade 13	4.87 (0.91)	4.42 (0.83)	6.64 (1.24)	3.92 (0.73)	5.34
Grade 12	11.63 (0.95)	11.70 (0.96)	11.43 (0.93)	10.92 (0.89)	12.24
Grade 11	7.48 (0.97)	6.62 (0.86)	5.85 (0.76)	6.72 (0.87)	7.71
Grades 9, 10	13.79 (0.79)	13.67 (0.78)	9.23 (0.53)	13.45 (0.77)	17.53
Elementary	16.56 (0.87)	17.88 (0.94)	11.11 (0.59)	14.29 (0.75)	18.93
No Schooling	0.41 (0.64)	0.66 (1.03)	0.24 (0.38)	0.28 (0.44)	0.64
Total percent	100%	100%	100%	100%	100%
Number	9,755	2,265	35,825	1,785	200,000

Highest parental education was selected to maximize the number of persons reporting parental education. Recall that only those classed as children at home are included. In addition to the parental educational breakdown of the different groups, the ratio of representativeness (cf. Porter, 1965) is presented. A figure of 1 indicates representation equal to the proportion of persons in the population. A figure greater than 1 indicates overrepresentation, and a figure less than 1, underrepresentation. Such figures provide the same type of information as the participation rates used previously. The tables in this section are reported in this manner in order to focus on differences in the composition of part-time and full-time students.

The totals (Numbers) at the bottom of Table 5.10 show that the proportion of part-time students aged 18 to 21 is very small for university, compared with PSNU, students. In 1976, part-timers comprised 2265 or 18.8 percent of all PSNU students, an absolute increase of 5.1 per cent over the 1971 figures. The university rates remained stable around 4.7 per cent.

Part-time university students aged 18 to 21 tended to come from lower parental educational backgrounds than full-time students, in both 1971 and 1976. This is especially clear (from the ratios of representativeness) at parental education below Grade 11 and also at the university degree level. It is noteworthy that males whose parents had some university education are the most highly overrepresented group among part-time university students. Perhaps a parental modelling pattern similar to that noted earlier in conjunction with PSNU attainment also works for part-time students who may take longer to reach their degrees - and may, in fact, never do so.

Has there been a change in the parental educational background of part-time students from 1971 to 1976? One way of examining the trends in parental educational background of part-time university students is to compare the ratios of representativeness in 1971 and 1976. These ratios control for the gradual rise in the proportion of students with higher parental education. Category-by-category comparisons suggest that there has been a small trend towards equalizing the ratios of representativeness for groups of different educational backgrounds. The trends for full-time students have already been discussed in previous sections where university attainment was the dependent variable. They are not discussed further here.

Relative to full-time PSNU males, the part-timers tend to have slightly lower parental education (see Table 5.10). This is particularly noticeable at the highest levels of parental education, where it is rare for persons to attend PSNU institutions part-time. In terms of trends, there was no clear-cut change in the degree to which different parental educational categories contributed to part-time PSNU enrolment from 1971 to 1976.

Losers and Winners

Looking at full-time and part-time male enrollees in post-secondary education, the general pattern is for part-time PSNU students to have the lowest parental education, followed by full-time PSNU students, part-time university students, and finally, full-time university students. Part-time and full-time students at the same type of institution tended to resemble each other more than they did students at different institutions.

Table 5.11 shows the composition of part-time and full-time post-secondary student populations and ratios of representativeness among women aged 18 to 21 living at home. The pattern shown for males, that part-timers have slightly lower levels of parental education for both the university and PSNU students, holds for women. No sharply discernible narrowing or widening of inequalities in enrolment by parental education categories was observed.

Summary

- Among men and women aged 18 to 21, part-time students tend to have slightly lower parental educational background than full-time students. This held for university students and PSNU students.

- There was no significant pattern of change in the parental educational composition of part-time post-secondary students (either university or PSNU) over the five years.

Mother-tongue Background

How do part-time students differ from full-time students in mother tongue? Table 5.12 shows the results for males. First, though, the figures from Table 5.12 (and also Table 5.13) need some discussion. As noted earlier, most people have English as their mother tongue. The number of persons with Native Indian, Netherland, and Scandinavian mother tongue is already quite small, even in this large sample, and the corresponding number of persons with, say, part-time university education is sometimes vanishingly small. In addition, Statistics Canada rounds numbers to the nearest five, a fact that especially affects proportions based on low total populations. This means that for these ethnic groups, the figures may be subject to some variation, and ratios of representativeness may also fluctuate randomly. Also, the caveats mentioned earlier, such as the trend towards fewer people claiming a non-English mother tongue, need to be considered. For these reasons, only general trends with the larger mother-tongue groups are mentioned.

Looking first at male part-time university attenders (Table 5.12) the following general pattern is evident. Compared with their proportion in the population, German, French, and Italian

TABLE 5.11: PROFILE OF FULL- AND PART-TIME UNIVERSITY AND POST-
SECONDARY NON-UNIVERSITY STUDENTS AND POPULATION
18-21 AT HOME, BY HIGHEST PARENTAL EDUCATION,
FEMALES 1971 AND 1976

HIGHEST PARENTAL EDUCATION (Ratio of Representativeness)	Post-secondary Non-university		1 9 7 1 University		Population 18-21 At Home
	Full-time	Part-time	Full-time	Part-time	
University Degree	6.83 (0.72)	6.28 (0.66)	23.63 (2.50)	14.00 (1.48)	9.46
Some University	8.10 (1.15)	5.86 (0.77)	11.40 (1.61)	15.50 (2.19)	7.07
Post-secondary Non-university	22.14 (1.41)	25.94 (1.65)	18.17 (1.19)	20.50 (1.30)	15.71
Grade 13	6.41 (0.98)	5.44 (0.83)	8.20 (1.25)	8.50 (1.30)	6.55
Grade 12	12.45 (1.06)	12.55 (1.07)	11.22 (0.95)	8.50 (0.72)	11.78
Grade 11	9.75 (1.06)	8.79 (0.95)	7.21 (0.78)	8.50 (0.92)	9.24
Grades 9, 10	17.43 (0.92)	17.15 (0.90)	10.39 (0.55)	11.50 (0.61)	18.98
Elementary	16.68 (0.80)	17.57 (0.85)	9.57 (0.46)	13.50 (0.65)	20.75
No Schooling	0.32 (0.71)	--	0.11 (0.24)	0.50 (1.11)	0.45
Total percent	100%	100%	100%	100%	100%
Number	9,440	1,195	22,370	1,000	126,120

TABLE 5.11:   PROFILE OF FULL- AND PART-TIME UNIVERSITY AND POST-
(contd.)   SECONDARY NON-UNIVERSITY STUDENTS AND POPULATION
                18-21 AT HOME, BY HIGHEST PARENTAL EDUCATION,
                FEMALES 1971 AND 1976

| HIGHEST PARENTAL EDUCATION (Ratio of Representativeness) | 1976 | | | | Population 18-21 At Home |
| | Post-secondary Non-university | | University | | |
	Full-time	Part-time	Full-time	Part-time	
University Degree	9.02 (0.82)	7.25 (0.66)	23.43 (2.13)	16.18 (1.47)	11.02
Some University	10.77 (0.96)	11.18 (0.99)	16.04 (1.42)	17.80 (1.58)	11.27
Post-secondary Non-university	24.95 (1.36)	28.40 (1.55)	19.51 (1.06)	19.74 (1.07)	18.37
Grade 13	5.40 (1.00)	4.23 (0.78)	6.46 (1.20)	4.53 (0.84)	5.40
Grade 12	13.57 (1.09)	9.67 (0.78)	10.88 (0.88)	11.97 (0.96)	12.43
Grade 11	7.80 (1.04)	7.85 (1.05)	5.16 (0.69)	6.80 (0.91)	7.48
Grades 9, 10	14.14 (0.89)	13.90 (0.87)	9.19 (0.58)	11.00 (0.69)	15.97
Elementary	14.18 (0.81)	16.92 (0.97)	9.20 (0.53)	11.33 (0.65)	17.52
No Schooling	0.08 (0.15)	0.30 (0.56)	0.11 (0.20)	0.32 (0.59)	0.54
Total percent	100%	100%	100%	100%	100%
Number	12,305	1,655	31,670	1,545	150,750

TABLE 5.12:   MOTHER TONGUE PROFILE OF FULL- AND PART-TIME
UNIVERSITY AND POST-SECONDARY NON-UNIVERSITY
STUDENTS AND POPULATION 18-21, MALES, 1971 AND 1976

MOTHER TONGUE[1] (Ratio of Representativeness)	1 9 7 1				Population 18-21
	Post-secondary Non-university		University		
	Full-time	Part-time	Full-time	Part-time	
English	82.47 (1.02)	81.33 (1.00)	85.45 (1.06)	82.84 (1.02)	80.98
French	5.38 (0.81)	3.90 (0.59)	3.98 (0.60)	4.24 (0.64)	6.62
German	1.73 (1.11)	2.27 (1.46)	1.64 (1.05)	0.64 (0.41)	1.56
Italian	3.27 (0.82)	2.92 (0.74)	2.20 (0.55)	3.39 (0.85)	3.97
Netherlandic	0.75 (0.95)	2.27 (2.87)	0.53 (0.67)	1.69 (2.14)	0.79
Scandinavian	0.08 (0.80)	0.16 (1.60)	0.08 (0.80)	0.21 (2.10)	0.10
Polish	0.98 (1.24)	0.65 (0.82)	0.94 (1.19)	1.06 (1.34)	0.79
Ukrainian	1.13 (1.66)	0.32 (0.47)	1.25 (1.84)	0.85 (1.25)	0.68
Native Indian	0.08 (0.21)	0.32 (1.05)	0.07 (0.18)	--	0.38
Other	3.91 (0.94)	5.68 (1.37)	3.82 (0.92)	5.08 (1.23)	4.14
Total percent	100%	100%	100%	100%	100%
Number	13,290	3,080	37,570	2,360	267,405

[1]The rounding technique used by Statistics Canada renders small percentages (and thus the corresponding ratios of representativeness) subject to instability. This is especially true for the Native Indian, Scandinavian and Netherlandic mother tongue groups, and for part-time students. See note in text as well.

123

TABLE 5.12: (contd.) MOTHER TONGUE PROFILE OF FULL- AND PART-TIME UNIVERSITY AND POST-SECONDARY NON-UNIVERSITY STUDENTS AND POPULATION 18-21, MALES, 1971 AND 1976

MOTHER TONGUE[1] (Ratio of Representativeness)	1976 Post-secondary Non-university Full-time	Post-secondary Non-university Part-time	University Full-time	University Part-time	Population 18-21
English	83.68 *(1.00)*	85.60 *(1.03)*	84.66 *(1.02)*	81.76 *(0.98)*	83.34
French	5.12 *(0.88)*	4.92 *(0.85)*	4.03 *(0.69)*	5.41 *(0.93)*	5.80
German	1.22 *(1.28)*	1.05 *(1.11)*	1.14 *(1.20)*	0.93 *(0.98)*	0.95
Italian	3.34 *(1.25)*	2.81 *(1.05)*	2.31 *(0.87)*	2.47 *(0.93)*	2.67
Netherlandic	0.38 *(1.36)*	0.35 *(1.25)*	0.20 *(0.71)*	0.31 *(1.11)*	0.28
Scandinavian	0.03 *(0.75)*	0.23 *(5.75)*	0.06 *(1.50)*	0.15 *(3.75)*	0.04
Polish	0.49 *(1.40)*	0.35 *(1.00)*	0.55 *(1.57)*	0.31 *(0.89)*	0.35
Ukrainian	0.73 *(1.55)*	0.35 *(0.74)*	0.83 *(1.77)*	0.62 *(1.32)*	0.47
Native Indian	0.07 *(0.28)*	--	0.04 *(0.16)*	0.31 *(1.24)*	0.25
Other	4.98 *(0.85)*	4.45 *(0.76)*	6.18 *(1.06)*	7.42 *(1.27)*	5.85
Total percent	100%	100%	100%	100%	100%
Number	14,365	4,270	46,765	3,235	

[1]The rounding technique used by Statistics Canada renders small percentages (and thus the corresponding ratios of representativeness) subject to instability. This is especially true for the Native Indian, Scandinavian and Netherlandic mother tongue groups, and for part-time students. See note in text as well.

TABLE 5.13:   MOTHER TONGUE PROFILE OF FULL- AND PART-TIME
UNIVERSITY AND POST-SECONDARY NON-UNIVERSITY
STUDENTS AND POPULATION 18-21, FEMALES,
1971 AND 1976

MOTHER TONGUE[1] (Ratio of Representativeness	1 9 7 1				
	Post-secondary Non-university		University		Population 18-21
	Full-time	Part-time	Full-time	Part-time	
English	86.92 (1.07)	80.83 (1.00)	86.11 (1.06)	79.54 (0.98)	81.03
French	4.30 (0.67)	5.79 (0.90)	3.93 (0.61)	7.59 (1.19)	6.40
German	1.29 (0.88)	1.27 (0.86)	1.48 (1.01)	2.07 (1.41)	1.47
Italian	1.66 (0.44)	2.35 (0.62)	1.34 (0.35)	1.84 (0.48)	3.80
Netherlandic	0.95 (1.14)	1.81 (2.18)	0.54 (0.65)	0.46 (0.55)	0.83
Scandinavian	0.16 (1.14)	0.54 (3.86)	0.08 (0.57)	0.23 (1.64)	0.14
Polish	1.13 (1.36)	0.72 (0.87)	0.90 (1.08)	1.15 (1.39)	0.83
Ukrainian	0.90 (2.71)	1.08 (1.59)	1.49 (2.19)	0.92 (1.35)	0.68
Native Indian	0.11 (0.31)	0.18 (0.51)	0.05 (0.14)	--	0.35
Other	2.58 (0.58)	5.79 (1.29)	4.07 (0.91)	5.98 (1.34)	4.47
Total percent	100%	100%	100%	100%	100%
Number	18,960	2,765	29,485	2,175	263,930

[1]The rounding technique used by Statistics Canada renders small
percentages subject to instability. This is especially true
for the Native Indian, Scandinavian and Netherlandic mother
tongue groups and for the part-timers. See also note in text.

TABLE 5.13:   MOTHER TONGUE PROFILE OF FULL- AND PART-TIME
(contd.)   UNIVERSITY AND POST-SECONDARY NON-UNIVERSITY
              STUDENTS AND POPULATION 18-21, FEMALES,
              1971 AND 1976

| MOTHER TONGUE[1] (Ratio of Representativeness) | 1 9 7 6 | | | | |
| | Post-secondary Non-university | | University | | Population 18-21 |
	Full-time	Part-time	Full-time	Part-time	
English	87.67 (1.06)	82.07 (0.99)	84.93 (1.03)	79.03 (0.96)	82.61
French	4.33 (0.74)	4.88 (0.83)	4.43 (0.75)	6.76 (1.15)	5.87
German	0.87 (0.87)	1.83 (1.83)	1.23 (1.23)	1.24 (1.24)	1.00
Italian	1.60 (0.58)	2.20 (0.80)	1.81 (0.66)	1.93 (0.70)	2.76
Netherlandic	0.26 (0.93)	1.10 (3.93)	0.16 (0.57)	0.04 (0.14)	0.28
Scandinavian	0.39 (1.03)	0.12 (0.32)	0.52 (1.37)	0.69 (1.82)	0.38
Polish	0.03 (0.60)	0.12 (2.40)	0.10 (2.00)	--	0.05
Ukrainian	0.57 (1.27)	0.24 (0.53)	0.98 (2.18)	0.55 (1.22)	0.45
Native Indian	0.10 (0.42)	0.12 (0.50)	0.05 (0.21)	--	0.24
Other	4.18 (0.66)	7.07 (1.11)	5.76 (0.91)	8.83 (1.39)	6.36
Total percent	100%	100%	100%	100%	100%
Number	19,385	4,100	43,435	3,625	310,820

[1]The rounding technique used by Statistics Canada renders small percentages subject to instability. This is especially true for the Native Indian, Scandinavian and Netherlandic mother tongue groups and for the part-timers. See also note in text.

mother-tongue groups were underrepresented in the part-time
population in 1971, but much less so (though still to a small
extent) in 1976. This pattern was similar to that described
earlier in terms of university attainment. The Polish and
Ukrainian groups were overrepresented among part-time students
in 1971, but Poles were underrepresented in 1976.

In 1971, the French and Italian mother-tongue groups as
well as the Polish and Ukrainian categories were underrepresented in part-time attendance at PSNU institutions. However, there
was a levelling out of ethnic differences in terms of representativeness for part-time enrollees over the five-year period. For
example, the ratio of representativeness for the French rose from
.59 in 1971, indicating substantial underrepresentation among
part-time community college attenders to .85 or slight underrepresentation in 1976. There was a general movement towards unity,
that is, part-time participation proportioned to the size of the
group in the population.

The pattern of part-time versus full-time university enrolment by mother tongue for women (Table 5.13) is somewhat
different. In 1971, all the major non-English mother-tongue
groups showed higher representation among part-time students
than among full-time students. This pattern did not change much
in 1976, though there was a slight trend for the proportion of
part-time women university students to reflect more closely the
proportion of mother-tongue groups in the larger population.

There was no clear-cut pattern of difference between
mother-tongue groups in terms of part-time non-university enrolment. Nor was there any especially strong pattern of change
noted over the period from 1971 to 1976.

Summary

-       Among males, there was a levelling-out of mother-tongue
        differences in that, in 1971, those groups with lower educa-
        tional attainment than the English group increased their
        enrolment rate and those groups originally with higher
        educational attainment decreased their enrolment.

-       Non-English mother-tongue women tended to attend uni-
        versity part-time more than English mother-tongue women.
        There was no major change in this pattern from 1971 to
        1976.

127

CONCLUSIONS

The results of this chapter enable us to draw a number of conclusions. For one, it is clearly feasible, practical, and valuable
to employ special runs of the full census to monitor changes in
patterns of post-secondary participation among different subgroups in the population, albeit a number of limitations and
restrictions need to be kept in mind. With the full census of
1981 becoming available to researchers in the near future, we
expect that a more extensive analysis of changes in enrolment
patterns will be possible, by comparing 1971, 1976 and 1981 data.

The findings from the census analysis emphasize the value of
the social-stratification perspective which underlies this book.
This perspective points to a number of different dimensions of
structured inequality (i.e., gender, social class, ethnicity).
Indeed, the findings indicate that patterns of post-secondary
participation or attainment depend on which dimension of stratification one selects, what level–university or PSNU - one focuses
on, and what type of enrolment - full-time or part-time - one
wishes to examine.

The most intractable problem from an equality-of-results perspective is clearly the inequality of university attainment by social
class. From 1971 to 1976, there has been little reduction in the
gap in university participation rates between the social classes for
either men or women. Universities in 1976 still attracted a much
higher proportion of people from advantaged sectors of society
than from disadvantaged sectors. PSNU institutions, on the other
hand, draw from a much wider social-class base. Different levels
of parental education had roughly equal PSNU attainment rates.

Women have made substantial gains in attainment of PSNU education and especially university education during the 1971 to
1976 period. Thus, it appears that inequality of educational results based on gender differences have been more amenable to
change than inequalities based on social class. This is undoubtedly due at least in part to the attention drawn to gender inequalities by the various women's organizations over the last
decade. Of course, we do not suggest that gender inequalities
have been completely eliminated in post-secondary education.
Women still tend to go to community colleges in larger numbers
than men, are still underrepresented in university, and (although
not shown in our data) tend to take different courses from men.

Most of the ethnic groups considered in this chapter have
experienced significant gains in the proportion attaining university and PSNU education. Indeed, some groups have surpassed the dominant English mother-tongue group in this respect.
Thus, with the notable exception of Native Indians, ethnic-
group-based inequality in post-secondary educational participation
is less apparent than social-class inequalities.

Notes

1. A more detailed analysis would consider participation rates among smaller subdivisions, programs, and perhaps even institutions. For example, one could ask, "Does the participation rate in professional courses among different groups differ from the participation rate in the arts?" Such questions are clearly important, but in most cases are beyond the scope of the present report, given data limitations. (For example, type of program enrolled in university or community college was not asked in the 1976 census.)

2. Some data from the special runs did allow for multiple variable analysis, but could not be included in this book.

3. To the extent that those of lower social class or minority ethnic status attend post-secondary educational institutions after a period of work force experience or delay their enrolment for some other reason (e.g., stopping out), there will be a bias in our sample in favour of elitist attendance.

4. Recent research has questioned the use of a single dimension of social class as adequate to portray the effects of social class. Hauser (1972) disaggregated an index of social class and found that each component; mother's and father's education and occupational prestige, had approximately equal effects on educational achievement for a large sample of Wisconsin students. Moreover, there is some question as to whether parental education is the best indicator of social class. Indeed, a study done for the Ontario government recommended that the Blishen socio-economic index based on parental occupation be employed to assess social-class trends in accessibility (Stevenson and Kellogg, 1979). In fact, parental occupational status or prestige, not education, is the measure of social class most commonly used by sociologists. Furthermore, it is not just a matter of selecting the "best" operational definition of social class. Some researchers have pointed out that there are divergent conceptions of social class. For example, Wright and Perrone (1977) and others (e.g. Horan, 1978) suggest that one's choice of conceptions is related to theoretical preferences. These issues aside, however, parental educational attainment is a frequently reported and increasingly available (von Zur-Muehlen, 1978:7), if imperfect, measure of socio-economic background.

5. It may be possible to examine trends in accessibility by birthplace of parents and period of immigration when the 1981 census data are available.

6. The special runs obtained for this study did include a country breakdown, so in the future it will be possible to

examine urban-rural factors as they affect the relationship between mother tongue and post-secondary educational attainment.

7.   In other demographic studies, researchers have inferred Jewish ethnicity from the census through religion.

CHAPTER 6

Conclusions and Recommendations

THE SOCIAL-STRATIFICATION PERSPECTIVE

Throughout this book a social-stratification perspective has been applied in reviewing literature and analysing census data that deal with inequalities in educational opportunity. This choice of perspective is important in that it implies an equality-of-results orientation. Further presumed is the notion that equal opportunity is attained only when groups of persons varying along important social dimensions (e.g., social class, ethnicity, gender) have equal participation rates. This focus on collective measures of behaviour is an appropriate strategy, in our view, for evaluating the extent to which equality of access to post-secondary institutions has been attained.

The social-stratification perspective has the additional merit of focusing attention on the reasons why some groups are less equal than others. We have suggested that early socialization experiences are potent forces in producing strong attitudinal and motivational differences across important social and cultural groups. A realistic appraisal of equality of post-secondary accessibility should, therefore, not overlook what is known about the impact of early socialization experiences on subsequent educational participation rates.

Our analysis indicates that both concern with specific dimensions of post-secondary educational stratification and actual patterns of inequality have altered over time. In Ontario, women, compared with men, have made fairly substantial gains in reducing the post-secondary education gap. Many ethnic groups (excluding Native Indians) can be comparably proud of their progress in reducing inequalities in post-secondary participation. Social-class differences in post-secondary participation remained stable in the 1970s, and no measurable reduction of strong class inequalities could be observed in our trend analysis of census data. As we noted in Chapter 1, social class is a crucially important feature of all social-stratification systems. Thus, the intransigence of class to rapid educational expansion in Ontario raises questions concerning the possible "interventionist" role government can play in substantially reducing inequalities in educational opportunity.

In the following section we consider the limits of government response to unequal access. We also attempt to place this issue into perspective by examining the changing post-secondary context of accessibility in the 1980s. Particularly relevant to this discussion is the phenomenal growth and diversity of post-secondary non-university (PSNU) education. Equally important is the growing trend towards vocational or technical emphasis in post-secondary education (e.g., employment considerations). Societies around the world are in the process of making post-secondary education more efficient, and "system rationalization" is becoming an increasingly common phrase. Underfunding of post-secondary institutions, then, must be taken into account in considering accessibility in the 1980s.

A final component we consider before making a number of recommendations designed to reduce inequalities in educational opportunity for disadvantaged groups is that of demographic changes. More specifically, we examine changes in age distribution in the 1980s, with the objective of evaluating their impact on accessibility.

The recommendations made at the end of this chapter fall into the areas of compensatory education, monitoring accessibility, and early financial intervention. We believe many of these recommendations can feasibly be implemented within the social context of the 1980s. Furthermore, social science research indicates their workability.

LIMITS OF THE GOVERNMENT RESPONSE

In spite of an expressed, long-term commitment to equal accessibility to post-secondary institutions in Ontario, the government's response has been to provide physical facilities and adjust tuition fee levels and loan/ grant formulas as a cure-all approach to ensuring accessibility at the university level. The development of the Colleges of Applied Arts and Technology (CAATs), located in many smaller towns as well as larger cities, in Ontario was in part a means of increasing access to post-secondary institutions among rural and less academically proficient students, but this must not be seen as increasing university accessibility, since CAATs were designed to be occupation-oriented and have no established transfer arrangement with universities. The other major government action with regard to the commitment to accessibility has been the funding or striking of commissions to explore accessibility further and make recommendations.

Over the last decade, commissions, advisory boards, and legislators themselves have shown increasing awareness of social, cultural, and even physical barriers (e.g., for the handicapped) to post-secondary accessibility as documented by social science literature. Indeed, the <u>Report of the Committee on the Future Role of Universities in Ontario</u>, formed in 1980 at the request of Premier Davis, acknowledged the limitation of the traditional approach towards the objective of equalizing accessibility:

> The committee considers that some progress toward this objective can be made by increasing the resources available to the universities for the purpose. For example, accessibility could be improved for Franco-Ontarians, residents of northern Ontario, native peoples, part-time students, the handicapped, women, and those who live a long distance from any university. At the same time, the committee notes that increasing resources to the universities will not guarantee that all social and economic groups will be adequately represented among the students enrolled in our universities. Interest in university education is affected by many attitudinal and motivational factors that cannot directly be influenced by the universities. These include family attitudes, peer group pressure, adequacy of early schooling, and other broad social issues that will not be addressed in this report (pp. 11-12).

Although the committee rightfully indicated the importance of social, attitudinal, and motivational factors in discussing equality of access, it posited increased resources to universities as a strategy for achieving progress towards this public objective. This recommendation is consistent with that of other government committees and commissions reviewed in Chapter 2.

As we have indicated throughout this book, financial considerations do play an influential role in determining who goes on to university or community college. However, our review of literature leads us to conclude that if inequalities in access to post-secondary education are to be significantly reduced, strategies of a compensatory nature must be introduced at a much <u>earlier</u> stage in the life cycle. Before presenting our own recommendations along this line, however, a brief discussion of the context in which our recommendations are made is necessary.

ACCESSIBILITY CONCERNS IN THE 1980s

In Chapter 2, we argued that the nature of concern for post-secondary accessibility in the last two decades was a reflection, in part, of the social, political, and economic climate in the wider society. This is no less true for the present.

Losers and Winners

Perhaps the most important aspect of concern is the changing view of education as a means of social mobility and progress for both individuals and society. During the 1960s, spurred on by research such as John Porter's The Vertical Mosaic (1965) which called for more post-secondary facilities to meet growing needs for highly qualified manpower, Canada witnessed an extraordinary growth in post-secondary facilities. Expenditures on higher education grew from $273 million nationally in 1960-61 to $1767 million in 1970-71, a growth nearly three times the increase of GNP in the same decade. This increase constituted 9 per cent of GNP and placed Canada first with respect to the proportion of GNP devoted to education (Lockhart, 1979: 224-37). Among the explanations generally offered in accounting for this rapid growth are the themes of equality of educational opportunity and the theories of post-industrial society and human capital (Turrittin, 1980). Equality of educational opportunity caught the popular imagination in the 1960s and was viewed as society's primary mode of social mobility. As Husén indicated, schools were thought of as "Great Equalizers" (1979:74). Indeed, Lockhart (1975) speaks of an implicit agreement, pointing out that:

> . . . the state became increasingly committed to a binding contract with those who accepted the new mobility norms. The terms of this contract, though unwritten, were well understood. On the one hand, those who wished to succeed within the institutional norms of the corporate state agreed to accept a narrow, sometimes irrelevant, often alienating and increasingly prolonged educational confinement as the price paid in youth for privilege in later life. On the other hand, the state not only guaranteed access to higher education on demand . . . but . . . also implicitly underwrote the availability of the appropriate jobs to all those who achieved certification (p. 197).

As everyone now knows, the situation changed drastically in the recessive economy of the 1970s as the number of new positions (especially highly qualified manpower positions) failed to keep up with the massive increases in post-secondary graduates (see Zsigmond et al., 1978). This seemingly gloomy situation led one social scientist to comment: "Thus, to almost everyone's surprise, the 1970s were ushered in not with the happy statistics of high rates of educationally-propelled mobility, but rather with the bitter evidence of graduate underemployment spilling over into outright unemployment" (Lockhart, 1977:80).

The "broken promises" (cf. Bowles and Gintis, 1976) of higher education have had a number of important ramifications in terms of both student behaviour and public perceptions of and priorities regarding higher education. In the 1960s and early 1970s the relationship of program expansion within universities to the labour market was largely unquestioned. The development of less autonomous community college systems were designed to meet more technical and vocational labour market demands. Universities were given leeway to fulfil the promises of human capital theories. Decreases in prestige of jobs held by university graduates in the 1970s (Anisef, 1982), when coupled with negative media exposure on graduate underemployment, led to an increasing demand for vocationally relevant education. As we indicated in our description of educational expansion in Canada, the growth of the PSNU sector and declining undergraduate enrolments in Arts and Science faculties are reliable indicators of this growing vocational trend. Very recently a federal Employment and Immigration Department Task Force on Labour Market Development in the 1980s has recommended a reallocation of post-secondary resources to place more emphasis on technological training done by community colleges (The Financial Post, 1981:4).

This increased emphasis on "employment considerations" in the 1970s will surely continue into the 1980s. Higher education in Canada in the 1980s will be significantly more responsive to changes in the size and composition of the labour force than in the 1970s (OECD, 1981:53). Given the escalating costs of higher education in the 1970s and projected costs for the 1980s, provincial and federal governments are underscoring the value of efficiency and rationality in their allocation of monies to the post-secondary sector. Universities especially are feeling the impact of "system rationalization" prompted by the underfunding of universities by provincial and federal governments. Such under-funding results in the need to streamline or actually cut university programs. A quote which appeared in a recent newsletter from the Ontario Confederation of University Faculty Associations illustrates this concern:

> The 1980's are not, on preliminary evidence, going to be comfortable for many of the world's universities. Indeed, only a naive observer would expect stability for the next few years. The universities, central as they are to the economic, cultural and social processes of their countries, cannot escape the shocks and strains of the world economy, and the interplay of those shocks at the national and local levels (1981:1).

What effects do these changes have on our examination of post-secondary accessibility? First, it is now even more important to recognize the diversity of institutions that are labelled by "post-secondary." In our analysis, we separated university from PSNU institutions; the latter category includes community colleges, trade schools, private vocational schools, apprenticeship training programs, etc. Given the vocational nature of Ontario's CAATs (which form the bulk of the PSNU category) and the lack of formal university transfer arrangements, it is necessary to maintain this distinction. The relatively egalitarian recruitment of PSNU institutions should not be confused with university recruit-

135

ment. Indeed, some have argued that PSNU institutions have served a safety-valve function, preventing universities from being inundated by a large number of lower-social-class and otherwise disadvantaged students (e.g., Karabel and Halsey, 1977).

The effect of more stringent government funding of universities on patterns of recruitment to university have been noted by several writers. Peter M. Leslie in a recent policy study for the Association of Universities and Colleges of Canada (1980) admits that the present fiscal crisis mentality by government can bring "hardship to academically talented young people whose life chances depend on their having access to university education of the highest quality" (p. 319).

Some groups in Canada are currently arguing that universities may be in the process of becoming more rather than less elite, given the impact of tuition-fee increases and inflation. For example, the Ontario Federation of Students takes this stance:

> Beginning in 1977, however, real family incomes did decline, and this most likely amplified the impact of the $100 fee increase in 1977. It would not be an exaggeration to say that the combination of higher fees and lower real incomes sent Ontario's participation rate into a tailspin from which it has yet to recover. . . . Without a doubt then, there is a substantial body of evidence which suggests that declining participation rates takes its greatest toll from potential students who do not have access to the necessary financial resources (1980a:12-19).

Clearly, in making our recommendations, policies which are aimed at equalizing social-class participation in university will serve to counteract a potential regressive tendency in social-class recruitment if the real cost of tuition increases. Indeed, recommendations like ours become even more important if social justice needs are to be met under present economic conditions in relation to university funding.

Demographic considerations are important for assessing the social context of accessibility in the 1980s. After the original period of massive expansion during the 1960s and early 1970s, it appears that in the mid-1980s we will experience a loss in absolute numbers of persons in the 18 to 24 age group usually associated with post-secondary participation (Anisef, 1981:9), and possibly a decline in the university participation rate. However, since 1978-79 there has been a sharp jump in Ontario university enrolments for persons aged 24 or 25 and older. Insofar as Canada's population is aging, this upswing in "older" students illustrates the present and future importance of "recurrent" or lifelong education. At the present time nearly 23 per cent of Ontario universities draw their full-time enrolments from the population 25 and over. This percentage is likely to increase in the future (Committee on the Future Role of Universities in Ontario, 1981:5).

Changes in the age distribution of students in post-secondary education are also influenced by recurrent education. Many older persons are interested in resuming their studies as reflected in the fact that there were over 216,000 part-time undergraduate and graduate enrolments in Canada in 1978-79 (Anisef, 1981).

Our view of the effect of such changes is that they allow for policies that can have a positive effect on equalizing participation rates. Maintaining physical plants in an era of decreasing numbers of traditional full-time students suggests that policies of increasing participation rates of low-participation groups might be seen as more feasible. The sponsorship of part-time education for mature students could be viewed as a strategy for increasing lower-social-class participation. Indeed, our own statistics, like those of others, indicate that part-time university students have lower social-class backgrounds than full-time ones. However, for such changes to take place, it is necessary to implement changes that affect the attitudes and motivation of disadvantaged "target" groups. The importance of this is especially clear once we recognize that the rapid expansion of post-secondary facilities in the 1960s did not reduce the gap in participation rates between social classes from 1971 to 1976.

Importantly, policies that recommend increasing the proportion of disadvantaged persons in post-secondary institutions (especially universities) may be seen to perpetuate economic inequalities, since a B.A. is no longer a guarantee (if it ever was) of desirable employment. However, some observers have provided convincing documentation that a university education should not be discounted in securing a competitive edge in today's brutal labour market. For example, Turrittin (1980) comments:

In brief, the findings are very clear: in spite of the tight labour market since 1975, university graduates have had low rates of unemployment compared to the overall rate of unemployment for the 15 to 24 year old age group. It is also true that community college graduates on average have had somewhat lower rates of unemployment than university graduates until very recently (p. 25).

Research by social scientists has also had a significant impact on the climate in which we make our recommendations. In our own analysis of accessibility to Ontario post-secondary institutions, we have documented the progress made by women and most mother-tongue groups in terms of university accessibility. These groups are also well represented in PSNU institutions (Anisef, 1981). In terms of priorities, it appears that the social-class dimension is the one that most significantly affects post-secondary participation and is the hardest to alter. Thus, without denying the importance of the need to continue to strive for gender equality (especially in terms of program selection and graduate and professional school participation) and ethnic equality (especially for Native Indians), most of the recommendations in the following section deal with the problem perceived to be most significant in the 1980s - continuing or worsening social-class stratification in our universities.

RECOMMENDATIONS

Though changes in educational policy are largely in the hands of legislators and those with influence on them, social science research (e.g., Coleman, 1968; Jencks et al., 1972) has had an impact on government policy and modes of thinking about concepts like equality of opportunity. At a general level, our review of the public debate on accessibility and of the social science litera-ture is valuable in setting the stage for a discussion of policies concerning accessibility. Clearly, acceptance of particular defini-tions of accessibility or equality of opportunity entail the accep-tance of a number of related assumptions concerning the nature of intelligence, social justice, and the belief in the influence of nature and/or nurture. This suggests, at a minimum, the need to translate implicit assumptions into explicit ones if policy changes are to make sense.

In making our specific recommendations for increasing the participation rates of disadvantaged groups in Ontario, we have attempted to keep in mind (1) what social science research in-dicates might work, (2) the social context in which we make these recommendations, as indicated in the previous section, and (3) our perception of what recommendations can most feasibly be implemented by the government. With regard to this last point we recognize that recommendations we have made concerning early financial intervention would require the consent of other depart-ments or levels of government. It should also be noted that our recommendations are generally applicable to other provinces in Canada.

COMPENSATORY EDUCATION

Our top priority (Recommendations 1 and 2) is compensatory education. Recent sociological research has suggested that social and cultural barriers to equality of educational opportunity are harder to remove than previously thought. Present systems of education may serve to reinforce existing social inequalities rather than equalize differences. Facile solutions such as lowering financial barriers at the post-secondary level are probably insufficient to effect important changes. Social science research has documented a variety of child-raising and family-life factors associated with early socialization processes which result in lower academic performance, expectations, and aspirations for some social and cultural groups. Unfortunately, the research is not conclusive in the sense of identifying one factor or even a set of factors which, if altered, would clearly increase the cognitive development or motivation of offspring of the disadvantaged. Be that as it may, social science literature does indicate the types of areas (e.g., linguistic styles, self-concept of ability, achievement values) that form the negative basis for becoming disadvantaged in school. The following recommendations, all related to the use of schools as agents of change, are consistent with our reading of the social science literature.

Recommendation 1

THE GOVERNMENT SHOULD IMPLEMENT COMPENSATORY EDUCATION PROGRAMS AT THE PROVINCIAL LEVEL. THESE PROGRAMS WOULD BE DESIGNED TO PROVIDE ECONOMICALLY DISADVANTAGED CHILDREN WITH A "HEAD START" AT THE PRE-KINDERGARTEN LEVEL, EXTENDING INTO ELEMENTARY AND SECONDARY LEVELS IF NECESSARY.

In spite of early negative evaluations of Head Start, subsequent research indicates that pre-school programs employing a relatively structured curriculum oriented to cognitive development do result in superior academic performance for low-status students compared with control groups (Havighurst and Levine, 1979:224-25). Longitudinal research indicates that the benefits of such programs are lasting; they were particularly effective at younger ages (one to three years) and when they were of long duration. Results appear especially remarkable for persons in a concentrated poverty (slum) environment given massive early family intervention.

Reviews of research of school-based compensatory education projects (e.g., Follow Through, a continuation of Head Start in the United States) indicate that continuing emphasis in curricula on basic skills and definite instructional objectives in the cognitive and conceptual domains had positive effects on academic performance. The role of principals in providing leadership is one of the most important factors in the success of compensatory education programs. Evaluations of the results of "Title I," the U.S. government's program for improving the academic achievement of low-status students, justify "cautious optimism" according to some researchers (cf. Havighurst and Levine, 1979:236). However, going beyond the mastery of basic skills needed for functional literacy to the development of comprehensive, problem-solving abilities may require different sorts of compensatory programs.

Recommendation 2

THE GOVERNMENT SHOULD INSTITUTE SUMMER LEARNING PROGRAMS AIMED AT ECONOMICALLY DISADVANTAGED CHILDREN OF ELEMENTARY SCHOOL AGE.

Research in the United States indicates that disadvantaged students show a higher rate of relative achievement during the school year than during the summer. The cognitive achievement gap between low- and high-income children widens during the time when school is not in session (Heyns, 1978:187). Though a precise specification of the causal processes is not yet available, a small number of factors, such as the amount that children read seemed to make a difference. Though Heyns (1978:195) reported the difficulty in isolating the effects of school-related variables from family-related ones, the general finding that disadvantaged children lose ground over the summer supports our general recommendation. Further research, of course, will be needed to specify what sorts of programs may be most effective and feasible to implement.

Recommendations 3 and 4 can be seen as adjuncts to the previous two recommendations. In our view, they are steps that need to be taken to ensure, to the highest degree possible, that a solid empirical base for the pure recommendations exists and that new programs instituted are adequately evaluated.

Recommendation 3

THE GOVERNMENT SHOULD PERIODICALLY HIRE EXTERNAL CONSULTANTS TO REVIEW THE STATE OF RESEARCH WITH REGARD TO EARLY SOCIALIZATION EFFECTS ON POST-SECONDARY ENROLMENT ATTITUDES. THE PURPOSE WOULD BE TO ASSESS THE EFFECTIVENESS OF ONGOING EXPERIMENTS AND POLICIES AIMED AT EQUALIZING ACCESS TO UNIVERSITIES AND COMMUNITY COLLEGES. THIS REVIEW SHOULD INCLUDE COMPARABLE RESEARCH IN COUNTRIES OTHER THAN CANADA, INSOFAR AS THIS WOULD FACILITATE CROSS-CULTURAL COMPARISONS OF THE RELATIVE EFFECTIVENESS OF COMPENSATORY EDUCATION STRATEGIES.

Recommendation 4

FUNDING SHOULD BE MADE AVAILABLE TO ENSURE A SYSTEMATIC EVALUATION OF THE EFFECTIVENESS OR SUCCESS OF PROGRAMS THAT ARE INTRODUCED TO HELP ECONOMICALLY DISADVANTAGED CHILDREN. THESE PROGRAMS SHOULD BE EVALUATED IN TERMS OF THEIR SPECIFIC OBJECTIVES.

Recommendations 5, 6 and 7 should be seen as indirect but important attempts to alter the motivation of students at the elementary and secondary school level.

Recommendation 5

IN VIEW OF DIFFERENCES IN HIGH SCHOOLS IN RETEN-TION RATES AND SUCCESS IN PLACING PERSONS IN HIGHER EDUCATION, INCENTIVE PROGRAMS (e.g., AWARDS) SHOULD BE ESTABLISHED FOR STAFF AND ADMINISTRATION IN ORDER TO INCREASE POST-SECONDARY EDUCATIONAL PARTICIPATION.

Public schools feeding into high schools can share these "neighbourhood" awards. The rewards can be financial and symbolic (e.g., favourable publicity to the winning school, its students and staff, etc.). Recent research (e.g., Ravitch, 1981) indicates that schools do make a difference in terms of student achievements and other cognitive results of schooling. We there-fore anticipate that school incentive programs will positively affect students' academic achievement.

Recommendation 6

VOCAL FEMINIST ADVOCATES HAVE DOCUMENTED THE PRESENCE OF STEREOTYPED AND SEXIST IMAGES OF WOMEN'S SOCIAL AND OCCUPATIONAL ROLES IN TEXT-BOOKS AND TEACHING AIDS. THE SAME STEREOTYPING OCCURS IN TEXTBOOKS THAT FOCUS ON MINORITY-GROUP MEMBERS. SHOWING NATIVE INDIANS AS TEACHERS OR ETHNICS AS DOCTORS IS AN EASY FIRST STEP IN CHANGING CONCEPTIONS ABOUT IMPORTANT SOCIAL ROLES.

Recommendation 7

> GUIDANCE COUNSELLING IN HIGH SCHOOL SHOULD NOT
> ONLY BE A SOURCE OF FACTUAL INFORMATION, BUT
> SHOULD ALSO ENCOURAGE EDUCATIONAL ATTAINMENT TO
> THE LIMIT OF A CHILD'S ACADEMIC POTENTIAL. IN
> ADDITION, PROGRAMS THAT BRING LOCALLY-KNOWN
> SUCCESSFUL GRADUATES OF HIGHER EDUCATION INTO
> THE SCHOOL COULD BE IMPORTANT SOURCES OF EN-
> COURAGEMENT IN REGIONS WHERE FEW ATTEND COLLEGE
> OR UNIVERSITY.

MONITORING ACCESSIBILITY

The findings reported in Chapter 5 illustrate the use of census
data for monitoring the accessibility to post-secondary education
of different social and cultural groups. This is one research area
that government should continue to sponsor insofar as trend
information is provided.

Recommendation 8

> THE GOVERNMENT SHOULD CONTINUOUSLY MONITOR
> TRENDS IN ACCESSIBILITY TO POST-SECONDARY INSTI-
> TUTIONS IN ONTARIO.

This is especially necessary in view of the opinions (e.g.,
OFS, 1980a) that accessibility has decreased for disadvantaged
groups in recent years. In this regard, the 1981 census
analysis, which is in the planning stage by the authors of this
book, should provide valuable insights. An attempt at developing
and employing a standardized or common measure of social class
(e.g. the Blishen socio-economic index) and ethnicity would also
prove most useful in comparing findings across various data sets.
In contrasting the 1971 and 1981 censuses, comparisons of socio-
economic status employing family income, father's occupation, and
the above-mentioned Blishen socio-economic index would become
possible. In addition, data on ethnicity, gender, and regional
origins of students should be collected.

Recommendation 9

> THE USE OF THE CENSUS COULD BE EXTENDED TO
> DESCRIBE ADOLESCENTS BETWEEN THE AGES OF 15 AND

20 WHO ARE EITHER IN SCHOOL OR HAVE DROPPED OUT. THIS COMPARISON OF ATTENDERS AND NON-ATTENDERS IN TERMS OF SOCIO-ECONOMIC STATUS AND CULTURAL GROUP CHARACTERISTICS WOULD PROVE VALUABLE TO EDUCATORS AND GOVERNMENT OFFICIALS ALIKE.[1]

Recommendation 10

GIVEN THE DRAMATIC INCREASES IN PARTICIPATION RATES FOR SOME ETHNIC GROUPS, RESEARCH SHOULD BE UNDERTAKEN TO ISOLATE THE CIRCUMSTANCES, CONDI-TIONS, AND FACTORS RELATED TO SUCH SHARP IN-CREASES IN PARTICIPATION RATES. IN PARTICULAR, CULTURAL VALUES REGARDING THE DESIRABILITY OF UNIVERSITY EDUCATION, RATES OF ASSIMILATION, URBAN-RURAL FACTORS, AND THE DEGREE OF FAMILY SUPPORT AND ENCOURAGEMENT (FINANCIAL AND NON-FINANCIAL) SHOULD BE INVESTIGATED.

EARLY FINANCIAL INTERVENTION

Our book shows that strategies of financial intervention by various levels of government are aimed at the student who has successfully completed secondary school. In terms of the effects of altering financial arrangements (fee, loan, or grant schemes) for post-secondary education, raising the cost of higher education is likely to deter some disadvantaged persons even if they have the requisite motivation and marks. Higher loans will still have a differential effect because of the debt load incurred. Lowering the costs of higher education will help some disadvantaged students to attend, but since such decisions are usually made well before senior high school, the overall increase in participation rates will likely not change much. Strategies of informing younger children of the availability of aid in the form of loans and grants begin to "get at" the problem of motivation.

Recommendation 11

A SCHEME SHOULD BE DEVELOPED WHEREBY RECIPIENTS OF FAMILY ALLOWANCE BENEFITS ARE GIVEN THE OPTION OF PLACING MONEY RECEIVED INTO A SPECIAL GOVERN-MENT ACCOUNT WHICH WOULD ACCRUE INTEREST AND BE PAYABLE TO THE CHILD IN THE EVENT THAT HE/SHE ATTENDS A POST-SECONDARY EDUCATIONAL INSTI-TUTION.

Thus, in economically disadvantaged families, a regular procedure would be instituted for saving for a child's future educational needs, much as wealthier families normally do today. In addition, the government should publicize this option and send monthly reminders to families accepting the option as a means of encouraging the development of the expectation of post-secondary education. For families below a given income, this "scholarship fund" could be a supplement rather than substitute for the allowance. Therefore, lower-income families would not be forced to sacrifice further to encourage their children's post-secondary aspirations.

Recommendation 12

AN INCOME TAX DEDUCTION (REGISTERED HIGHER ED-UCATION SAVINGS PLAN) SHOULD BE INTRODUCED AND PUBLICIZED.

The rationale for this recommendation is similar to that explained in the previous recommendation.

Our assumption in developing Recommendations 11 and 12 is that parents will be fully informed concerning the nature of the program. Once parents understand the program, they can elect to participate on a voluntary basis.

Notes

1. An accessibility steering committee was recently constituted in the Ministry of Education/Ministry of Colleges and Universities. Recommendation 9 is one proposal generated by that committee. However, the Ministries have decided not to sponsor this research at the present time.

Bibliography

Anisef, Paul.
  1980   "A Study on Women's Accessibility to Higher Educa-
          tion."   University and College Placement Association
          Journal 14, no. 2:9-12.

  1981   "The Pursuit of Tomorrow: Accessibility to Higher
          Education in Canada and Elsewhere," Paper presented
          at the International Symposium, Beersheva, Israel
          (December).

  1982   "Higher Education and the Labor Market: Occupational
          Attainments of University Graduates." Interchange, Vol
          13(2):1-19.

Anisef, P., Paasche, J. G.; and Turrittin, A. H.
  1980   Is the Die Cast? Educational Achievements and Work
          Destinations of Ontario Youth. Toronto: Ministry of
          Education/Ministry of Colleges and Universities.

Beaujot, Roderic, and MacQuillan, Kevin.
  1982   Growth and Dualism: The Demographic Development of
          Canadian Society. Toronto: Gage, forthcoming.

Bernstein, B., and Henderson, D.
  1974   "Social Class Differences in the Relevance of Language
          to Socialization." In Contemporary Research in the
          Sociology of Education, edited by John Eggleston.
          London: Methuen.

Boocock, Sarane.
  1980   Sociology of Education: An Introduction, 2nd ed.
          Boston: Houghton Mifflin.

Bowles, S., and Gintis, H.
  1976   Schooling in Capitalist America. New York: Basic
          Books.

Breton, Raymond.
  1972   Social and Academic Factors in the Career Decisions of
          Canadian Youth. Ottawa: Manpower and Immigration.

Brim Jr., O. G.
   1966   "Socialization Through the Life Cycle." In <u>Socialization</u> <u>After Childhood</u>, edited by O. G. Brim, Jr. and S. Wheeler. New York: John Wiley.

Bronfenbrenner, Urie.
   1958   "Socialization and Social Class through Time and Space." In <u>Readings in Social Psychology</u>, edited by E. E. Maccoby et al. New York: Holt, Rinehart & Winston.

Buttrick, John.
   1977   <u>Who Goes to University from Toronto</u>? Toronto: Ontario Economic Council.

Cameron, D. M.
   1977   <u>The Northern Dilemma: Public Policy and Post-secondary Education in Northern Ontario</u>. Toronto: Ontario Economic Council.

Carlton, R. A.; Colley, L. A.; Mackinnon, N. J.
   1977   <u>Education, Change and Society</u>. Toronto: Gage.

Cassie, J. R. B., et al.
   1980   <u>Sex-Role Stereotyping: Incidence and Implications for Guidance and Counselling of Students</u>. Toronto: Ministry of Education.

Clark, Edmund; Cook, David; Fallis, George; and Kent, Michael.
   1969   <u>Student Aid and Access to Higher Education in Ontario</u>. Toronto: Institute for Quantitative Analysis of Social and Economic Policy, University of Toronto.

Clark, S. D.
   1976   <u>Canadian Society in Historical Perspective</u>. Toronto: McGraw-Hill Ryerson.

Clark, W., and Zsigmond, Z.
   1981   <u>Job Market Reality for Post-secondary Graduates</u>. Ottawa: Statistics Canada.

Clausen, J. A., et al.
   1968   <u>Socialization and Society</u>. Boston: Little, Brown & Co.

Clement, Wallace.
   1975   <u>The Canadian Corporate Elite: An Analysis of Economic Power</u>. Toronto: McClelland and Stewart.

Losers and Winners

Coleman, James S.
  1961   The Adolescent Society. New York: Free Press.

  1968   "The Concept of Equality of Educational Opportunity."
         Harvard Educational Review 68:7-22.

  1966   Equality of Educational Opportunity.   Washington,
         D.C.:   U.S. Government Printing Office.

Collins, Randall

  1971   "Functional and Conflict Theories of Educational Strati-
         fication."   American Sociological Review 36:1002-19.

  1979   "Where are Educational Requirements for Employment
         Highest? Sociology of Education 47:419-42.

Commission on Post-secondary Education in Ontario.
  1971   Draft Report.   Toronto: Ministry of Government
         Services.

  1972   The Learning Society.   Report of the Commission.
         Toronto: Ministry of Government Services.

Committee of Presidents of Universities of Ontario.
  1970   Undergraduate Student Aid and Accessibility in the
         Universities of Ontario.   Toronto: Subcommittee on
         Student Aid.

  1971   Towards 2000.   Toronto: Subcommittee on Research
         and Planning.

Committee on the Future Role of Universities in Ontario.
  1981   Report.   Toronto: Ministry of Colleges and Uni-
         versities.

Cook, Gail C. A.; Dobell, Rodney; and Stager, David A. A.
  1969   "Student Aid Programs." Policy Paper Series: Number
         7.   Toronto: Institute for the Quantitative Analysis of
         Social and Economic Policy, University of Toronto.

Coopersmith, S.
  1967   The Antecedents of Self Esteem.   San Francisco: W.
         H. Freeman and Co.

Council of Ontario Universities.
  1971   Accessibility and Student Aid.   Report by the Sub-
         committee on Student Aid.

  1976   "Statement on the Principles Which Should Govern the
         Setting of Tuition Fees." Toronto: Special Committee
         on Access to University Policies and Plans.

Curtis, James E., and Scott, W. H.
  1979   Social Stratification: Canada, 2nd ed. Scarborough, Ontario: Prentice-Hall of Canada.

Dahrendoret, Ralf
  1959   Class and Class Conflict in Industrial Society. Stanford, California: Stanford University Press.

Deosaran, Ramesh.
  1975   Educational Aspirations, What Matters? A Literature Review, No. 135. Toronto: Toronto Board of Education.

Economic Council of Canada.
  1965   Second Annual Review. Ottawa: Information Canada.

  1971   Design for Decision Making: An Application to Human Resources Policies. Eighth Annual Review. Ottawa: Information Canada.

  1978   A Time for Reason. Fifteenth Annual Review. Ottawa: Information Canada.

Evetts, Julia.
  1973   The Sociology of Educational Ideas. London: Routledge and Kegan Paul.

Federal-Provincial Task Force on Student Assistance.
  1980   "Summary of Existing Student Assistance Programs." Ottawa: Council of Ministers of Education.

Fleming, W. G.
  1974   Educational Opportunity: The Pursuit of Equality. Scarborough, Ontario: Prentice-Hall of Canada.

Forcese, Dennis.
  1975   The Canadian Class Structure. Toronto: McGraw-Hill Ryerson.

Forcese, Dennis, and Stephen Richer
  1975   Issues in Canadian Society: An Introduction to Sociology. Scarborough, Ontario: Prentice-Hall of Canada.

Gilbert, S., and McRoberts, H. A.
  1975   "Differentiation and Stratification: The Issue of Inequality." In Issues in Canadian Society, edited by D. Forcese and S. Richer. Scarborough, Ontario: Prentice-Hall of Canada.

Hall, Oswald, and McFarlone, B.
  1962   Transition from School to Work. Report No. 19 of the Interdepartmental Skilled Manpower Training Research

Committee, Department of Labour. Ottawa: Queen's Printer.

Harvey, Edward.
1977 "Accessibility to Post-secondary Education–Some Gains, Some Losses." University Affairs 18:10-11.

Harvey, Edward B., and Lennards, J. L.
1973 Key Issues in Higher Education. Toronto: The Ontario Institute for Studies in Education.

Hauser, R.M.
1972 "Disaggregating a social-psychological model of educational attainment." In Structural Equation Models in the Social Sciences, edited by A. S. Goldberger and O. D. Duncan. New York: Seminar Press.

Havighurst, Robert, and Levine, Daniel U.
1979 Society and Education, 5th ed. Boston: Allyn and Bacon.

Herrnstein, Richard.
1973 IQ in the Meritocracy. Boston: Little, Brown & Co.

Hess, R., and Shipman, V.
1965 "Early Experience and the Socialization of Cognitive Modes in Children." Child Development 36:869-86.

Heyns, Barbara.
1978 Summer Learning and the Effects of Schooling. New York: Academic Press.

Horan, P.
1978 "Is Status Attainment Research Atheoretical?" American Sociological Review 43:534-41.

Humphreys, Elizabeth, and Porter, John.
1978 "Part-time Studies and University Accessibility." Unpublished report, Carlton University, Department of Sociology.

Husén, Torsten.
1975 Social Influences on Educational Attainment. Paris: Centre for Educational Research and Innovation, Organization for Economic Co-operation and Development.

1979 The School in Question. Oxford: University Press.

Hyman, H. H.
1953 "The Value Systems of Different Classes: A Social Psychological Contribution to the Analysis of Social Stratification." In Class, Status and Power, edited by R. Bendix and S. M. Lipset. New York: Free Press.

Information Canada.
1974   Perspective Canada: A Compendium of Social Statistics.
Ottawa: Information Canada.

Ishwaran, K., ed.
1979   Childhood and Adolescent Canada. Toronto: McGraw-
Hill Ryerson.

James, Carl E.
1980   "Peer Influence on Educational and Occupational Aspirations and Achievements." Master's thesis, York University.

Jencks, Christopher, et al.
1972   Inequality: A Reassessment of Family and Schooling in
America. New York: Basic Books.

Jensen, Arthur.
1969   "How much can we boost I.Q. and Scholastic Achievement?" Harvard Educational Review 39:1-123.

Johnstone, J. C.
1969   Young People's Images of Canadian Society.   Ottawa:
Queen's Printer.

Kahl, J. A.
1953   "Educational and Occupational Aspirations of 'Common
Man' Boys." Harvard Educational Review 23:186-203.

Kalbach, W. E., and McVey, W. W.
1979   The Demographic Bases of Canadian Society, 2nd ed.
Toronto: McGraw-Hill Ryerson.

Kalbach, Warren E., and Richmond, Anthony H.
1980   Factors in the Adjustment of Immigrants and their
Descendants. Ottawa: Statistics Canada.

Karabel, Jerome, and Halsey, A. H.
1977   Power and Ideology in Education. New York: Oxford
University Press.

Kerckhoff, Allan C.
1972   Socialization and Social Class. Englewood Cliffs, New
Jersey: Prentice-Hall.

Kitagawa, E. M.
1955   "Components of a Difference Between Two Rates."
American Statistical Association Journal 50:1169-94.

Kohn, M. L.
1969   Class and Conformity. Homewood, Illinois: Dorsey
Press.

Losers and Winners

Kohn, M. L.
    1977   Class and Conformity: A Study in Values,   2nd ed.
            Chicago: University of Chicago Press.

Kralt, John.
    1976   Ethnic Origins of Canadians. 1971 Census of Canada
            Profile Studies. Ottawa: Statistics Canada.

Lawr, D. R., and Gridney, R. D.
    1973   Educating Canadians: A Documentary History of Public
            Education. Toronto: Van Nostrand Reinhold.

Lennards, Jos.
    1980   "Education." In Sociology, edited by Robert Hagedorn.
            Toronto: Holt, Rinehart & Winston of Canada.

Leslie, Peter M.
    1980   Canadian Universities 1980 and Beyond: Enrollment,
            Structural Change and Finance. Study no. 3. Ottawa:
            Association of Universities and Colleges of Canada.

Lipset, Seymour M.
    1964   "Canada and the United States--A Comparative View."
            Canadian Review of Sociology and Anthropology 1:173-
            85.

Lockhart, Alexander.
    1975   "Future Failure: The Unanticipated Consequences of
            Educational Planning." In Socialization and Values in
            Canadian Society, edited by R. Pike and E. Zureik,
            vol. 2. Toronto: McClelland and Stewart.

    1977   "Educational Policy Development in Canada: A Critique
            of the Past and a Case for the Future." In Education,
            Change and Society, edited by Richard Carlton, L. A.
            Colley, and N. J. Mackinnon. Toronto: Gage.

    1979   "Educational Opportunities and Economic Opportunities--
            The 'New' Liberal Equality Syndrome." In Economy,
            Class and Social Reality, edited by John A. Fry.
            Scarborough, Ontario: Butterworth.

Mackinnon, N. J., and Anisef, P.
    1979   "Self Assessment and the Early Educational Attainment
            Process."   The Canadian Review of Sociology and
            Anthropology 16, no. 3:305-19.

Marsden, L., and Harvey, E. B.
    1971   "Equality of Educational Access Reconsidered: The
            Post-secondary Case in Ontario." Interchange 2,
            4:11-26.

McIntyre, Gail.
  1975 Women and Ontario Universities. Toronto: Ministry of Colleges and Universities.

Medsker, Leland L.
  1972 The Global Quest for Educational Opportunity. Berkeley Center for Research and Development in Higher Education, University of California.

Mehmet, O.
  1978 Who Benefits from the Ontario University System. Occasional Paper 7. Toronto: Ontario Economic Council.

Ministry of Colleges and Universities.
  1973 1970-1973 Statistical Summary. Toronto: Ministry of Colleges and Universities.

  1979a Study of Tuition and Incidental Fees, 1977/1978. Main report. Toronto: P. S. Ross & Partners.

  1979b "Ontario Student Assistance Program: 1978-79 Program Review." Toronto: Student Awards Branch.

  1980-81 Financial Assistance for Students. Ontario Student Assistance Program. Information and Instructions.

Murphy, Raymond.
  1979 Sociological Theories of Education. Toronto: McGraw-Hill Ryerson.

Neatby, H. Blair.
  1972 The Politics of Chaos: Canada in the Thirties. Toronto: Macmillan of Canada.

Okihiro, Norman R.
  1981 "Community Colleges and Early Occupational Stratification." Paper presented at the annual meeting of The Canadian Sociology and Anthropology Association, Halifax, Nova Scotia.

Ontario Confederation of University Faculty Associations.
  1981 Newsletter no. 1, October.

Ontario Council on University Affairs.
  1975 First Annual Report, September 25, 1974 to February 28, 1975. Toronto: Ministry of Colleges and Universities.

  1976 Second Annual Report, March 1, 1975 to February 29, 1976. Toronto: Ministry of Colleges and Universities.

1977   Third Annual Report, March 1, 1976 to February 28,
       1977.   Toronto: Ministry of Colleges and Universities.

1978   Fourth Annual Report, March 1, 1977 to February 28,
       1978.   Toronto: Ministry of Colleges and Universities.

1979   Fifth Annual Report, March 1, 1978 to February 28,
       1979.   Toronto: Ministry of Colleges and Universities.

1980   Sixth Annual Report, March 1, 1979 to February 29,
       1980.   Toronto: Ministry of Colleges and Universities.

Ontario Economic Council.
   1975   Issues and Alternatives: 1976, "Education."   Toronto.

   1977   Emerging Problems in Post-secondary Education.   Dis-
          cussion Paper Series.   Toronto.

Ontario Federation of Students.
   1979   "The Unequal Pursuit of The Golden Fleece: A Reas-
          sessment of Social and Cultural Barriers to Universal
          Accessibility."   Toronto: Research Department.

   1980a   "Swimming Against the Current."   Brief to the Federal/
           Provincial Task Force on Student Assistance, Toronto
           (June).

   1980b   "Where Do Access Studies Come From?   Equalizing the
           Pursuit of the Golden Fleece Revisited."   Toronto:
           Research Department (September).

Ontario Status of Women Council.
   1974   Annual Report # 1.   Toronto.

   1975   Annual Report # 2.   Toronto.

   1977   Annual Report # 3.   Toronto.

   1978   Annual Report # 4.   Toronto.

   1979   Annual Report # 5.   Toronto.

Organization for Economic Co-operation and Development.
       Development of Higher Education 1950-67.   Paris.

   1976   Review of National Policies in Canada.   Paris.

   1979   Equal Opportunities for Women.   Paris.

   1981   Access to Higher Education in the 1980s.   Paris.

Osadchuk, Michael.
1980   Untitled paper. Department of Sociology, York University.

Peng, Samuel S.
1977   "Trends in the Entry to Higher Education: 1961-1972." Educational Researcher 6:15-19.

Persell, Caroline Hodges.
1977   Education and Inequality: A Theoretical and Empirical Synthesis. New York: Free Pess.

Picou, S. J., and Carter, T. M.
1976   "Significant-Other Influence and Aspiration". Sociology of Education 49:12-22.

Pike, R. M.
1970   Who Doesn't Get to University--and Why? A Study on Accessibility to Higher Education in Canada. Ottawa: Association of Universities and Colleges of Canada.

Pike, R. M., and Zureik, E.
1978   Socialization and Values in Canadian Society, Vol 2. Toronto: Macmillan of Canada.

Pike, Robert.

1970   Who Goes to University and Why? AUCC. Ottawa.

1979   "Equality of Educational Opportunity: Dilemmas and Policy Options." Interchange 9, no. 2:30-39.

1980   "Education, Class, and Power in Canada." In Power and Change in Canada, edited by Richard Ossenberg. Toronto: McClelland and Stewart.

Porter, John.
1965   The Vertical Mosaic: An Analysis of Social Class and Power in Canada. Toronto: University of Toronto Press.

1971   Toward 2000. Toronto: McClelland and Stewart.

1979   The Measure of Canadian Society. Toronto: Gage.

Porter, Marion R.; Porter, John; and Blishen, Bernard R.
1979   Does Money Matter? Prospects for Higher Education in Ontario. Toronto: Macmillan of Canada.

Rabinovitch, Robert
1966   An Analysis of the Canadian Post Secondary Student Population. Part I A Report on Canadian Undergraduate Students. Ottawa: Canadian Union of Students.

Ramu, G. N., and Johnson, S. D.
1976   Introduction to Canadian Society: Sociological Analysis.
        Toronto: Macmillan of Canada.

Ravitch, Diane.
1981   "The Meaning of the New Colemen Report." Phi Delta
        Kappan 62:718-720.

Rawls, John.
1971   A Theory of Justice.   Cambridge, Mass.:   Harvard
        University Press.

Richardson, James C.
1977   "Education and Social Mobility: Changing Conceptions
        of the Role of Educational Systems." Canadian Journal
        of Sociology 2 (April):417-433.

Richer, S.
1977   "The Kindergarten as a Setting for Sex-Role Socializa-
        tion." Department of Sociology, Carlton University.

Rosen, B. C.
1959   "Race, Ethnicity and the Achievement Syndrome."
        American Sociological Review 24:47-60.

Schaar, John H.
1967   "Equality of Opportunity and Beyond." In Equality,
        Nomos II, edited by J. R. Pennock and John W.
        Chapman. New York: Atherton.

Secretary of State.
1976   Some Characteristics of Post-secondary Students in
        Canada. Ottawa: Education Support Branch, Depart-
        ment of Secretary of State.

Selleck, Laura.
1980   "Equality of Access to Ontario Universities." Toronto:
        Council of Ontario Universities.

Sewell, W. H., and Hauser, R. M.
1980   "The Wisconsin Longitudinal Study of Social and Psycho-
        logical Factors in Aspirations and Achievements."
        Research in Sociology of Education and Socialization
        1:59-99.

Shibutani, I., and Kwam, K. M.
1965   Ethnic Stratification. New York: Macmillan Co.

Squires, Gregory D.
1979   Education and Jobs: The Imbalancing of the Social
        Machinery. New Brunswick, N.J.: Transaction Books.

Spring, Joel
  1976   The Sorting Machine. New York: David MacKay C.

Statistics Canada.
  1972   Dictionary of the 1971 Census Terms. Catalogue no.
          12-540. Ottawa.

  1976   "Users Guide to the 1976 Census Data on Education."

  1978   A User's Guide to 1976 Census Data on Education.
          Working paper. Catalogue no. 8-2400-529. Ottawa.

  1979   Education in Canada. Catalogue no. 81-229. Ottawa.

  1981   Education in Canada. Catalogue no. 81-229. Ottawa.

Stevenson and Kellogg, Management Consultants.
  1979   Evaluation of Methods for Collecting Socio-economic Data
          on Post-secondary Students. Report prepared for the
          Ontario Ministry of Colleges and Universities (January).

Stodolsky, S. S., and Lesser, G. S.
  1967   "Learning Patterns in the Disadvantaged." Harvard
          Educational Review 37:546-93.

Tawney, R. H.
  1931   Equality. London: Allen & Unwin.

Tepperman, L.
  1975   Social Mobility in Canada. Toronto: McGraw-Hill
          Ryerson.

The Financial Post.
  1981   "Community Colleges Health." November 7.

The Globe and Mail.
  1977   Tuesday, February 22.

The University Students' Council.
  1980   "Student Employment and Income Backgrounds: A
          Statistical Survey and Report." University of Western
          Ontario (March).

Turrittin, Anton H.
  1980   "The Employment Problems of the Highly Trained in
          Canada with Special Reference to Ontario." Paper
          presented to the International Conference on Intellectual
          Employment and Unemployment, 5-8 December, Uni-
          versity of Sienna, Italy.

Turrittin, A.; Anisef, P.; and MacKinnon, N. J.
   1980   "Gender Differences in Educational Achievement: A
          Study in Social Inequality."   Department of Sociology,
          York University.

Vallee, F., and Shulman, N.
   1969   The Viability of French Groupings Outside Quebec.
          Toronto: University of Toronto Press.

Von Zur-Muehlen, Max.
   1978   The Educational Background of Parents of Post-secon-
          dary Students in Canada.   Ottawa: Statistics Canada
          (Second Draft).

Western News.
   1977   February 24.

Wright, E. O., and Perrone, L.
   1977   "Marxist Class Categories and Income Inequality."
          American Sociological Review 42:32-55.

Zsigmond, Z. E., and Wenaas, C. J.
   1970   Enrollment in Educational Institutions by Province 1951-
          52 to 1980-81.   Staff Study no. 25, Economic Council of
          Canada.   Ottawa: Information Canada.

Zsigmond, Z.; Picot, G.; Clark, W.; and Deveraux, M. S.
   1978   Out of School--Into the Labour Force.   Ottawa:
          Statistics Canada.

Functional and Conflict Perspectives in the Sociology of Education

A number of writers have identified two major theoretical perspectives in the sociology of education for analysing the role of education in modern society (c.f. Persell, 1977; Murphy, 1979; Collins, 1979; Squires, 1977; Karabel and Halsey, 1977).[1] Until recently, the dominant framework (that is, human capital theory) was provided by economists; in sociology this perspective is referred to as the functional theory of social stratification (Lennards, 1980: 498).[2]

THE FUNCTIONALIST PERSPECTIVE

During the 1950's and 1960's one of the key societal concerns in the United States was with the "cold war" between the United States and Russia. This involved not only an armaments race, but a general competition in terms of economic production and technology. One result was a concern for an adequate flow of engineers and scientists through the educational system (Spring, 1976). In Canada, a similar educational concern centred around nationalist fears that an inadequate number of domestically trained scientists and engineers would lead to even more dependence on foreign technology (Lockhart, 1977; Porter, 1965). This concern for human resources, especially the desire to optimally utilize what was conceived to be a limited pool of talent and ability, provided the social context in which functionalist theory in the sociology of education developed and thrived.

At a very general level, the key underlying assumptions of the functionalist orientation relate to the nature of society. Functionalists implicitly view society as a system composed of integrated, interdependent parts, each of which contributes to the maintenance and equilibrium of the whole. Adaptation to the environment, or survival, depends on the ability to meet the needs or imperatives of society. The system is held together largely through a consensus of values which controls the personality development and channels the energies of individuals (Murphy, 1979).

Losers and Winners

A variant of functionalism described by Karabel and Halsey (1977) as "technological functionalism" has been the most established theoretical orientation in the area of the sociology of education. The key idea is that the educational system has functional ramifications for the occupational structure. Education acts as a democratizing force on occupational stratification, creating opportunities, reducing poverty, and facilitating upward mobility. The rationale for this view is that the technological economy of modern industrial societies requires more and more skilled, cognitively proficient workers. Able, skilled workers are the key to the economic productivity that comes with higher technology, and this technology creates a further need for able, skilled workers. A scarcity of such persons results in inefficiency in the economy and calls for a lessening of ascriptive barriers which prevent able but poor workers from developing high levels of skills through formal education. The labor market for skills is seen as a neo-classical, competitive free market where individuals' placement depends on individual qualities, particularly cognitive skills and training.

The Functionalist basically views education as a rational means of selecting and preparing people for adult statuses (e.g., occupational roles) in a complex, organizational society (Husén, 1979:73). Education, from the functionalist perspective, becomes a crucial social institution as society moved from a preindustrial to postindustrial stage. The family became inadequate for socializing children for new, specialized roles. Moreover, urbanization became associated with a variety of social problems in growing cities, and education was increasingly perceived as the "solution." Thus, the belief that the new technological society required an educated work force to rationally achieve efficiency and the public recognition of unique types of social problems resulted in a strong commitment to public education in European and North American societies.

The ideological goal for those operating in the functionalist perspective is one of equality of opportunity. Those who attain higher statuses and better jobs in society are selected on the basis of achieved statuses, obtained via the cognitive and technical skills learned in schools open to everyone, not on the basis of ascribed statuses like race, sex or social class background. Fundamental is the belief that <u>society should reward persons according to their merit and not on the basis of their birth or wealth</u>. The underlying ideal is <u>equality as meritocracy</u>, in a society where the pre-dominant ethical mode is <u>individualism</u>. It therefore follows that educational systems should be organized so that external barriers (e.g., geographic location, socio-economic background) are eventually removed. John Porter points out that liberal reformers conceived of education as an equalizer at the beginning but not throughout the life cycle. Education would not eliminate the structure of inequality, rather it would allow for some additional movement of individuals up and down the class structure (1979:250).

Losers and Winners

The Functionalist vision of equal opportunity was dominant in most Western industrial societies until the late 1960s. Education as an investment paying high dividends to the individual and society was perceived as a worthy goal. Canada witnessed remarkable growth in post-secondary institutions in the 1960s and sharp increases in upper secondary school participation rates.

Starting in the 1960s, a series of important research studies, conducted in different countries, began to question the individual and societal payoffs to higher education and the role of formal education as a means of reducing societal inequalities. In his keynote address to the OECD Conference in 1970, the Swedish Minister of Education reflected this change in sentiment:

> It is possible that we have been too optimistic, par-
> ticularly perhaps concerning the time it takes to bring
> about changes. On the other hand, it is hardly
> possible to change society only through education. To
> equalize educational opportunities without influencing
> working conditions, the setting of wage rates, etc. in
> other ways, would easily become an empty gesture.
> The reforms in educational policy must go together with
> reforms in other fields: labour market policy, economic
> policy, social policy, fiscal policy, etc. (OECD,
> 1971b:69)

THE CONFLICT PERSPECTIVE

The recognition that schools could not possibly serve as "Great Equalizers" was widely accepted by the early 1970s. Functionalism was challenged strongly by those who endorsed Marxist or Weberian conflict views. These latter perspectives present the image of schools as "Great Sorters" rather than "Great Equalizers."

At a general level, the conflict approach postulates that society is composed of groups which have opposing interests. As a result , society is in constant change and flux. Order is possible only through the coercion or co-optation of one element in society by another, and is rarely sustained over a long period of time (Dahrendorf, 1959:162; Murphy, 1979). Educational systems serve primarily to reproduce and legitimate the existing stratification system in society.

The education system, according to Bowles and Gintis, is best understood as an institution whose major purpose is to perpetuate the social relations of economic life (1976:11-13). Schools accomplish this through subtle forms of indoctrination and

160

by emphasizing the ethical principle of individualism. This becomes a primary mechanism in legitimizing inequalities in a capitalistic system insofar as success or failure is accepted as an individual responsibility; thus, if they are truly effective, schools produce an acceptance of authority that, when translated to productive sectors of society, results in acceptance of a division of labor paralleled by a gradient of unequal rewards. To accomplish this objective, schools must themselves act efficiently and emphasize a "sorting and allocation" to work objectives. The causes of inequality are not to be located in education per se but in the very structure of society. Clement thus comments: "education is treated here as a consequence of inequality which appears elsewhere in the society and as an institution which further reinforces inequality but is not itself the cause of, that inequality" (Clement, 1975:4).

In contrast to Bowles and Gintis, who emphasize the crucial role played by capitalistic employers in business and commercial concerns, Randall Collins (1971), in his early work, developed a non-Marxist conflict approach which allowed for groups formed on non-economic criteria to have large instrumental roles in the development of education in general.

For Collins, society is composed of status groups, or groups sharing common cultures—"styles of language, tastes in clothing and decor, manners and other ritual observances, conversational topics and styles, opinions and values, and preferences in sports, arts and media" (1971: 1009). Status groups can derive from class or economic differences, power differences, or differences stemming from cultural conditions, geographic origin, ethnicity, religion and so on.

Collins envisages a continuous struggle in society for societal rewards—wealth, power and prestige—among these groups, as opposed to individuals. The struggle takes place primarily within organizations in modern societies.

The main activity of schools, as seen by Collins, is to teach particular status cultures, both within and outside of the school. Insofar as a particular status group controls education, education can be used to foster control of work organizations, be it through demanding educational credentials to ensure new elite recruits have the elite culture, or through hiring of persons at lower levels who have acquired respect for elite values and styles.

The dramatic alteration in the conception of how individuals, education, and society are related as exemplified in Bowles and Gintis, Clements and Collins' work was brought about, in large part, by a series of major research studies (or reanalysis of previous surveys) by American sociologists. The work of James Coleman and Christopher Jencks has had, perhaps, the largest impact in terms of challenging the functionalist view that education was the Great Equalizer. A brief summary of their work is therefore in order.

THE COLEMAN REPORT

In 1964, the President and Congress commissioned a report the objective of which was to assess "the lack of availability of equal educational opportunities for individuals by reason of race, color, religion, or national origin in public educational institutions. . . ." (Coleman, 1966: iii). The report, published in 1966, was called Equality of Educational Opportunity. Based on a comprehensive survey of American elementary and high schools, it included information on over 645,000 pupils. Six groups of students (whites, blacks, Mexican-Americans, Oriental Americans, Puerto Ricans, Indians Americans) were tested on achievement (e.g., verbal and non-verbal factors), with items designed to measure motivation and interest in learning also incorporated into the research instrument. Coleman and his associates fully anticipated that finding gross differences in the quality of school characteristics (i.e., age of buidings, instructional facilities, class size, teacher background) would explain differences in achievement test scores among pupils of different backgrounds. However, Coleman came up with "unexpected" findings. First, white and black schools were not as unequal in "quality" as had been expected. Secondly, and more controversially, school differences in resources did not account for much of the variation in achievement among students. Thus, presumably, increasing expenditure on teacher training, school buildings, and new pedagogy would not noticeably reduce the relatively poor showing in achievement levels among poverty-struck children. The characteristics that counted most were those involving the composition of the student body. Another way of saying this is that there was more variation in test scores within any one school than across schools; Coleman's findings were obviously disheartening to educators and social planners who sought to ignore them as much as possible. The most important impact of Coleman's research was to severely challenge the notion of schools as "equalizers." The degree of academic success of students entering schools reflected structural inequalities in society at large, specifically, minority group and socioeconomic status. These initial social background differences promote inequalities in performance, unmediated or influenced by school factors.

What resulted from this challenge to traditional assumptions was an emphasis on "compensatory" educational programs in the United States, one of the most famous and important initiatives being the Office of Economic Opportunity's Head Start Program. The primary purpose of this program was to raise the cognitive skills of lower socioeconomic students to give them a starting point equivalent to other students. This program was eventually judged by most a failure; its critics frequently complained that an attempt to alter individual children and not the middle-class schools accounted for the program's failure. However, as we argue in Chapter 6, there is evidence that certain types of compensatory education programs do raise cognitive scores effectively.

Christopher Jencks and Colleagues

In 1972, Christopher Jencks and his associates at the Harvard School of Education published <u>Inequality: A Reassessment of Family and Schooling in America</u>. This book collects a wide array of research findings (including a reinterpretation of Coleman's findings) on the inheritability of intelligence, the effects of family structure on IQ, tests of cognitive ability, school marks, level of formal education, the jobs people get, and, subsequently, the effects of all these factors on income. After an elaborate and sophisticated reanalysis of data, Jencks argues that inequality is composed of different dimensions (e.g., inequality of opportunity, cognitive skills, occupational status and income) and that the associations among these dimensions are weak:

> . . . While occupational status is more closely related to educational attainment than to any other thing we could measure, there are still enormous status differences among people with the same amount of education. This remains true when we compare people who have not only the same amount of schooling, but the same family background and the same test scores. Anyone who thinks that a man's family background, test scores and educational credentials are the only things that determine the kind of work he can do in America is fooling himself. At most, these characteristics explain about half the variation in men's occupational statuses. This leaves at least half the variation to be explained by factors which have nothing to do with family background, test scores or educational attainment. (Pp. 190-91)

Jencks not only deals with occupational status and income but also with the relationship between schooling and inequality. He concluded that education has failed in this area as well, insofar as cognitive skills are not equalized by formal schooling (Jencks, 1972:109).

In speculating on what might account for occupational success besides educational attainment and other background factors, Jencks unfortunately described the residual factors using the term "luck." This resulted in much heated and severe criticism of his work. Importantly, Jencks's view stressed that

163

educational reform could not alter the distribution of rewards in society. Schools were not democratizing influences, but rather allocative ones. Although, strictly speaking, Jencks could not be described as a Marxist, he expresses the belief that only a redistribution of wealth would overcome inequality in American society. It is important to note that Jencks's reanalysis of existing data bases begins to swing the pendulum from schools as an equalizing force to schools as a sorting institution, perpetuating already existing inequalities in society.

Notes

1.   Some sociologists (e.g., Murphy, 1979) identify a third major perspective, symbolic interactionism. However, this perspective tends to focus on behaviour at the micro, rather than macro level and is thus of limited relevance to the present concern. Our discussion of sources of structural inequality, with its emphasis on the importance of perceptions of reality, however, has been influenced by research utilizing the interactionist framework.

2.   Some material in this section is excerpted from Okihiro (1981).

Detailed Notes to Chapter 5

1.   There have been several studies which have examined temporal trends in accessibility to post-secondary education in
Canada.   They have largely focused on social-class trends in
enrolment and have used a variety of data-presentation methods
to indicate changes in accessibility.

Von Zur-Muehlen's and Harvey's Analyses

Max von Zur-Muehlen and Edward Harvey, working indepen-
dently, employed the large and nationally representative samples
of post-secondary students in Canada surveyed by Statistics
Canada in 1968-69 and 1974-75 to examine trends in post-
secondary enrolment.   Though the surveys were not explicitly
designed to examine trends in the background of post-secondary
students, both researchers (Harvey, 1977:10; Von Zur-Muehlen,
1978:67-68) felt that there was enough comparable data to warrant
temporal trend analysis.

The general strategy for analyzing socio-economic trends in
Canadian post-secondary enrolment was the same for both
researchers.   They examined the "relative" shift in the socio-
economic composition of students (Von Zur-Muehlen, 1978:36) or,
more specifically, changes in the proportion of post-secondary
students from higher socio-economic backgrounds to students from
lower backgrounds.   For example, Harvey found that the proportion of undergraduate students with higher social class (as
measured by the father having at least some post-secondary
education) changed from 53.0 percent in 1968-69 to 50.8 percent
in 1974-75, a 3.8 percent decrease.

In their analyses, both researchers recognized a major
problem associated with simply comparing such percentages.   Over
the six-year period, the general level of educational attainment of
the Canadian population increased, and we can expect an upward
trend in the attainment of students' parents.   Thus, we should
expect an increase in the proportion of students with higher
educational attainments even if, within each level of parental
education, the proportion going to post-secondary educational
institutions remained stable.   Clearly, a meaningful assessment of

changes in equality of educational opportunity needs to take into account shifting patterns of parental social class in the larger population.

Von Zur-Muehlen dealt with this by comparing the educational attainment of parents of 18 to 21-year-old students with the educational attainment of persons aged 45-64, obtained from the 1969 and 1975 Labour Force Surveys. Though he noted the gradual rise in educational attainment of the age 45 to 64 Canadian population in this period, the dramatic difference between the educational attainment of the general population and parents of post-secondary, especially university students, remained. He concluded that hopes of achieving greater equality in educational opportunity have not been realized. Harvey did not attempt to deal with changing proportions of parents with higher education.

In spite of their common data source, there were several differences in the methods employed by the researchers. In measuring social class, Harvey looked specifically at father's education, which he considered the "best single indicator of socio-economic background" (1977:10), although the post-secondary-student surveys employed contained information on mother's education, father's occupation, and combined parental income as well. Von Zur-Muehlen also concentrated on the educational attainment of parents of post-secondary students, but examined the effects of mother's education as well as father's. He noted (1978:8) an Economic Council of Canada study that indicated father's influence on female educational accomplishments was substantially less than that of the mother.

There were some other important differences. Harvey dichotomized respondents' educational attainment, while Von Zur-Muehlen employed five separate categories from elementary schooling to university degree. Von Zur-Muehlen focused on full-time undergraduate and community college students, with the caveat that some part-time 1968-69 students were included in the tabulations. Harvey also considered full-time students, but divided them into five categories: college terminal and college transfer, undergraduate university, professional and postgraduate students. Though both studies were Canadian-wide, Von Zur-Muehlen alone (1978:63) included a provincial breakdown in the composition of full-time university undergraduate students by father's educational attainment.

Von Zur-Muehlen was pessimistic about the inaccessibility of post-secondary education to students with lower parental education in the 1969-75 time period. He wrote (1978:51) that "hopes of achieving greater equality in educational opportunity have not been realized; social barriers seem to have been more formidable than originally anticipated". Harvey was more equivocal, choosing to argue that there have been some gains in the proportions of students with fathers having lower educational attainment, but the gains have been smaller than those made by women relative to men in the same period (1977:10).

Pike's Analysis

In The Vertical Mosaic, John Porter (1965) examined the representation of social classes in terms of university enrolment. The Canada-wide data are presented as percentage breakdowns of university students in terms of social class, and like Von Zur-Muehlen, the percent breakdown of the relevant larger population (in this case, male heads of families with children) is presented for comparison purposes.

Pike's (1970) work is built on Porter's, and is the major Canadian study based on the census that examined temporal trends in the social-class background of students. Unlike Harvey or Von Zur-Muehlen, and following Porter, Pike used occupational prestige as the measure of social-class background. He argued that a growth in university enrolments does not ensure a reduction of class bias unless the expanded facilities are made pro-portionately more accessible to the disadvantaged (1970:59). Consequently, he wished to examine the changes in the likelihood of school attendance for persons from different social classes. By examining the proportion of university participants of each social class, a more direct comparison can be made between social classes in terms of accessibility than can be obtained by comparing the social-class composition of the university population and the larger population. The data is based on both Porter's (1965) analysis of 1951 census data and Pike's own calculations for 1961.

It is important to note that only indirect measures of university enrolment trends are possible with Pike's data. Rather than university enrolment, the percentage at school is the key dependent variable, and since the age range of the population studied was 14-24, secondary as well as university enrolment was included. Pike also reported problems in replicating the Blishen Socio-economic Index for the 1961 census (1970:60) and excluded those who were not classed as children living at home at the time of the census. Given all this, he felt that his analysis should be treated as only a "very rough guide" (Pike, 1970:60) to trends in educational participation. He did hazard a couple of informed guesses regarding trends in access to universities, however. First, children of all social classes were more likely to attend university at the time of his writing than fifteen years previously. There might even have been a narrowing in the accessibility gap between children of highly paid professional workers and children of relatively well-off white-collar and skilled blue-collar workers. However, he doubted that the accessibility gap between these groups and those at the bottom–children of semiskilled and unskilled manual workers–had lessened, and felt, in fact, that the gap may have widened. These tentative observations can be compared with the findings of our census analysis in this chapter.

2. The usual way of calculating a participation rate is to divide the full-time university or post-secondary non-university enrolment by the relevant age group, usually 18 to 24 inclusive (Leslie, 1980:13). This is an easy calculation, since statistical reports of educational institutions and population figures are readily available. Statistics Canada publishes such data annually.

Table B1 compares the participation rates calculated from the PUST data with institutional statistics from Statistics Canada and the 1974-75 Post Secondary Student Survey conducted by the federal government (Secretary of State, 1976).

There are a number of observations. Regarding census (PUST) estimates, there was no question in the 1971 census sufficiently close in meaning to college or post-secondary non-university to warrant inclusion of a figure.

In 1976, the census term "post-secondary non-university" was employed, a term which is generally broader in its coverage than community colleges. This term was admittedly wide in its possible application (the census was self-reported) since it could include private vocational courses, recreation or leisure courses, arts and crafts courses, and so on (User's Guide to 1976 Census Data on Education: Statistics Canada, 1978:29) and it also included a number of unique educational institutions such as the National Ballet School, Chiropractic Colleges, Shaw Business Schools and so on. The wider applicability of the term is probably reflected in the greater full-time participation rate in post-secondary non-university institutions from 1976 census data compared to 1976 college enrolment figures from Statistics Canada. This is a serious discrepancy because the Statistics Canada college enrolment figures are derived by taking all enrollees, regardless of age, in career college program and thus, itself, overestimates college enrolment. Indeed, in 1978, 15.8% of college enrollees were over 24 or under 18.

For comparison sake, we shall examine university enrolment rates. There are some reasons for expecting fall enrolment statistics from Statistics Canada to be slightly higher than PUST data. First, institutional enrolments often include persons who have come to study in Ontario from other provinces and countries. In 1967-68, 5,675 students enrolled full-time in Ontario universities (including teachers' colleges) were from other parts of Canada, and another 5,578 from outside of Canada. They comprised 13.1% of the total enrolment of about 86,000 students (Zsigmond and Wenaas, 1970:219).

168

Losers and Winners

On the other hand, institutional enrolment figures like those from Statistics Canada omit Ontarians who study outside of the province. In 1967-68, Zsigmond and Wenaas (1970:75) found that 4.9% of Ontario residents attending university attended university in a different province. Ontario, it is clear, is a net importer of university students, so that the raw institutional figures inflate the participation rate by Ontario domiciles. Zsigmond and Wenaas' study also clearly shows fluctuations in students coming into Ontario to study, and those leaving the province, a factor which would clearly affect computations regarding accessibility of Ontario universities to Ontario residents if institutional figures were employed. Statistics Canada publishes statistics on these patterns, but they are not crosstabulated separately for the 18 to 24 age group.

While it does not affect the comparison of sources of partici- pation rates for Ontario, a comment on the denominator–the number of persons aged 18 to 24 from the census–is in order. Participation rates are affected by changes in this base. An emigration of persons not attending school to other provinces or countries may reduce the denominator and hence result in an apparent increase in post-secondary participation rates. (Leslie, 1980: 34-37). Differential economic prospects (for example, the recent relative prosperity of western provinces compared to Ontario) may influence migratory patterns of 18- to 24-year-olds seeking employment, and thus affect participation rates.

Census statistics from the PUST and from special runs are based on self-reports of attendance during the previous year and employ different categorizations of institutions. The inclusion of a question asking the type of institution attended (university or post-secondary non-university) in the 1976 census suggests that the data on post-secondary non-university attendance should yield figures equivalent to those from institutional statistics but it is important to note that this category is more vaguely defined than the university category (see footnotes 4 and 7, Table B1).

In comparing enrolment rates from the censuses and from institutional enrolments between 1971 and 1976, a slightly divergent pattern emerges. Statistics Canada enrolment statistics show an increase in participation of 1.1%, while there is a slight decrease (0.1%) according to the census figures. Part of the difference is no doubt due to the fact that the type of academic institution attended was inferred from highest educational attain- ment in the 1971 census. Consequently, in forming the table, it was assumed that all 18- to 24-year-olds with at least some uni- versity education who said they were attending school or uni- versity full-time were attending university. In fact, some may have been attending high school (again) or, more likely, a com- munity college or other post-secondary non-university institution. The 11.4% 1971 university participation rate is probably inflated slightly. Given this, the two sources do not seem to show diver- gent general patterns.

TABLE B1: FULL-TIME PARTICIPATION RATES OF 18-24 YEAR OLDS BY DIFFERENT SOURCES

SOURCE	Population 18-24	University		College		Total	
		Enrolment	Rate	Enrolment	Rate	Enrolment	Rate
1. PUST 1971	933,300	106,300	11.4[1]	—[2]	—	—	—
2. Statistics Canada 1971	946,235	108,373[3]	11.5[3]	37,981[4]	4.0	—[5]	—
3. Secretary of State 1974-75			12.5[6]		4.5		
4. PUST 1976	1,057,800	119,700	11.3	62,700[7]	5.9[7]	182,400[7]	17.2[7]
5. Statistics Canada 1976	1,058,220	132,815[3]	12.6[3]	58,915[4]	5.6[4]	—[5]	—

[1] In 1971, type of school attendance was not asked. Persons who indicated some university education were classed as attending university, though this may overestimate their numbers. For example, some may have quit university and were attending a CAAT, but they were classed as full-time university enrollees.

[2] Not available from Public Use Sample Tape data from 1971.

[3] Based on Fall enrolments at degree-granting post-secondary institutions. Statistics Canada, August 1981.

[4] Based on Fall enrolments in post-secondary *career* programmes at community colleges. The latter include post-secondary non-degree granting institutions and establishments providing training in specialized fields of agriculture, fisheries, marine technology, surveying and para-medical technologies but exclude hospital schools of nursing and trades-level vocational courses. However, students over 24 and under 18 are also counted.

[5] Not calculated due to different numerators (see notes 4 & 5).

[6] Based on figures from *Some Characteristics of Post-secondary Students in Canada* (Secretary of State, 1976: 6 and 9). Professional students were assumed to be full-time university students.

[7] Includes enrolment at a number of post-secondary non-university institutions other than community colleges. (User's Guide to 1976 Census Data on Education: Ottawa, 1979:29).

TABLE B2: EDUCATIONAL ATTAINMENT OF MALES 18-21 AT HOME BY HIGHEST PARENTAL EDUCATIONAL ATTAINMENT, 1971 AND 1976

		SON'S EDUCATION							
HIGHEST PARENTAL EDUCATION		Grade 13 or less		Post-secondary Non-university		At Least Some University		Row Total	Percent of Total Population
		Number	Percent	Number	Percent	Number	Percent		
University with Degree	71	7,585	52.89	620	4.32	6,135	42.78	14,340	8.14
	76	9,755	50.81	1,055	5.49	8,390	43.70	19,200	9.60
Percent change			-2.08		+1.17		+0.92		(+1.46)
Some University	71	7,155	62.87	835	7.33	3,390	29.79	11,380	6.46
	76	12,455	59.84	1,765	8.48	6,595	31.68	20,815	10.40
Percent change			-3.03		+1.15		+1.89		(+3.94)
Post-secondary Non-university	71	16,845	65.29	3,055	11.84	5,900	22.87	25,800	14.64
	76	22,150	62.80	4,975	14.11	8,145	23.09	35,270	17.63
Percent change			-2.49		+2.27		+0.22		(+2.99)
Grade 13	71	7,495	65.06	1,020	8.85	3,005	26.09	11,520	6.54
	76	7,035	65.83	800	7.49	2,850	26.67	10,685	5.34
Percent change			-0.77		-1.36		+0.58		(-1.20)
Grade 12	71	14,840	71.62	1,830	8.83	4,050	19.55	20,720	11.76
	76	17,505	71.49	1,950	7.96	5,030	20.54	24,485	12.24
Percent change			-0.13		-0.87		+0.99		(+0.48)
Grade 11	71	12,055	75.60	1,330	8.34	2,560	16.06	15,945	9.05
	76	11,475	74.39	1,290	8.36	2,660	17.24	15,425	7.71
Percent change			-1.21		+0.02		+1.18		(-1.34)
Grades 9, 10	71	27,940	79.18	2,845	8.06	4,500	12.75	35,285	20.02
	76	27,940	79.65	2,555	7.28	4,585	13.07	35,080	17.53
Percent change			+0.47		-0.78		+0.32		(-2.49)
Elementary None	71	33,495	81.18	3,280	7.95	4,485	10.87	41,260	23.41
	76	30,125	76.96	3,640	9.30	5,380	13.74	39,145	19.56
Percent change			-4.22		+1.35		+2.87		(-3.85)
Total	71	127,390	72.28	14,820	8.41	34,035	19.31	176,245	100.0
	76	138,425	69.18	18,035	9.01	43,640	21.81	200,100	100.0
Overall percent change: 1971 to 1976			-3.10		+0.60		+2.50		

171

3.   Table B2 shows the educational attainment of males 18-21 by highest level of parental education, for both 1971 and 1976. The key figures in Table B2 are the percentages in the columns post-secondary non-university or university degree under son's education. These figures, labelled "percent", simply tell us the percent of the subgroup of, in this case, parent's educational attainment, which attained a given level of education. For example, in 1971, 42.78% of the 14,340 males whose highest parental education was a university degree had attained at least some university. In 1976, the equivalent figure was 43.70%, giving an absolute increase of 0.92% from 1971.

     Going down the column showing the rate of attainment of at least some university, the first observation is that the proportion of 18 to 21 year-olds at home attaining this level of education decreases strongly and systematically with lower levels of parental education in both 1971 and 1976. For example, while almost 43% of those whose highest-educated parent had a university degree attained at least some university in 1971, only 11% of those whose highest parental education was elementary, or no schooling, attained university.

     Examining attainment <u>rates</u> for each level of parental education in both 1971 and 1976 allows us to compare equivalent parental educational categories for changes over the five-year period.

     The figures in the margins to the right of the table show the total number of persons in each category of parental education, and the percentage they comprise of all single 18 to 21 year-olds living at home. Two observations are relevant. First, the absolute size of the 18 to 21 male cohort living at home has increased from 176,245 to 200,100 over the five-year period. This represents, then, part of the post-war baby boom reaching the post-secondary age range. The second is that the educational attainment of parents has increased gradually over the five-year period, as expected. In 1971, only 8.14% of the male sample had at least one parent who had a university degree, but in 1976 this increased to 9.60%. Larger proportions of parents had some university education, and post-secondary non-university as well. Of course, this meant that the proportion of parents having lower levels of education decreased in 1976 relative to 1971.

4.   Tables B3 through B6 summarize the trends in university and PSNU attainments of different parental education and mother tongue groups, by sex. More detailed tables like Table B2 following and a more detailed technical discussion of our methodological procedures are available on microfiche from the Ontario Ministry of Colleges and Universities/Ministry of Education. Refer to order number ONO2384 (A/TR).

5. It is clear from Table B3 that in looking at university attainment rates for a particular parental educational level, it matters whether mother's, father's, or highest parental education is employed. The results for mother's education appears to be particularly different from the other two at higher levels of educational attainment. For example, 46% of females whose fathers had a university degree attained at least some university, compared to 55% of those whose mothers had a university degree. Why the difference? To answer this, we have to look at the more detailed information (not shown here). Only 2.7% of the mothers of females at home in 1971 had a university degree. On the other hand, 8.45% of the fathers had a university degree. Clearly, to have a mother with a university education placed one into a more elite social-class position than having a father with an identical education, and this is indeed reflected in the higher educational attainments of the former group. The same principle accounts for the fact that when highest parental education is employed, the university-attainment level of offspring is lower than when mother's or father's education is used.

6. The overall change in the post-secondary attainment rates over the five-year period can be partitioned into its two major components (see Kitagawa, 1955): the change in the attainment rates for each level of parental education and the shift in proportion of the population in each category of parental education. The independent effect of these two components on overall attainment rates is clearest at the extremes. Suppose that there were no changes between 1971 and 1976 in, say, the university attainment rates for any of the categories of parental education. It is still possible for the overall rate of university attainment to increase if the distribution of people between parental educational categories has changed. With more people in categories where their chances of university attainment are better, the overall university attainment rate will increase in spite of no change in the rate of university attainment within the different categories of parental education. Figure B7 illustrates how this can come about.

A few simple calculations allow us to partition the overall change in the percentage of persons with post-secondary attainment into its component parts. Consider Table B2. The overall change in the percentage with at least some university is 2.50%. We also have information on the change in university attainment rates for each parental educational category. For example, the percentage of persons with some university education whose highest-educated parent had a university degree increased 0.92%. The percentage whose parents had only some university increased 1.89%, etc. The weighted average of these figures yields the percentage increase in university attainment if there were no change in the distribution of people within categories (the percent change due to increased subgroup participation). Using the 1971 population figures as weights, the weighted average increase in

TABLE B3: PERCENT OF 18-21-YEAR-OLDS AT HOME WITH AT LEAST SOME
UNIVERSITY BY THREE MEASURES OF PARENTAL EDUCATION,
1971 AND 1976

EDUCATIONAL LEVEL		SONS Highest Parental Education	Father's Education	Mother's Education
University	71	42.78	43.15	47.66
with Degree	76	43.70	44.73	46.88
Percent change		+0.92	+1.58	-0.78
Some	71	29.79	30.46	35.38
University	76	31.68	31.86	35.75
Percent change		+1.89	+1.40	+0.37
Postsecondary	71	22.87	23.00	27.67
Nonuniversity	76	23.09	23.56	26.92
Percent change		+0.22	+0.56	-0.75
Grade 13	71	26.09	28.29	28.84
	76	26.67	28.99	31.90
Percent change		+0.58	+0.70	+3.06
Grade 12	71	19.55	22.52	23.27
	76	20.54	23.30	24.21
Percent change		+0.99	+0.78	+0.94
Grade 11	71	16.06	20.16	20.00
	76	17.24	20.92	19.75
Percent change		+1.18	+0.76	-0.25
Grades 9, 10	71	12.75	15.82	14.53
	76	13.07	16.70	15.55
Percent change		+0.32	+0.88	+1.02
Elementary	71	10.87	11.84	11.85
None	76	13.74	13.55	14.28
Percent change		+2.87	+1.71	+2.43
Total	71	19.31	19.13	18.87
	76	21.81	21.61	21.22
Overall percent change:1971 to 1976		+2.50	+2.48	+2.37

Losers and Winners

TABLE B3: PERCENT OF 18-21-YEAR-OLDS AT HOME WITH AT LEAST SOME
(contd.) UNIVERSITY BY THREE MEASURES OF PARENTAL EDUCATION,
1971 AND 1976

PARENTAL EDUCATIONAL LEVEL	DAUGHTERS		
	Highest Parental Education	Father's Education	Mother's Education
University 71	46.88	46.44	54.91
with Degree 76	49.64	49.79	55.68
Percent change	+2.76	+3.35	+0.77
Some 71	32.74	34.45	39.87
University 76	36.83	35.64	43.96
Percent change	+4.09	+1.19	+4.09
Post-secondary 71	22.86	22.94	28.29
Non-university 76	25.92	27.01	30.41
Percent change	+3.06	+4.07	+2.12
Grade 13 71	24.32	27.26	30.67
76	29.67	32.75	34.94
Percent change	+5.35	+5.49	+4.27
Grade 12 71	18.61	21.82	23.15
76	22.63	25.45	26.18
Percent change	+4.02	+3.63	+3.03
Grade 11 71	16.19	20.59	19.25
76	18.05	22.53	22.24
Percent change	+1.86	+1.94	+2.99
Grades 9, 10 71	11.22	14.19	13.82
76	16.01	19.81	18.58
Percent change	+4.79	+5.62	+4.76
Elementary 71	9.83	11.38	10.70
None 76	14.25	15.43	15.51
Percent change	+4.42	+4.05	+4.81
Total 71	19.83	19.66	19.43
76	25.28	25.12	24.77
Overall percent change:1971 to 1976	+5.45	+5.46	+5.34

TABLE B4: PERCENT OF 18-21-YEAR-OLDS AT HOME WITH POST-SECONDARY
NON-UNIVERSITY BY THREE MEASURES OF PARENTAL EDUCATION
1971 AND 1976

PARENTAL EDUCATIONAL LEVEL	SONS		
	Highest Parental Education	Father's Education	Mother's Education
University 71	4.32	4.19	3.19
with Degree 76	5.49	5.30	5.13
Percent change	+1.17	+1.11	+1.94
Some 71	7.33	7.16	6.08
University 76	8.48	8.16	7.45
Percent change	+1.15	+1.00	+1.37
Postsecondary 71	11.84	11.91	10.78
Nonuniversity 76	14.11	14.20	12.63
Percent change	+2.27	+2.29	+1.85
Grade 13 71	8.85	8.87	7.93
76	7.49	7.54	7.35
Percent change	-1.36	-1.23	-0.58
Grade 12 71	8.83	8.83	8.61
76	7.96	8.40	8.47
Percent change	-0.87	-0.43	-0.14
Grade 11 71	8.34	8.47	8.40
76	8.36	8.58	9.16
Percent change	+0.02	+0.11	+0.76
Grades 9, 10 71	8.06	8.53	8.57
76	7.28	8.03	7.72
Percent change	-0.78	-0.50	-0.85
Elementary 71	7.95	8.27	8.04
None 76	9.30	9.29	9.51
Percent change	+1.35	+1.02	-1.47
Total 71	8.41	8.39	8.37
76	9.01	8.98	9.07
Overall percent change:1971 to 1976	+0.60	+0.59	+0.70

TABLE B4:   PERCENT OF 18-21-YEAR-OLDS AT HOME WITH POST-SECONDARY
(contd.)   NON-UNIVERSITY BY THREE MEASURES OF PARENTAL EDUCATION
              1971 AND 1976

PARENTAL EDUCATIONAL LEVEL		DAUGHTERS		
		Highest Parental Education	Father's Education	Mother's Education
University	71	8.13	8.23	6.29
with Degree	76	9.57	9.41	5.97
Percent change		+1.44	+1.18	-0.32
Some	71	12.11	11.80	10.05
University	76	12.25	11.65	10.23
Percent change		+0.14	-0.15	+0.18
Post-secondary	71	17.06	16.16	16.61
Non-university	76	18.63	17.44	18.24
Percent change		+1.57	+1.28	+1.63
Grade 13	71	11.31	11.07	10.56
	76	12.54	11.68	12.08
Percent change		+1.23	+0.61	+1.52
Grade 12	71	12.32	12.59	12.46
	76	14.03	14.54	14.21
Percent change		+1.71	+1.95	+1.75
Grade 11	71	12.40	12.33	12.26
	76	14.41	13.17	14.39
Percent change		+2.01	+0.84	+2.13
Grades 9, 10	71	11.34	13.00	12.02
	76	12.46	14.37	13.01
Percent change		+1.12	+1.37	+0.99
Elementary	71	10.32	11.07	10.91
	76	12.50	13.45	15.51
Percent change		+2.18	+2.38	+4.60
Total	71	11.98	11.97	12.00
	76	13.60	13.54	13.57
Overall percent change:1971 to 1976		+1.62	-1.57	+1.57

TABLE B5:   PERCENT OF 18-21 COHORT WITH AT LEAST SOME UNIVERSITY
BY THREE MEASURES OF MOTHER TONGUE, 1971 AND 1976.

MOTHER TONGUE		Self	Sons Father's[1]	Mother's[1]
English	71	17.58	19.87	19.38
	76	19.37	21.39	20.93
Percent change		+1.79	+1.52	+1.55
French	71	10.91	12.95	13.81
	76	15.16	16.34	16.47
Percent change		+4.25	+3.39	+2.66
German	71	16.93	19.20	19.71
	76	24.69	23.73	24.09
Percent change		+7.76	+4.53	+4.38
Italian	71	10.22	14.37	13.85
	76	17.66	21.56	20.68
Percent change		+7.44	+7.19	+6.83
Netherlandic	71	14.01	14.87	15.27
	76	17.05	16.92	17.92
Percent change		+3.04	+2.05	+2.65
Scandinavian	71	15.09	22.81	17.24
	76	29.17	32.39	32.05
Percent change		+14.08	+9.58	+14.81
Polish	71	18.87	19.59	21.46
	76	28.31	27.27	32.11
Percent change		+9.44	+7.68	+10.65
Ukrainian	71	28.80	23.69	26.01
	76	33.45	29.84	31.60
Percent change		+4.65	+6.15	+5.59
Native Indian	71	3.90	4.05	3.09
	76	3.80	3.30	6.48
Percent change		-0.10	-0.75	+3.39
Other	71	16.67	22.04	22.56
	76	22.02	25.66	25.20
Percent change		+5.35	+3.62	+2.64
Total	71	16.80	19.15	18.87
	76	18.16	21.61	21.22
Overall percent change:1971 to 1976		+1.36	+2.46	+2.35

[1]Includes only those living at home

178

TABLE B5:   PERCENT OF 18-21 COHORT WITH AT LEAST SOME UNIVERSITY
(contd.)   BY THREE MEASURES OF MOTHER TONGUE, 1971 AND 1976.

MOTHER TONGUE		Daughters	
	Self	Father's [1]	Mother's [1]
English 71	14.52	20.37	20.13
76	19.05	25.41	25.00
Percent change	+4.53	+5.04	+4.87
French 71	10.25	13.97	14.58
76	17.03	21.06	20.98
Percent change	+6.78	+7.09	+6.40
German 71	14.73	20.38	19.86
76	21.97	24.29	25.63
Percent change	+7.24	+3.91	+5.77
Italian 71	5.93	11.38	10.97
76	13.19	20.69	20.43
Percent change	+7.26	+9.31	+9.46
Netherlandic 71	10.55	13.29	13.78
76	15.52	21.33	20.83
Percent change	+4.97	+8.04	+7.05
Scandinavian 71	10.96	17.07	15.63
76	29.41	37.29	36.07
Percent change	+18.45	+20.22	+20.44
Polish 71	14.19	21.56	20.60
76	27.66	34.51	34.58
Percent change	+13.47	+12.95	+13.98
Ukrainian 71	27.58	26.33	27.65
76	37.94	34.76	34.98
Percent change	+10.36	+8.43	+7.33
Native Indian 71	2.15	3.06	0.09
76	4.05	7.46	7.69
Percent change	+1.90	+4.40	+7.60
Other 71	14.82	24.04	23.00
76	20.27	26.77	26.58
Percent change	+5.45	+2.73	+3.58
Total 71	13.94	19.65	19.42
76	17.26	24.63	24.77
Overall percent change:1971 to 1976	+3.32	+4.98	+5.35

[1] Includes only those living at home

TABLE B6:   PERCENT OF 18-21 COHORT WITH POST-SECONDARY NON-UNIVERSITY
            EDUCATION BY THREE MEASURES OF MOTHER TONGUE, 1971 AND 1976

MOTHER TONGUE		Males		
		Self	Father's[1]	Mother's[1]
English	71	8.80	8.18	8.22
	76	10.04	8.53	8.55
Percent change		+1.24	+0.35	+0.33
French	71	8.03	8.03	7.89
	76	10.87	9.70	10.02
Percent change		+2.84	+1.67	+2.13
German	71	11.16	8.97	8.17
	76	13.24	10.26	10.23
Percent change		+2.08	+1.36	+2.06
Italian	71	8.34	9.56	10.04
	76	11.81	11.43	11.80
Percent change		+3.47	+1.87	+1.76
Netherlandic	71	12.83	9.83	9.48
	76	14.20	12.82	13.09
Percent change		+1.37	+2.99	+3.61
Scandinavian	71	7.55	7.22	5.75
	76	12.50	7.79	8.97
Percent change		+4.95	+0.57	+3.22
Polish	71	11.08	8.91	8.22
	76	11.42	10.21	11.64
Percent change		+0.34	+1.30	+3.42
Ukrainian	71	11.08	10.34	10.28
	76	11.60	9.75	9.92
Percent change		+0.52	-0.59	-0.36
Native Indian	71	2.93	4.05	4.32
	76	3.80	4.40	3.70
Percent change		+0.87	+0.35	-0.62
Other	71	10.26	9.03	8.92
	76	9.89	8.72	9.01
Percent change		-0.37	-0.31	+0.09
Total	71	8.87	8.39	8.37
	76	10.15	8.73	9.07
Overall percent change:1971 to 1976		+1.28	+0.34	+0.70

[1]Includes only those living at home.

TABLE B6:   PERCENT OF 18-21 COHORT WITH POST-SECONDARY NON-UNIVERSITY
(contd.)   EDUCATION BY THREE MEASURES OF MOTHER TONGUE, 1971 AND 1976

MOTHER TONGUE		Females		
	Self	Father's[1]	Mother's[1]
English 71	14.79	12.25	12.21
76	14.97	13.75	13.69
Percent change	*+0.18*	*+1.50*	*+1.48*
French 71	11.64	10.96	11.12
76	12.89	12.03	13.27
Percent change	*+1.25*	*+1.07*	*+2.15*
German 71	15.12	11.06	11.35
76	14.54	14.15	13.74
Percent change	*-0.58*	*+3.09*	*+2.39*
Italian 71	8.12	11.06	10.97
76	10.51	13.28	13.06
Percent change	*+2.39*	*+2.22*	*+2.09*
Netherlandic 71	19.72	15.48	15.08
76	19.54	16.54	17.28
Percent change	*-0.18*	*+1.06*	*+2.20*
Scandinavian 71	17.81	10.98	15.63
76	14.71	11.86	9.84
Percent change	*-3.10*	*+0.88*	*-5.79*
Polish 71	16.25	13.56	14.56
76	13.19	14.32	12.06
Percent change	*-3.06*	*+0.76*	*-2.50*
Ukrainian 71	16.16	13.06	13.33
76	12.77	15.80	15.84
Percent change	*-3.39*	*+2.74*	*+2.51*
Native Indian 71	4.30	3.06	5.41
76	4.73	2.99	6.41
Percent change	*+0.43*	*-0.07*	*+1.00*
Other 71	9.65	9.74	9.77
76	11.75	11.78	12.08
Percent change	*+2.10*	*+2.04*	*+2.31*
Total 71	14.14	11.97	12.00
76	14.49	13.55	13.57
Overall percent change:1971 to 1976	*+0.35*	*+1.58*	*+1.57*

[1]Includes only those living at home

FIGURE B7: SCHEMATIC REPRESENTATION OF THE EFFECT OF POPULATION
COMPOSITION CHANGES ON OVERALL PARTICIPATION RATE
DESPITE EQUAL SUBGROUP PARTICIPATION RATES

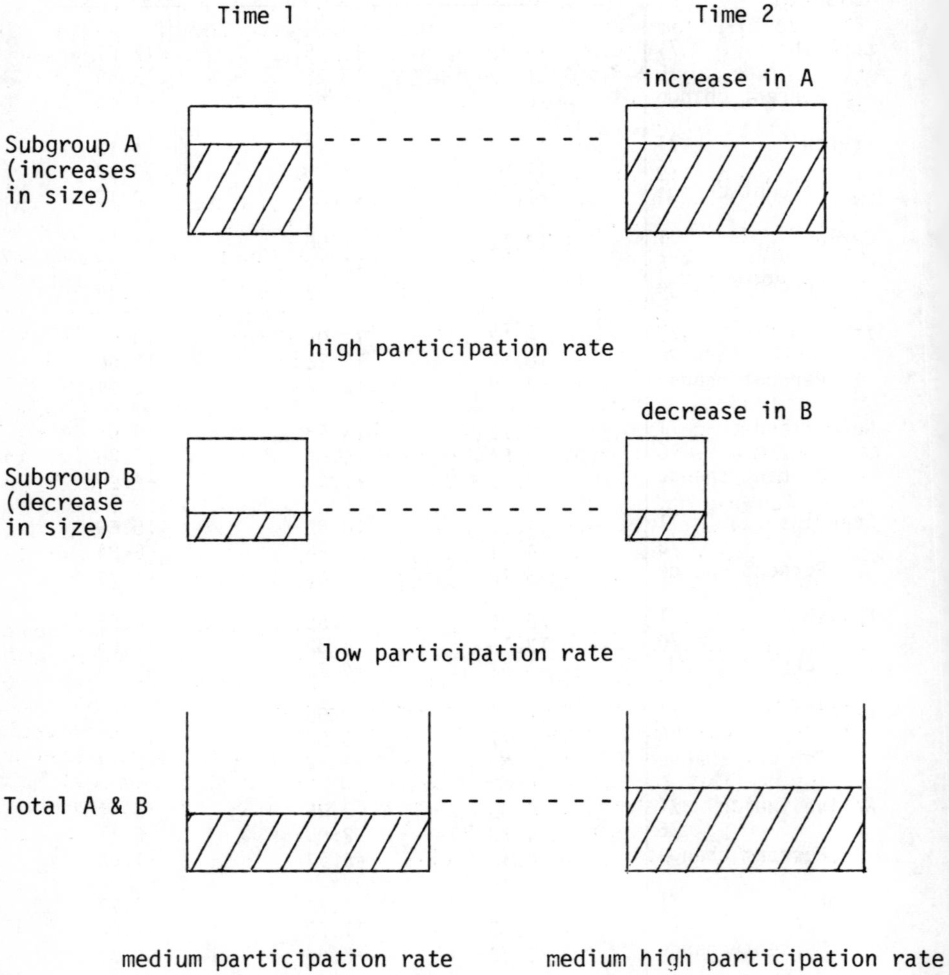

182

university attainment for the categories was 1.26 percent. Since the overall increase in the percent of males at home attaining some university was 2.50, the remainder, 1.24, or almost exactly half of the overall increase in males attaining university between 1971 and 1976 is due to the shift in population resulting from an increase in people with parents in educational brackets where the chances of going to university are higher (see Kitagawa, 1955: 1182-83 especially). While Kitagawa (p. 1178) suggests using the average of the two populations being compared as weighting factors, the general similarity in the figures led us to use the 1971 census counts as weights. We expect no substantive difference in our results by employing this simplification.

7.   Examination of detailed tables (not shown here) shows that the proportion of the the total population that each non-English mother-tongue group comprises has diminished from 1971 to 1976 for every group except "other." In some cases, the proportion has diminished by more than one-half. For example, the Netherlandic group comprised 0.79% of the 18 to 21 year-old males in 1971, but only 0.28% in 1976. It is not clear why so many fewer persons claim a non-English mother tongue, nor to what extent the persons claiming a particular mother tongue are similar across the censuses. Thus, the trends noted in this section need to be viewed cautiously. In some cases (notably the Scandinavian and the Native Indian groups), the total population is so low as to raise questions about the precision and validity of the percentage with varying levels of education. This is particularly so because of the effect of the rounding procedure used by Statistics Canada. For these groups, extra caution must be exercised in examining trends in post-secondary accessibility.

8.   Table B5 and B6 show rates of attainment of at least some university and PSNU among different subgroups, for males and females. Note that there is often a fairly large difference in the percent of a mother-tongue group attaining at least some university, depending on which mother-tongue variable is employed. Mother's and father's mother tongue generally show similar patterns, but there is often a discrepancy between parental and respondent's mother tongue, just as for university attainment. For small groups like the Scandinavian one, this may be an artifact of the tiny numbers involved.

Annotated Bibliography of Canadian Accessibility Studies

In this Appendix we present an annotated bibliography consisting primarily of journal articles or excerpts from books. Several criteria were employed in selecting articles for inclusion. First, the work should enhance our understanding of equality of educational opportunity and accessibility to post-secondary education. Second, the work should be Canadian in perspective. Third, the work should be empirical or data based, rather than exclusively philosophical in nature. Finally, the work should be relatively recent. The reader should note, therefore, that most articles reviewed were written within the last decade.

Anisef, Paul (1975). "Consequences of Ethnicity for Educational Plans Among Grade 12 Students." In Aaron Wolfgang (ed.) Education of Immigrant Children, Toronto: Ontario Institute for Studies in Education.

In an effort to understand whether "ethnicity and future educational plans were truly related and whether aspects of an adolescent's social background and present experiences could aid us in explaining the nature of this relationship," Anisef re-examined data which he had collected earlier to analyze the educational plans and career objectives of students. In the representative survey done, 2,555 Ontario-wide Grade 12 students from 97 schools filled out questionnaires (an 87% response rate). For this particular study, ethnic origin was defined in terms of respondent's birthplace and father's birthplace ("mixed" means that father is foreign-born while the student is Canadian-born). Educational plans were based on student's desire to continue education past the high-school level.

Anisef reported that "mixed" students, more than foreign-born and native-born expected to enroll in post-secondary education. However, foreign-born students were more likely to continue with part-time studies or enroll in trade schools, apprenticeship programs, etc. Ethnicity was definitely associated with students' intentions and aspirations after high school. Social class background and residency (i.e., live in urban or rural areas) influenced educational plans. More students from urban areas compared to those from rural areas planned to enroll in universities and CAATs. When sex, residence, social class and grade average were each controlled, it was found that the relationship between ethnicity and educational plans held for males but not for females; there was no significant relationship when residence was controlled; ethnicity related to educational plans only for working-class adolescents; and the relationship between ethnicity and educational plans only held for adolescents with C+ or lower grades.

Anisef, Paul (1982). "University Graduates Revisited: Occupational Mobility, Attainments and Accessibility," Inter-change vol 13(2):1-19.

The paper extends, into the late seventies, an analysis of social mobility among male and female university cohorts. The author compares his own data on university graduates (1977-79) gathered in 1979 as part of a six-year follow-up of 2,555 former grade 12 students in Ontario with historical cohorts data on university graduates (1960, 1964, 1968) as collected by Harvey. The analysis is divided into two sections: firstly, a descriptive application of a social mobility classification and secondly, an examination of gender differences in first full-time job attainments through the application of a status-attainment model. Further dramatic declines in economic prospects for university graduates are revealed and the role of accessibility is elaborated. Significant variations in recruitment patterns among Ontario universities are identified. These variations help in comprehending occupational attainment. The continued disadvantaged position of female graduates is established and policy-oriented recommendations directed toward producing desirable changes are noted.

Ashworth, Mary (1975). Immigrant Children and Canadian Schools. Toronto: McClelland and Stewart Ltd.

By using data collected through a questionnaire which was sent to 117 teachers and by examining data on students in books and articles in Canada and Britain, Ashworth analyzed the issues faced by immigrant children in Canada. Children of different ethnic backgrounds were divided into those which had the most difficulty (East Indians, Greeks, Italians and Portuguese); and students who faced problems of discrimination (viz., West Indians).

Ashworth stated that although facilities to teach immigrant students are available, limitations often exist, some of which include insufficient time, lack of curriculm materials, space and equipment. There is also a shortage of administrators and classroom teachers. Furthermore, the makeup of classes (i.e., difference in students' ages) and class sizes present problems. Teachers are also not sufficiently aware of the student's culture and often lack sensitivity in dealing with the problems immigrant

Losers and Winners

students face in adjusting to a new environment. Cultural shock and racism were two factors cited as contributing to immigrant students' problems in school. Non-English immigrant students from lower socio-economic backgrounds face the same problems as other immigrant students but have the additional problem of having to cope with overcrowded living conditions, poor diet and overcrowded schools.

Immigrant students who reside in communities with high immigrant population will often retreat into a non-English environment thus blocking their acquisition of English-language skills and their assimilation into the mainstream of Canadian society.

Ashworth also examined parental expectations of immigrant students. Due to differences in cultural background, family expectations will often clash with what is expected of the adolescent by his Canadian-born peers. This is particularly true of families from cultures where there are strict roles for children, especially females. Ashworth identified the need for more communication between ESL teachers, regular teachers, and school administrators concerning immigrant students. She also recommended that the federal and provincial governments should bear the cost of ESL and not the school boards, and that the latter should be allowed to determine which programs are necessary, depending on the concrete needs of the area.

Bancroft, George W. (1962). "Socio-economic Mobility and Educational Achievement in Southern Ontario," The Ontario Journal of Educational Research Vol 5(1):27-31.

In this article the author discussed the complex relationship that exists between equality of opportunity and social process by examining the equality of educational achievement and the improvement in the social and economic status of 522 southern Ontario male students. He questioned the extent to which upward and downward mobility exists; the extent to which individuals with similar educational backgrounds are equally mobile; and what conclusions might be drawn by the relationship between their educational achievement and change in occupational status. Social class was measured by the type of occupation selected; mobility was defined as the change between the occupational status of the respondent and that of his father; and educational achievement was defined as the amount of education gained.

Although mobility was generally high it was differentially distributed across social classes. Greater mobility was observed among sons whose fathers were in clerical or skilled occupations than in higher groups, while sons whose fathers were in semi-skilled or unskilled occupations were most likely to inherit that status level. Occupation status of father strongly determined son's educational attainment. For example fully 65 percent of sons who attended university originated from the professional group; this decreased to 30 percent for those originating from the unskilled labor group. A direct link between educational attainment of sons and their occupational attainment was also identified. Thus, over 9 in 10 who entered professional or management positions were university graduates, compared with slightly over 1 in 10 who entered clerical or semiskilled jobs.

Breton, Raymond (1970). "Academic Stratification in Secondary Schools and Educational Plans of Students," The Canadian Review of Sociology and Anthropology 7:(1): 17-34.

This paper was based on the results of a larger study in which 360 Canadian secondary schools (representing 8.3 percent of the total number of secondary schools) and 151,252 students (respesenting 13.3 percent of the total number of students) participated. The paper examined how the internal stratification of schools affected the educational plans of students by looking at programs of study within schools, students' experience of failure, and the rate of failure within schools. To determine the educational plans of students, they were asked: "Do you think you will leave school soon, leave later, or stay until finished?" and "Do you think you will continue your education after high school, on a full-time or part-time basis or not at all?" Weighted samples were used so that different types of schools would be reflected in proportion to their existence in the Canadian educational system.

It was found that the school curriculum or program of study had the greatest impact on the educational intentions of students. Students in terminal programs were less likely to continue their education after high school, while those in nonterminal programs were more likely to continue. Students' "class of destination" (i.e., position they would like and expect to occupy in society) was a function of the position that the students occupied in the school stratification system rather than of their families' social-class position. Breton found that students of higher socio-economic backgrounds were more likely to be in academic nonterminal programs compared to students from lower socio-economic backgrounds who were more likely to be in terminal programs. A student's experience of failure was also found to influence his academic plans. Specifically, if a student's experiences were positive, continuation was more likely.

The importance of examining the formal organization of the school rather than simply analyzing informal factors such as student subcultures and peer relations was also stressed. The author questioned the mechanisms responsible for allocating students to different programs and thought that they might be somewhat arbitrary and unreliable.

Buttrick, John (1977). <u>Who Goes to University from Toronto</u>. Toronto: Ontario Economic Council.

Buttrick reported that students' secondary school outcome was largely affected by family background, residential neighborhood, and genetic endowment. These findings were the results of a study conducted in metropolitan Toronto schools which tested the extent to which students' chances of acquiring university education were affected by social-class background, ethnicity, geographic location of school, (i.e., neighborhood effects), characteristics of schools, and parental influence.

Further findings showed that students' success in education was influenced by family background and neighborhood characteristics. Specifically, "wealthier" students were more academically successful in school. Middle-class students who attended schools in higher social-class neighborhoods achieved better grades than those who attended schools in lower social-class neighborhoods. The author claimed that the schools into which students are streamed help to determine possible educational outcomes. For example, he mentioned that some students were granted diplomas when they should not have received them and some received only a Grade 12 diploma when they had the potential to obtain a Grade 13 diploma. This, Buttrick states, undermines the intended purpose of the public, tax-supported educational system which is supposed to compensate for differences in family backgrounds and neighborhoods and provide equal opportunity for all children. Current practices allow some intellectually weak students to attend university, while at the same time many highly capable students are directed into occupations that require little ability, and thus never realize their full potential.

Clark, Barbara S. (1971). "Pre-School Programs and Black Children," <u>Minority Canadians 2: Immigrant Groups</u>, Jean Leonard Elliott, (ed.). Scarborough: Prentice-Hall of Canada Ltd. 106-19.

The author reports on an experimental preschool program carried out in a poverty-stricken, racially-mixed area of Halifax, Nova Scotia. The program had two major purposes: to offer planned experiences which would prevent academic retardation, characteristic of culturally disadvantaged children–and to provide an interracial environment to reduce racial prejudice. Small groups (4-5 children) met for twenty minutes every day in a school setting which emphasized adult-child interaction. Children were encouraged to express information and relate it to the past, present and future. They were also encouraged, through the careful selection of books and the employment of both black and white staff, to view people of different races with respect and dignity. The results reveal that this enriched preschool program not only provided the individualized attention and intense learning necessary to raise IQ scores, but it also contributed to the modification of racial attitudes and social behaviors.

Clark, Edmund; Cook, David; Fallis, George (1975). "Socialization, Family Background and the Secondary School," Socialization and Values in Canadian Society: Socialization, Social Stratification and Ethnicity, V. 2. Robert M. Pike & Elia Zureik (eds.).

This study was undertaken to examine the interaction between students and the school system to discover who proceeds to post-secondary education. The authors attempted to determine if students from low-income families placed less value on post-secondary education and if low income remained a significant barrier to the continuance of one's education. Information was derived from questionnaires given to Grades 9-13 students in Ontario urban high schools during April 1969.

The results of the study indicated that most students valued post-secondary education however, students entering high school professed widely divergent desires and expectations for continuing to post-secondary education. Approximately 38 percent of students from Class 1 (defined as family income under $5,000 per year) desired a university education compared to 69 percent from Class 4 (incomes over $10,000 per year). The authors noted that students' expectations differed from their desires. For example, more than three times as many students from Class 4 compared to Class 1 actually expected a university education. Curriculum choices in high school were looked at to aid in determining the school's effect on the students. Students from Class 4 almost exclusively entered a 5-year Arts and Science program (university preparation) and only about 1:10 entered a 4-year program, whereas 4:10 of Class 1 entered the 4-year program. There was very little difference in the Grade 12 dropout rates between the classes but only about half as many students from Class 1 enter Grade 13 as compared to those from Class 4. Students with high IQ's generally chose a 5-year course in high school, but ability wasn't the only determinant. As family income rose, students of any given IQ tended to stay in school longer, except with those of IQ over 120.

The authors feel that the school system does little to alter the fact that the selection of courses is closely linked to the student's socio-economic status. Students are forced early on to make choices which limit them in the future. The survey found that the cost of future post-secondary education had little effect on these early choices. Student aid, then, is valuable but not the answer. There is still a challenge for society in its "pursuit of its goal of equality of opportunity to ensure that educational socialization is not affected by family background."

Losers and Winners

Clifton, Rodney A. (1980). "Ethnicity, Teachers' Expectations and the Academic Achievement Process," <u>Educational Administration and Foundations</u>, University of Manitoba (April).

This study examines the extent to which differences in achievement between German- and French-speaking students are accounted for by the expectations of their teachers. The data used was obtained from the Carnegie Human Resources Data Bank, a five-year panel study of 90,719 students who were enrolled in the first year of Ontario high schools at the beginning of the 1959-60 academic year. The subjects for this study represented students who spoke either French or German as their main language at home.

The findings suggest that expectations play a significant role in understanding the differences between students' potential and actual achievement. Teachers appear to engage in discrimination based more upon past performance and intellectual ability rather than upon ethnicity or socio-economic status (SES measured by father's occupation and education and mother's education). They evaluate student achievement on the basis of both normative (i.e., teacher's rating of student's reliability) and cognitive (i.e., teacher's rating of student's chance of completing Grade 13) expectations, whereas performance on standardized achievement tests are influenced by cognitive expectations. However, it was noted that there was some evidence of ethnic bias influencing teachers' expectations. Clifton found that teachers had higher expectations of the German than of the French students even when socio-economic status, intellectual ability, assigned grades and academic aspirations were equal.

The effects of ethnicity on normative and cognitive expectations are "moderately strong" when socioeconomic status, intellectual ability, and ethnicity are included in the analysis. When assigned grades and academic aspirations are included, the effects decrease substantially--more so for males than females. It was found that teachers assign grades to males on the basis of both normative and cognitive expectations, while for females, grades are assigned to a greater degree on the basis of cognitive expectations than of normative expectations.

The author recognizes that the data is 20 years old and may not hold up today. Also interpretations of the present data must be limited to high school students and further research should examine these processes within the elementary school.

Losers and Winners

Clifton, Rodney A. (1981) "The Effects of Students' Ethnicity and Sex on the Expectations of Teachers," Interchange, 12(1):31-38.   Educational Administration and Foundations.

Using the Carnegie Human Resources data, Clifton studied the differences in teachers' expectations of Yiddish-, German-, French- and English-speaking students. The data was obtained through a five-year panel study of Grade 9 students in Ontario in 1959-60. Students were questioned on their educational plans and the education of their parents. Tests were given to measure students' intellectual ability and their academic performance. Teachers evaluated each student according to: (1) student's reliability (i.e., performance in curricular and extracurricular activities); (2) cooperation with teachers and students; (3) industry in school work; and (4) chances of completing Grade 13. A covariance approach was used in the analysis in order to remove bias because groups were not matched on all variables.

It was found that both ethnicity and sex had significant effects on the expectations of teachers. This was consistent across the four expectation measures for both males and females. Ethnic-group differences were apparent with respect to intellectual ability, academic performance, educational plans, and parents' education. Teachers' expectations for female students in each ethnic group were consistently higher than those for male students. Using a control of covariates, Yiddish- and German-speaking students had the most positive scores. French-speaking students were the lowest on the scales.

The results imply that teachers may not necessarily base their expectations of students on past performances, intellectual ability or educational plans. Instead ethnicity, sex, and for certain types of expectations, the educational level of the students' mothers have some influence. Clifton stated that teachers have important influences upon the performances and eventual achievement of students. The result of this comparison demonstrates the relative position of each ethnic group within Canadian society. Thus, it seems that educational institutions may be allocating people to positions within society based on ascribed characteristics like sex and ethnicity. This allocation may be linked to expectations of teachers.

Clifton suggests that in order to ensure that children of all ethnic groups and both sexes have equality in school, it is not only important to acknowledge that texts, tests and books may be biased but that teachers may also be biased. Therefore, it may be necessary to do something during teacher training and in-service education to ensure that teachers do not develop expectations conditional upon the ascribed characteristics of their future students. Inequality and injustice results, and some children could suffer.

Losers and Winners

Crysdale, Stewart, (1975). "Aspirations and Expectations of High School Youth: an action research project in a workers' area," International Journal of Comparative Sociology 16(1,2):19-36.

This study took place during 1969 through 1972 on a project in Riverdale, a working-class area of downtown Toronto. Three hundred and thirteen students drawn from graduates of a senior elementary school and 304 chief wage earners who lived in the same area were selected for the study. Preliminary findings were presented that illustrated the influence of the variables (intelligence test scores, sex, family income, father's and mother's education) on students' aspirations, expectations, values, curriculum and standing. Each student was interviewed and a ranking mobility potential score was assigned.

The study showed that a strong relationship exists between IQ scores and students' educational aspirations and expectations. Students with high IQ scores, were more likely to aspire to obtain university degrees compared to low-IQ students. Twice as many students suggested that they would like to graduate from university as compared to students who expected to graduate. Family income was somewhat consistently related to both aspirations and expectations. More students from families with incomes of $8,000/yr. or more said that they would like to graduate from university than those from families with less than $5,600 per year. More than twice as many youths from families having higher incomes actually expected to graduate than those from low-income homes.

In comparing job aspirations with more realistic job expectations, IQ scores in the former seemed to have the strongest impact, but gender made the greatest difference in the latter. Aspirations to white-collar and skilled blue-collar jobs positively correlated with IQ scores. Females, far more than males, thought they would actually achieve white-collar jobs; while fewer females than males thought they would obtain blue-collar jobs. The most common answer, in a predominantly low-income area to a question about the main purpose of education was "to get a better job" as reported by slightly less than half of the sample.

D'Abate, Dominic A. (1979). "Factors Affecting the Career Decisions of Youths in the Italian Community." Unpublished MSW Research Report, Social Work Library, Montreal.

The major aim of this study was to analyze the pattern of career development of youths of Italian origin. Several variables related to social and family background, school experience, and attitudes towards self, work, and the future were examined in terms of their impact on occupational preferences and educational intentions. Many of the theoretical concepts and research procedures used had been derived, in part, from a similar study conducted by Raymond Breton. Data was collected by means of a questionnaire administered to two groups of students enrolled in a local comprehensive high school situated in a predominantly Italian neighborhood. The findings indicated that a majority of students, especially males, expressed strong preferences for high-status occupations and intended to pursue education on a full-time basis. Program of study, sex, achievement level, failure in school, and parent support for education were found to be the most significant variables affecting career decisions. Socio-economic origin and attitudes towards self, work, and the future, on the other hand, played a minor role in determining future aspirations.

Danzinger, Kurt (1975). "Differences in Acculturation Patterns of Socialization Among Italian Immigrant Families." Socialization and Values in Canadian Society: Socialization, Social Stratification and Ethnicity, V. 2. Robert M. Pike and Elia Zureik (eds.).

Danzinger undertook this study in an Italian immigrant settlement area of Toronto in 1971 to determine if immigrant families valued education or supported their children in aspiring and achieving higher levels of education and occupation. Two groups were looked at: 1) nonimmigrants, defined as those in the sample who reported that English was spoken in their homes; and 2) immigrants, those who spoke Italian in their homes. The immigrant group was divided into two categories: high acculturation–those who had some facility in English and low acculturation–those who spoke no English or had only a rudimentary knowledge of the language.

Findings showed that the nonimmigrants had higher educational aspirations than immigrants. More nonimmigrants compared to high-acculturated and low-acculturated immigrants aspired to higher education. When actual expectations to attend post-secondary institutions were measured, again more nonimmigrants than high- and low-acculturated immigrants had such expectations. However, in choice of occupation, high-acculturated immigrants compared to nonimmigrants and low-acculturated immigrants chose the professional category as their first and second choices. Mothers of the high-acculturated immigrant students did not differ from nonimmigrant students in having lower aspirations. In comparing sons' aspirations with mothers' aspirations for sons, mothers from the low-acculturation immigrant group had a greater percentage of higher aspirations than their sons. This was seen as due to the mothers' underestimation of obstacles faced by their sons and the strong value placed on education. The study also revealed a strong sense of family solidarity among the immigrants and a belief that educational attainment would be a source of family honor.

Losers and Winners

The authors felt that the modest aspirations of immigrant children were not due to failure on the part of the family to act as a source of appropriate motivation, but that other factors in society had to be examined for appropriate reasons.

Danziger, Kurt (1974). "The Acculturation of Italian Immigrant Girls in Canada," International Journal of Psychology, Vol 9(2):129-137.

Data collected from interviews with Italian immigrant adolescents in Toronto indicate that Italian immigrant girls experience greater parental pressure in terms of "sex role socialization" than their male counterparts. According to Danziger's findings, there are heavy demands placed on recently arrived immigrant girls to maintain the traditional family culture which is felt to be threatened by migration to Canada. The Italian immigrant girl is allowed much less freedom in decision making and is required to take on more responsibilities within the home. In general, after a few years in Canadian society, Italian boys are allowed more independence to adapt to the competitive new society. Italian girls, on the other hand, are increasingly overprotected from cultural change.

D'Costa, Ronald B. (1971). "Post-Secondary Educational Opportunities for the Ontario Francophone Population." A study prepared for the Commission on Post Secondary Education in Ontario. Ottawa.

In this study D'Costa examined the major demographic characteristics of the Francophone population in Ontario by obtaining descriptions of existing French-language or bilingual post-secondary institutions and their programs of study. The 1961 census enumeration was employed to obtain information on the demographic and socio-economic features of Francophones. Information on post-secondary institutions was obtained from documents published by the institutions themselves. For the purpose of this study, a Francophone is defined as a person whose mother tongue is French.

In his analysis of educational attainment of Francophones in Ontario, D'Costa found that 64.5 percent of Francophone males attained only an elementary level of education and 0.9 percent obtained university degrees while the provincial figures were 40.3 percent and 2 percent. The author recommended that access to student housing should be more available to students coming from distant areas at Ottawa and Laurentian universities and Algonquin College (all located near sizeable Francophone population). Institutions should be in a position to offer students the possibility of pursuing their studies in French in all disciplines. The higher cost of providing these services must be accepted to make this education more accessible.

Losers and Winners

Denis, Ann B. "Wife and/or Worker: Sex Role Concepts of Canadian Female Students," in Eugen Lupri (ed.), The Changing Role of Women in Family and Society: A cross-cultural Comparison. Leiden: Brill (forthcoming).

A person's concept of appropriate sex-role behavior is influenced by socialization experiences in the home and in the school. Using this as a premise, Denis investigated the extent to which this applied to 666 female students in their first year at Toronto and Anglophone Montreal post-secondary institutions. The student's ethnic origin was also taken into consideration and was determined, using the Canadian census definition (i.e., father's ancestor or cultural origin). The data was translated into three scales: the degree of preference for mother or wife role; the degree of preference for holding jobs outside the home; and preference for combining family and work.

Denis reported that women strongly favored working while at the same time maintaining the role of wife and mother. However, the degree of preference was contingent on cultural origin; for example, British women perceived that it was incompatible to combine the distinct roles. But overall there was no great variation in preference for these roles among those of different socio-economic status and cultural background. It was found that women of Jewish, Eastern and Northern European origin, in that order, favored combining the roles. Women of low socio-economic status were more likely to favor labor-force participation for economic reasons and least likely to prefer combining family and work roles. On the other hand, women of high socio-economic status were more likely to favor a combining of the roles and their labor-force participation was based on economic reasons. Respondents whose mothers worked were significantly more likely to favor combining work with child rearing. Male student respondents were less enthusiastic than women about combining the roles.

Denis suggests that "the results show that there is likely to be an increasing incidence of women combining outside work and domestic responsibilities in one way or another. There is therefore likely to be increasing pressure to institutionalize more flexible career patterns," to optimize women's role in the labor force.

Denis, Ann B. (1979). "Educational Aspirations of Montreal Post Secondary Students: Ethnic, Sex and Social Class Differences," Two Nations, Many Cultures, J. L. Elliott, (ed.), 86-97.

In looking at the ethnic, sex and social-class differences in educational aspirations, Denis utilized a sample of 737 Montreal post-secondary students in her study of 1973. She defined ethnic

195

origin as the first ancestor on the male side to have come to Canada; and social class was defined as father's occupation (rated on the Blishen index) and the level of instruction of the most educated parent.

She found a positive relationship between father's occupation and aspiring to complete university for both sexes. Of those students of French origin whose father's occupational status was classified as low, 42.9 percent of the males and 33.3 percent of the females aspired to complete university, compared to 81.3 percent of males and 55 percent females whose fathers had a high occupational status. For those of British origin, 52.9 percent males and 40.5 percent females were from low status and 65.2 percent males, 58.6 percent females from high status. There was also a positive relationship between parental education (when at least one parent attended university) and student's aspiring to complete university. For students of French origin, 57.9 percent males and 39.6 percent females aspired to complete university when neither parent completed such, compared to 57.1 percent males and 83.5 percent females when at least one attended. For those of British origin, 58.5 percent males and 44 percent females aspired to complete university when neither parent completed university and 68.4 percent males and 67.6 percent females when at least one attended. In terms of ethnic origin the percentage of students aspiring to complete university ranked as follows: first, Jewish males (71.4%), second, Northern European females (65.4%), third, British males (59.8%) fourth, Southern European males (59.4%), fifth, French males (58.3%). Students who spoke French only or French and English were least likely to want to complete university, while women speaking English and another language and men speaking French and another language most likely aspired to do so. In all ethnic categories (with the exception of Northern European women) women ranked lower than men in percentage hoping to complete university. The positive relationship of father's occupation to hopes of completing university was more characteristic of men than women, while the relationship to parental education was stronger for women. Women who favored combining a career with child raising were also more likely to aspire to complete university.

W.G. Fleming (1957). "Background and Personality Factors Associated with Educational and Occupational Plans and Careers of Ontario Grade 13 Students," Atkinson Study of Utilization of Student Resources. Report No. 1.

This first report of the Atkinson study was set up to identify intellectual, personal and background characteristics of a large group of Grade 13 students in Ontario and to follow the students for two years into university, other post-secondary education and employment. It was hoped that this would reveal types of barriers to higher education encountered by deserving students.

Losers and Winners

The results of this survey document that family and school factors, on the one hand, and persons' attitudes on the other, are strongly associated with post-secondary enrolment patterns. Those who went to university tended to come from smaller families, as illustrated by the fact that almost 5 in 10 of those who attended university came from families where there was a maximum of two children. Socio-economic status counted strongly, in that nearly 5 in 10 students attending university had fathers who held managerial, professional or executive positions compared with 1 in 10 whose fathers held semiskilled and unskilled positions. Moreover, the better educated the parents, the more likely the children were to attend university. Nearly 7 in 10 students whose fathers attended high school went to university as opposed to 3 in 10 of those whose fathers did not. Students' intentions regarding university were strongly and positively related to their parents' attitudes. School achievement was positively related to university attendance as well as encouragement from school personnel and teachers' ratings.

Flowers, John F. (1964). "Some Characteristics of the Carnegie Students in Grades 10 and 11 in Ontario Schools," The Carnegie Study of Identification and Utilization of Talent in High School and College. Bulletin No. 7. Department of Educational Research, Ontario College of Education, University of Toronto.

In this study Flowers analyzed personal data obtained from students while they were in Grades 10 and 11, from 1960 to 1962, by examining questionnaires completed by the students and their teachers.

The Grade 10 student population was comprised of 45.4 percent males and 47.4 percent females. Most of the students were living in households with both parents and at least one sibling. In terms of their educational plans, slightly less than a third planned to complete secondary school and enter university. Approximately one in ten planned to enter teachers' colleges and trade schools upon finishing high school and slightly less than 2 in 10 students planned to work after finishing high school. Although post-secondary plans for the students as identified by the teachers, were largely similar to those identified by the students for themselves, students' post-secondary plans as suggested by their parents more closely approximated those suggested by the students. In terms of occupational goals 4 in 10 planned on entering a professional field, while nearly 2 in 10 planned on office work and 1 in 10 on a skilled trade.

The teachers rated the students on certain characteristics such as reliability, industriousness and chances of completing Grade 13 successfully. Most fell within the average range and the ratings were similar in Grades 10 to 11. For example, when rating "chances of completing Grade 13 successfully," fully 4 in 10 were rated by teachers as having average chances, while over 1 in 10 were rated above average, and almost 5 in 10 were rated as below average.

Gilbert, Sid and McRoberts, Hugh (1977). "Academic Stratification and Educational Plans: A Reassessment," Canadian Review of Sociology and Anthropology, 14(1): 34-46.

Using data from Porter and Blishen's Survey of Ontario Students' Aspirations, the authors examined the relative effect of school stratification as based on course selection and socio-economic status on the educational plans of secondary-school students. Moreover, they analyzed the effects of IQ, self-estimation of one's mental ability, academic achievement and familial influence on these educational plans. The sample included 2,722 Grade 8 students, 2,964 Grade 10 students and 2,862 Grade 12 students in Ontario schools.

Generally, the results showed that the higher the socio-economic status of a student the greater his chances of being in the university preparatory course. Approximately 6 in 10 working-class and over 7 in 10 upper middle-class students were enrolled in these courses. In addition, it was shown that the higher the socio-economic status of students already in the university preparatory course, the greater their expectations to actually enter university; i.e., 6 in 10 of upper-, nearly 5 in 10 middle- and over 3 in 10 working-class students expected to enter university. The data on female students revealed that fewer females than males in the preparatory course planned to enroll in university and more females of lower socio-economic-status level planned on other forms of post-secondary education. The authors found a significant relationship between mental ability, socio-economic status and program choice. Academic achievement was found to be weakly related to level-of-education expectation, while a strong relationship was identified for family influence and educational expectations. Finally, mental ability and socio-economic status of these students influenced their self-concept of ability.

Glaze, Avis. "Factors which Influence Career Choice and Future Orientations of Females: Implications for Career Education," Ph.D. Thesis, OISE, 1979.

This is a study of 1,167 girls from Grades 11 through 13 of Ontario's private and public schools examining the factors which influence the career choice of female students. Their ages ranged from 15-18 years. Almost half of the sample was middle class and the majority lived with both parents. An equal percentage of mothers and fathers had a high school education, but more fathers had completed post-secondary studies. Almost half of the parents wanted their daughters to attend university and slightly more than one-third of the daughters planned to do so. The daughters' grade level and academic averages contributed most to their educational plans (private-school girls had higher educational plans than public-school girls).

In terms of occupational choices, most had moderate career commitment. Their parents' plans for career involvement depended on the childrens' ages. More than half said they did not know enough about the occupations available to them to make a well-informed choice. About half of the girls aspired to have professional upper-class occupation but only 1 in 4 expected to have one. The daughter's position in the family was significantly related to both career aspirations and career commitment (the first-born had higher aspirations and stronger commitments). Also many of the girls contemplated nontraditional occupations, but they expected more traditional jobs.

It was recommended that Career Education Programs be implemented to help classroom teachers assist girls in career plans. Also that pre-high-school career counselling be developed to teach career information so that informed high-school program choices can be made.

Goyder, John C. (1980). "Trends in the Socio-Economic Achievement of the University Educated: A Status Attainment Model Interpretation," The Canadian Journal of Higher Education, 10(2):21-38.

This paper examined the hypothesis that a decline in university students' socio-economic background, a consequence of equalization of educational opportunity, accounts for some of the downward trends in prestige levels of first jobs obtained by university graduates.

Data from two surveys were examined: 1) Canadian mobility study done in July 1973 of 45,000 men and women over 18; and 2) Edward Harvey's survey of graduates from four Ontario universities in 1960, 1964, 1968 and 1972. In this paper only information on male students was used.

The results of the survey showed that the mean prestige occupational score (Blishen index) of the graduates' first job dropped from 65 in 1964 to 60 in 1968 and to about 55 in 1972. Attainment of high-status first occupations reached a peak between the late-1950s and the mid-1960s. The mean-status scores of first jobs among nonuniversity educated has risen steadily over the past 40 years. These people are still likely to have more education today than a generation ago (nonuniversity post-secondary education like CAATs being a major factor). Of the university educated, the mean occupational-prestige score of fathers dropped from 54.6 in 1960 to 50.5 in 1972. The educational mean score of fathers declined between 1960 and 1968 and recovered slightly by 1972.

Overall, the socio-economic status of the population has increased over the years and has generally remained the same among the university educated. The effects of family background on occupational attainment of university graduates has been small. The principal effect on status attainment appears to be educational differentiation within the university educated.

Hall, Oswald and McFarlane, Bruce (1962). Transition from School to Work, Report No. 10 of the Interdepartmental Skilled Manpower Training Research Committee, Department of Labor. Ottawa: Queen's Printer.

The purpose of this study was to examine the relationship between school and work experiences of secondary-school students. Data was collected from a sample of high-school students in a small southern Ontario community. The study focused on school-leaving patterns, occupational aspirations, current employment status of students, and how employment was obtained. The relationship of age, sex, and social class, as measured by father's occupation (manual or nonmanual) to students' goals and attainment was analyzed.

Results showed that boys, particularly those from manual-worker background, tended to drop out of school to a greater degree than did girls. Boys also tended to fail and repeat grades more often than girls. Girls seemed to view education as a means of obtaining higher social status than that of their parents. More girls whose parents were employed in manual occupations tended to be employed in nonmanual occupations than were boys. Occupations had different degrees of prestige for each social-class group. The authors suggest that family background was an important force in the development of students' occupational goals.

Harvey, Edward and Harvey, Lorna R. (1970). "Adolescence, Social Class and Occupational Expectations," The Canadian Review of Sociology and Anthropology, Vol 7(2):138-47.

A questionnaire survey of 345 Grade 10 students in a socio-economically heterogeneous, multiprogram urban high school was conducted to measure congruence between (a) a student's occupational values and choice; (b) a student's financial expectations of his work and actual likely earnings; and (c) a student's occupational choice and his parents' occupational choice for him.

Losers and Winners

Respondents were drawn from nine classes of students who were registered in programs geared toward university entry and six classes of students in vocational programs. Socio-economic status was measured in terms of father's occupation and grades were based on students' self-evaluation.

The overall findings show that students from higher socio-economic backgrounds experienced more congruence in all three dimensions than did students from lower socio-economic back-grounds. Students from higher socio-economic status, males more than females, tended to be more congruent with their values and occupational choices than lower-socio-economic status students. However, male students from lower socio-economic status were more likely to fall in the "very incongruent" category than were females when gender was controlled. Higher-status students' income expectations were more congruent to their actual likely earnings than lower-status students; but males more than females from the former group tended to overestimate their incomes. In the lower-status group, females were more likely to underestimate their income. When grades were controlled, it was found that except for lower-status males, the lower the students' grades, the more likely income would be underestimated.

Students from the higher-status group, who were more likely to have permissive parents than those from the lower-status group, tended to make occupational choices which were congruent to the choice of their parents, but this held slightly more for males than females. There was less agreement between students' choices and their parents', in the lower-status group. When gender was controlled, there was more disagreement among males than females, especially in the lower-status group.

Harvey, Edward (1977). "Accessibility to Post-Secondary Education–some gains, some losses," University Affairs, October.

This article examined the trends over time of student enroll-ment in various post-secondary programs according to students' gender and socio-economic status. The author sought to verify whether various post-secondary programs and fields of study were becoming more accessible. This was done by comparing the student population of 1968-69 to 1974-75, as reported by the Canadian census.

Harvey reported that while overall there were more males participating in post-secondary education, female participation had increased, especially in the area of law and commerce. The proportion of females in college transfer, undergraduate, pro-fessional, and postgraduate programs had increased on an average of 6-14 percent between 1968 and 1975. However, women still only constituted less than 50 percent of the enrolment in all programs with the exception of terminal college programs. As a result, women were still underrepresented in many professional and postgraduate programs. Two exceptions to this were nursing and pharmaceutical programs where, in 1974-75, more than 50 percent of the students were females.

The study showed that an increase in the proportion of students in college transfer programs and a decline in enrolment of terminal programs was evident for students whose fathers had a high level of education. A general increase of student enrolment in postgraduate, undergraduate and professional programs had brought about a corresponding increase in enrolment of students whose fathers had a low level of education. While there were significant increases in the areas of architecture, pharmacy, and agriculture, fewer gains were evident in other professional programs.

Humphreys, Edward H. (1971). "Equality? The Rural-Urban Disparity in Ontario Elementary Schools," Education Canada, Vol II:34-39.

In this study Humphreys investigated whether "the standard of educational personnel, facilities and sources available in or to an elementary school is related to the type of community in which the school is located. The more urban the community, the higher the standard of educational personnel, facilities and services" (p.24). Humphreys' key variables can be broken down into three–physical, staff, and service. The physical variables were size of school based on the number of teachers; the number of students to a class; and teaching aids available. The staff variables were teaching certificate held; years of experience and availability of consultants. The service variables were availability of special classes for atypical children; availability of special services and innovations employed.

The study was based on a reanalysis of data which was collected in 1967 and 1969. Originally, the data was collected from a random sample of urban and rural elementary school teachers throughout Ontario, and investigated the school system in an attempt to test the effectiveness of the amalgamation of school districts into larger units. There was an 80% response rate from the mailed questionnaires.

Findings showed that urban schools were much better served than rural schools, in that they were more likely to have more qualified, younger, and newly trained teaching staff. They were also more likely to have the services of consultants and medical and social service professionals available to them. In addition, it was found that there were differences between public and separate schools. In particular, the availability of consultants in separate schools was lower than in public schools, in both rural and urban areas. The lack of service factors in rural school contributed to a more conservative approach to education. Those who were best able to learn were taught in common groups, since the schools were curtailed by classroom resources.

In essence, Humphreys documented the disparities in urban/rural education. He pointed out that because of limited education, rural residents who migrate to urban areas because of economic reasons, were at a great disadvantage in acquiring jobs. Thus it was recommended that there be "more generous equalization grants for regions in economic difficulties," because it is better to support the educational needs of youth than to support them as adults.

Humphreys, Edward H. "Inequality and Rural Schools: Results of Surveys in 1967 and 1969," The Alberta Journal of Educational Research, Vol 17(2):111-23.

In this study, the author examined the relation between educational opportunity in terms of facilities, personnel and services, and the type of community in which a student lives. He utilized data obtained from questionnaires of Ontario's teachers by the Ontario Teachers' Federation in 1967 and again in 1969. His sample included 880 teachers in 1967 and 720 in 1969.

In terms of physical factors, the more urban an area the larger is its schools. Sixteen percent of all teachers reported working in schools with 27 or more colleagues and most of these schools were in urban areas. Twelve percent reported schools with eight or fewer teachers and these were in the farming areas. Urban areas were also better equipped with teaching aids. It was found that 59.9 percent of teachers in farming areas held standard 1 certificates (one year of professional training beyond Grade 13) as did 47.8 percent in large cities. Standard 4 certificates (one year professional training beyond a B.A. degree) were held by 22.6 percent of teachers in large cities and 5.9 percent in farming communities. Teachers in farming areas had more experience (49.3% had 11 years or more as compared to 31.4% in large cities). Consulting was more available in urban areas: three times as often for math and/or science, four times for reading and five times for speech. Generally more service factors were available in the urban areas than in the rural areas. For example, there were 20 percent more classes for slow learners in the city, 28 percent more access to physicians and 72 percent to psychologists; 37.1 percent of the urban as compared to 2.6 percent of the rural schools had access to social workers. However, innovative teaching methods were generally found as often in rural as in urban areas.

Losers and Winners

In general, the authors felt that Ontario must still find a way to equalize educational opportunities for the rural youth. They were most concerned with social mobility, particularly when it applied to the rural youth leaving the farming areas to look for jobs in the urban areas or to pursue higher education.

Humphreys, Elizabeth and Porter, John (1978). "Part-Time Studies and Universal Accessibility." Department of Sociology, Carleton University.

In this study the authors examined the selected characteristics of Carlton University's part-time students and their patterns of participation in part-time studies. A questionnaire was sent in February 1978 to undergraduate part-time students who had been enrolled in September of 1977 and those aged 26-35 years who had been enrolled in 1975. The authors felt that it was important to know the extent to which opportunities for part-time university education are contingent on characteristics that are not relevant to learning, for example socio-economic origin and sex.

Findings showed that the average age of part-time students was 30.8 years, which was higher than the average age of 21.2 years for full-time students. The majority of the part-time population (54%) was female and married, and had parents whose educational level was similar to those of full-time Canadian students. Fully 73 percent of the husbands of part-time students had some or had completed university education, but the wives of part-time students were not as well educated. The "desire for personal enrichment" was the most important reason to influence part-time study.

Other findings showed that a considerable proportion of Carleton University's large part-time student body came from advantaged circumstances, were already well educated, had experienced a considerable degree of upward occupational mobility, and had the motivational equipment necessary for educational success. Almost half (49%) of the part-time students were from families of upper middle-class origin as compared to 9 percent of a national sample of Canadians; 25 percent were from middle class; 25 percent from lower class, as compared to 25 percent and 66 percent of the national sample. The majority (58%) of part-time students had completed some post-secondary education before entering the labor force. However only 28 percent from lower-class origins had some university education when they entered the labor force. The vast majority (90%) of part-time students had entered the labor force and the average first job was a highly skilled blue-collar job or a low-level white-collar job. Most part-time students were employed (85% full time); however a greater percentage of males than females were working. The majority of males were employed in professional or managerial and administrative occupations. Although students

Losers and Winners

from lower-class origins had been in the labor force longer than those from more advantaged origins, the occupational status of their current jobs were virtually the same.

Although the present system of part-time studies is thought by many to offer a "second chance" to individuals who are educationally and socially deprived, the existing arrangements are used mainly by people who had a first chance but for some reason did not take it. But, the author warns, this should not obscure the fact that for some the existence of part-time studies can mean genuine opportunity. Attention should be directed to the social and organizational factors which might explain why those individuals from disadvantaged origins continue to remain largely unaffected by the opportunities that part-time studies are to provide them. In order to maximize accessibility of higher education, it is necessary not only to create educational opportunities and institutional arrangements, but to instill the requisite educational aspirations.

Lambert, W.E., Yackley, A., and Hein, R.N. (1971). "Child Training Values of English-Canadian and French-Canadian Parents," Canadian Journal of Behavioural Science, 3(3):217-36.

English-Canadian and French-Canadian working-class parents of six-year-olds were asked to listen and respond to tape recordings of a child's demands for attention, help and comfort, as well as his displays of anger, insolence and aggression. An analysis of the parents' reactions to these tapes revealed certain value orientations, some culturally distinctive and others cross-culturally common. For example, the findings suggest that both English-Canadian mothers and French-Canadian fathers are more active socializing agents and more punitive than their spouses. Both English-Canadian and French-Canadian parents generally agree on the childrearing treatment of their children, suggesting a general Canadian value orientation of conservatism. The variations in parents' modes of training children, as revealed in this study, provide an indication of their values and beliefs both within and among communities.

Lawlor, S.D. (1968). "Social Class and Achievement Orientation," The Canadian Review of Sociology and Anthropology 7(2):148-53.

Lawlor administered a questionnaire on value orientation to a sample of 301 Grade 9 boys in three high schools in Edmonton, Alberta. The fourteen items in the questionnaire dealt with areas of activism-passivism; present-future; and individualistic-familistic orientations. It was intended to test the extent to which social class made a difference to an individual's level-of-achievement

orientation. Social class was measured by using father's education and occupation. (Lawlor made reference to Rosen and
Reissman who used similar scales to measure the same item.)

Lawlor found that economically disadvantaged students were
not apathetic, submissive and withdrawn in all social situations.
He argued that lower-class students expressed achievement-
oriented values more readily when they perceived the opportunity
for material or tangible rewards, whereas middle-class students
were more committed to the intrinsic merits on holding achievement-oriented values as part of their value structure. The
findings have certain important policy implications for those
interested in understanding economically disavantaged classes and
motivating them to become more conventionally success-oriented.

Lee, Danielle Juteau and La Pointe, Jean (1979). "The Emergence
    of Franco-Ontarians: New Identity, New Boundaries,"
    Two Nations, Many Cultures, J. L. Elliott, (ed.),
    99-113.

Lee and La Pointe examined the definition of ethnic-group
boundaries, factors influencing fluctuation of those boundaries
and the impact of the fluctuations on collective identity.

The French-Canadian collectivity is seen as separated into
component parts, such as Quebecois, Franco-Ontarians, Franco-
Manitobans, Acadians, etc. When looking at the Franco-
Ontarians, two main reasons for the separation become apparent;
the emergence of the Quebecois and the industrialization and
urbanization of the French in Ontario. Initially it appeared that
the Quebecois excluded Francophones from other parts of Canada.
The Franco-Ontarians then banded together and felt the need to
rely on themselves and their provincial governments instead of
their French-Canadian identity. Also industrialization played a
part in this reorganization as urbanization accelerated and farm
life, religion, etc., became less important.

As people began to feel more as Franco-Ontarians than
French Canadians, their clubs, organizations and art began to
reflect their new identity. Clubs and organizations included
Franco-Ontarians in their names; poets and writers wrote and
sang about Franco-Ontarian realities. The term showed up in
political speeches and was used by community leaders.

The authors conclude that insofar as ethnic groups vary
over time, an understanding of collective identity requires an
understanding of their formation and transformation. Further
studies that would emphasize the viability of an ethnic community
must gather materials relating to the structural basis of the
ethnic group (e.g., social and political organization) rather than
exclusively dealing with cultural assimilation (e.g., language
spoken in the home).

Losers and Winners

Li, Peter S. (1978). "The Stratification of Ethnic Immigrants: in the case of Toronto," The Canadian Review of Sociology and Anthropology, 15(1):31-40.

This study focused on the stratification of ethnic immigrants in Toronto. It sought to evaluate the theory of differential opportunities with regard to occupational-status differences among eight European immigrant groups. A sample of 1,672 male heads of households, born outside of Canada, but living in Toronto was obtained from a large-scale survey of immigrant households in Toronto conducted by the Survey Research Centre of York University in 1970-71.

Findings indicated that a wide range of gross status differences exist among the various immigrant groups, and that inequality persists, despite adjusting for intergroup differences in social origin, education and prior achieved occupational status. The magnitude of status differences was reduced when intergroup variations in the father's occupation, the respondent's education and his first occupational status in Canada was statistically controlled. Although the English maintained the highest status in terms of current occupation, this status was attained mainly as a result of their advantage in formal levels of education and in initial occupational achievement when they first come to Canada. The Jews were least discriminated against in that they had the highest occupational status as a result of their ethnic origin when other factors in the career cycle were controlled. The Poles were the most discriminated against. Despite the fact that the Italians had the lowest occupational status, the low status achieved by the Italians was primarily due to their low educational attainments. The Germans, like the English, had some advantage over other groups because of their ethnic origin, though their occupational success was largely due to their educational level. The Ukrainians achieved slightly below the average, while immigrants from other Slavic origins (except Polish and Ukrainian) were about average. The data showed that the ethnic origin of the Ukrainians and other Slavic groups had little direct effect on their occupational status.

In general, the author concludes that occupational status is partially determined by one's ethnic origin. The entrenched status of some ethnic groups in Canada helps explain why immigrants from similar ethnic backgrounds are preferentially received.

Looker, Diane and Pineo, Peter C. "The Role of Parental Values in the Occupational Choice of Teenagers." Paper read at the Annual Meeting of the Canadian Sociology and Anthropology Association, London, Ont. Spring 1978.

Losers and Winners

In this study the authors examined the relationship between parental values in terms of self-directedness and conformity, socio-economic status and the occupational choices of teenagers. Four hundred teenagers and their parents were interviewed and asked to complete a questionnaire during the Spring of 1975 in Hamilton.

Correlations between orientation toward self-direction or conformity of parents and their teenagers was not statistically significant. A significant correlation was noted between status of father's job and parental orientation towards self-directedness. The authors interpreted this as indicating that class differences influence parental values. Further, the status of the father's job was positively related to the teenager's expectations of employment. The occupational status of the father had a definite influence on the son's values but not the daughter's. However, parental values had a greater influence on the vocational choice of daughters than sons, with self-directedness having a stronger influence. Those teenagers holding self-directed values expected to attain occupations higher in socio-economic status than those holding conformist values. Interestingly, mother's values appeared to have more influence on the son's occupational choice than fathers' values, while fathers has more influence on daughters choice than mother's. Also, it was shown that fathers were more likely to take socio-economic status into consideration when describing values they wish to see developed in a daughter than in a son.

Masemann, Vandra (1975). "Immigrant Students' Perceptions of Occupational Programs." In Education of Immigrant Students, Aaron Wolfgang (ed.). Toronto: The Ontario Institute for Studies in Education, 107-21.

Research conducted from 1968-72 in Toronto provided the data for this study which looked at particular experiences and characteristics of students in order to determine what influenced immigrant perception of occupational programs and their eventual entry into the labor market. Graduates and graduating students from seven schools in the inner-city and suburban areas were given questionnaires and in some cases personal interviews were conducted. Information was collected on students' backgrounds, school and work experiences. Differences between students who were born outside Canada and those born in Canada were noted.

In comparing immigrant and nonimmigrant students, it was found that many immigrants saw lack of proficiency in English as the main cause of their educational difficulties and employment problems; to them, English was seen as a passport to occupational success. Immigrant graduates were more likely to be employed immediately after leaving school. This was partly due to their determination to find work because of family pressures for them to start earning money. Immigrants aspired to higher-prestige jobs, and results showed that 80.9 percent of Canadian-born graduates compared to 60 percent of immigrant graduates, were employed in low-prestige occupations.

Immigrants perceived a clear link between school training and their subsequent employment. They were aware of the menial jobs held by their parents and were determined to achieve a higher level of employment. The time of arrival into the school system was critical for immigrant students. Depending on when they arrived, they might be placed in classes with "slow learners" emphasizing language and/or cultural differences and treated like the intellectually handicapped. Many first-generation immigrant students were found in occupational programs because they tended to settle in areas where schools offered occupational programs (e.g., inner city). Compared to Canadian students, immigrant students (e.g., Italians) tended to graduate at an older age (usually 1 year), mainly because they were put back one year in school upon arrival in Canada.

Mayovich, Minako K. (1975). "Ethnic Variation and Success Value," Socialization and Values in Canadian Society: Socialization, Social Stratification and Ethnicity, V. 2. Robert Pike and Eliza Zureik (eds.).

This study completed in 1966, compared Japanese Canadians, Italian Canadians and Canadian Mennonites in their pursuit of success values through educational and occupational aspirations. The study took place in Toronto and Kitchener and its environs. About 450 families with children in the age range of 10-15 years from each of the three groups were interviewed.

The study showed that Japanese Canadians measured success values by family reputation; Italian Canadians emphasized personal security; Traditional Canadian Mennonites measured success values by high agricultural productivity and ownership of land while Progressive Canadian Mennonites stressed personal security and religion (God's will). When the families were questioned on occupational aspirations, slightly more Japanese than Italian families expected their sons to secure professional, managerial or technical positions; with 10 percent more Japanese children aspiring to these occupations than Italian children. Japanese were found to have more realistic expectations of obtaining these positions compared to Italians. Also there was a great percentage difference (30%) between Japanese and Italian parents who expected their children to obtain at least a college education. The percentage difference was also evident when the researchers examined both groups' realistic expectations for college education.

Since Mennonites are against higher education, the importance placed on grades by parents was looked at in considering educational achievement. Naturally, a higher percentage of Progressive, compared to Traditional, Mennonites felt that grades were important. Discordance between high parental pressures and low achievement of children was also examined to determine how this frustration was displayed (i.e., covert symptoms such as colds, aches, trouble sleeping, loss of appetite, weight, etc., versus overt symptoms such as open hostility and rebellion). The Mennonite children generally displayed overt symptoms of dissatisfaction toward parental pressures, except when expectations were low and achievement high, then covert symptoms were displayed. Approximately the same number of Japanese and Italian children reacted negatively to parental pressures, but nearly five times as many Italian as Japanese children were openly rebellious. The authors concluded that Canadians share success values but that subgroups define success differently and that there is a need to recognize and accept these differences.

Pavalko, Ronald and Bishop, David (1968). "Socioeconomic Status and College Plans: A Study of Canadian High School Students," in <u>Sociology of Education: A Book of Readings</u>, Ronald Pavalko (ed.).

This study examined the relationships of socio-economic status to the college plans of Canadian youth. Questionnaires were administered to 889 Grade 12 students from six high schools in Port Arthur and Fort William, Ontario, and intelligence-score information was obtained from their school files.

The authors found that the percentage of students with college plans increased with socio-economic status. In the high socio-economic status category (father's occupation classified as nonmanual occupation) 52 percent of students planned to attend college as compared to 34.9 percent of low socio-economic status (father's occupation classified as manual). Males, irrespective of socio-economic status, more likely than females planned on attending college. Also, there was a direct relationship between measured intelligence and college plans. More students of the high-intelligence group as compared to those of the low-intelligence group planned on college. Slightly more than twice as many females of high intelligence than of low intelligence planned to enroll in college. The difference for males was smaller.

The author recommends that it would not be appropriate to generalize these findings to the whole of Canada because of Canada's high degree of cultural variation and regionalism. But a modest degree of generalization to some other urban areas seems justified. Overall, he feels that society should not fail in educating its most intellectually able (regardless of socio-economic status) and thereby losing talent and preventing social mobility.

Losers and Winners

Pavalko, Ronald M. and Bishop, David R. (1976) "Peer Influences on the College Plans of Canadian High School Students," in Ronald M. Pavalko (ed.), Sociology of Education: A Book of Readings.

In this study the authors were interested in examining the relationship of peer influences on the college plans of Canadian youth. They hypothesized that there is a greater probability that students whose friends plan to go to college will plan on college themselves than will students whose friends do not plan to go to college. In order to examine this, 889 Grade 12 students from six high schools in Port Arthur and Fort William, Ontario were given a questionnaire to complete, and intelligence test scores were obtained from their school files.

The results of the study show that a strong relationship exists between the future educational plans of high-school students and those of close friends. Those whose friends plan on college are themselves more likely to go to college (55.7%) than are those whose friends do not (27.4%). However, this may not operate uniformly across all socio-economic and gender groups. Students from a high socio-economic background and high-intelligence category are more likely to attend college and those whose friends plan on college are more likely to have college plans themselves. The effect of friends' plans persist among boys irrespective of socio-economic status but persist only among girls of high socio-economic status. This effect is stronger among boys of high intelligence and weakest among girls of low intelligence. The high relationship of educational plans of friends to one's own plans disappears among both girls of high and low intelligence and of low socio-economic status. The author recommends that there is a need to further investigate the dynamics of peer influence among different kinds of adolescent subgroups based on sex, intelligence, and economic background.

Pollard, Diane S. (1973). "Educational Achievement and Ethnic Membership," Comparative Education Review 17(3): 362-74.

Utilizing a sample of 420 Grade 7 pupils from five ethnic groups (Dutch, German, Irish, Italian and Polish) in private schools in a metropolitan area in Canada, Pollard examined ethnic differences in educational achievement. She looked at various personality and perceptual factors to determine their relationship to educational achievement for the five ethnic groups.

Some differences were found in these factors for the groups. In terms of general aspirations, the Italians were significantly higher than the other groups (in descending order: German, Dutch, Irish, Polish). For when fear of failure or test-anxiety was examined, the order varied significantly as follows: Polish,

Dutch, German, Irish and Italian. The Polish had the highest and the Italians the lowest test-anxiety scores. Certain factors were found to correlate positively with achievement and self-concept of ability; these associations held true for all ethnic groups. Certain variables were also found to differentiate between high and low achievers, one being perceived relationship with teachers, which held true for all groups. For example, aspiration and family background differentiated high and low achievers for the Polish, and motivation, self-concept of ability, scholastic aspiration for the Dutch.

Distinct patterns emerged for the Dutch and Poles and the authors attributed this to a strong sense of cultural identification. For the German and Irish, few patterns emerged. This was attributed to their early immigration and assimilation to the larger society. The Italians who are newer immigrants, are less assimilated but show a pattern similar to that of Germans and Irish.

Ramcharan, Subhas (1972). "Special Problems of Immigrant Children in Toronto Schools." In Aaron Wolfgang (ed.)., Education of Immigrant Students. Toronto: The Ontario Institute for Studies in Education.

Ramcharan's study specifically investigated the problems experienced by West Indian students in the metropolitan Toronto school system. The 290 students who responded through questionnaires provided information on their experiences with cultural conflict, adjustment to their new environment, emotional problems and discrimination.

It was found that within a sample of thirty students who were registered in secondary education, nineteen were in technical or vocational programs rather than academic programs. Of the nineteen students, sixteen were from working-class backgrounds and resided in areas of Toronto with a high West Indian population. The problem of cultural identity was a major factor to influence the educational process of the students. It was pointed out that the differences in cultural reference points of students and their parents presented problems in parent-child relations. That is, while students identified with the new culture, their parents identified with the old. This loss of cultural identity characterized all students. Those upwardly mobile students who proved successful in the school system largely abandoned or rejected their ethnic origin.

Black West Indian students also unjustifiably encountered, discrimination and were termed "slow learners." Teachers were accused of not showing enough interest in these students. Often coupled with discriminatory practices, they tended to discourage these students from entering academically-oriented programs. In many cases the lack of interest on the part of the teachers helped the students to foster resentment towards the school system.

Ratna, Ghosh (1978). "Ethnic Minorities and the School Curriculum," Multiculturalism, Vol II(1):24-26

Referring to curriculum materials, books, and media materials, Ratna examined the theme of multiculturalism as it affects students. He found that multiculturalism has not in itself provided an answer to the many problems of intergroup relations. However, Ratna mentioned that the introduction of multiculturalism to the school curriculum through academic and nonacademic activities could eliminate discrimination, alter values and attitudes towards different ethnic, racial, and immigrant groups, and create an attitude of goodwill and tolerance towards all minority groups. He felt that this would develop an understanding that to be different is not to be inferior, that every Canadian has a right to equal participation in every sphere of Canadian life, regardless of and in spite of differences in ethnic or racial membership, religious affiliation, sex, or social status.

The interpretation of the ideology of multiculturalism has major implications for education since cultural conflict affects school performance. The educational system has failed to appreciate the differences between people and cultures. The pressures of integration into the dominant culture and evaluation of performance in terms of standards set by the values, beliefs, and practices of this culture has resulted in education that is focused on the elimination of differences.

Richer, Stephen and LaPorte, Pierre (1979). "Cultural, Cognition and English French Competition," Two Nations, Many Cultures, (ed.) J. L. Elliott, 1979, pp. 75-85.

This article is based on a comparison of research studies and employs a status-attainment model developed to explain differences among Anglophones and Francophones.

French and English Canadians are generally found to vary significantly in status attainment. French Canadians are under-represented in professional and technical occupations as well as in the upper echelons of business and industry. In a sample of industrial firms in Quebec, French-Canadian presence in owner-ship and top-level management was weak. Only 27 percent of the firms were French-Canadian-owned, and only 37 percent had a French Canadian in a top-level management position.

Findings of one study showed that the stronger the French community the lower the occupational and educational success of its members. This strong sense of community was associated with high language retention. Conversely, high language loss was correlated with low in-group strength and high-status achievement. It was suggested that greater preoccupation with the family was partially responsible for lower French-Canadian success as entrepreneurs. Another study reviewed, this time in the area of family socialization, indicated that French Canadians appeared to be among the last ethnic groups to foster independence training for their children, whereas Anglo-Protestants were among the earliest. This review therefore suggests that the French-Canadian value or emphasis on community and family can act as a barrier to status attainment. The authors recommend that the government make a systematic effort to open up job opportunities for French Canadians and that this be done without cultural denial or loss.

Richmond, Anthony H. and Kalbach, Warren E. "Education, Training and School Attendance," Factors in the Adjustment of Immigrants and their Descendants. Census Analytical Survey, 1971, 243-74, Ottawa.

Utilizing 1971 census data, Richmond and Kalbach looked at the education, training and school attendance of Canada's immigrant population and their descendants. They used 1 percent of the immigrant population as their sample size and examined various ethnic groups, period and generation of immigration, and where they stood in terms of education and training.

Generally, after 1961, Canadian immigration policy became increasingly selective about the educational and vocational qualifications of immigrants. At the time of this census, recent immigrants were much younger than the immigrants just prior to and after World War II. Also the age distribution of Canadians born of foreign parentage differed from that of the population as a whole. So in order to interpret differences, distributions were standardized by age. When age was controlled, the native-born population was less likely to have some university education, some vocational training (12% compared to 16% foreign-born) and lower mean-educational levels (9.5 years compared to 10 years foreign-born males). Of those having at least some university education, there was a variation between the ethnic groups. Third-plus-generation Native Indians had the lowest percentage (2.2%), obtaining some university, with foreign-born of Italian origin the second lowest (4.6%). The highest educational attainment levels were held by those of Jewish descent (27%) and Chinese and Japanese (22%). The children of foreign-born family heads were more likely to be in school after age 19-24 than those of Canadian born (44.3% compared to 37.5%). Of those family heads born outside of Canada, 42.8 percent of the children from the United Kingdom and Ireland, 35.7 percent from Italy and 56.5 percent from Asia were attending school full time. Of those born inside Canada, the largest contrast was seen in the fact that the

214

Canadian-born Jewish population was three times as likely to be attending school than the Native Indian population.

Generally, educational opportunities were greater in large urban centers than in rural areas and small towns, and a large proportion of immigrants tended to locate in these large metropolitan areas. In Toronto and Montreal, the levels of education were higher than the national averages, though the tendency to remain in school at ages 19-24 was lower in Quebec (34.7%) than in Canada as a whole (39.6%).

Russell, C. Neil, Ed. D. (1979). "Post High School Outcomes of Manitoba High School Students," Manitoba Dept. of Education.

The purpose of this study was to validate post-high-school intentions as expressed in Grade 12 with actual outcomes. Information was provided as to why plans were or were not carried out. It identified factors which might have accounted for student behaviors differing from stated intentions, as well as identifying the historical and current labor-force status of students. A sample of 3,000 Manitoba high-school students was used for this analysis. The data was originally obtained between 1971-72 and 1976-77 from Grade 12 students who were surveyed during their last year of high school. Respondents were again interviewed in May-August 1978.

The results of the study showed that students who indicated in Grade 12 that they planned to enroll in a university were more likely to carry out that decision than students who had other post-secondary plans. The majority of students who were undecided about their plans after high school did not participate in post-secondary education. Major reasons for participating were to obtain a degree; to learn a trade; to get a better (interesting) job; or to get a general education. Major reasons for not participating were to start working; undecided about the future; limited finances. High-socio-economic-status students were more likely to participate in post-secondary education than students from medium- or low-socio-economic-status levels. Results indicated that both male and female students tended to carry out their father's and mother's educational expectations for post-secondary education, but females more than males seemed to be undecided about their future and wanted to break from school to think about their plans.

215

Losers and Winners

Samuda, Ronald J. and Crawford, Douglas H. (1980). Testing, Assessment, Counselling and Placement of Ethnic Minority Students Current Methods in Ontario. Ministry of Education, Toronto, Ont.

This study investigated the factors related to the reception and placement of immigrant minority students in the Ontario educational system. These factors were determined from discussions and interviews with school personnel and review of school documents including policies and procedures. For the purpose of this study, a sample of West Indian, Portuguese and East Indian students from 245 elementary and secondary schools in Ontario was used.

Students were evaluated mainly on academic history, personal demographic information and interviews. Most students were placed into grades which corresponded to their ages. The results showed that only one school in four did diagnostic assessments, four Metro Toronto boards made specific provisions for new Canadian students, while approximately one-third of the schools had a counselling-referral policy. Reassessment generally occurred upon referral by teachers, and testing was used much more at this time. The tests most frequently utilized were, teacher-made tests, Wechsler Intelligence Scale for Children, or the Wide Range Achievement Test. The Metro Toronto boards advised extreme caution in the use of intellectual-assessment tests in the first two years of Canadian schooling. Approximately 8 out of 10 schools modified the tests by extending the length of time, omitting items, and substituting words and phrases. Special placements did occur in almost all schools for students with poor language development and low achievement. Testing new immigrant students presented problems in that the assessment mechanism was sometimes questionable. Some school boards in Metro Toronto advised extreme caution when testing students and some utilized the tests following the "Guidelines for Testing Minority Group Children." Schools that did not adhere to this advice and guidelines used the tests which resulted in large numbers of students being placed in low- and medium-level classes. The need for appropriate training and retraining of teachers and counsellors was seen.

Taylor, D.M., Frasure-Smith, N. and Lambert, W.E. (1978). "Psychological Development of French and English Canadian Children: Child Rearing Attitudes and Ethnic Identity," The Canadian Ethnic Mosaic: A Quest For Identity. Leo Dreedger (ed.). McClelland and Stewart, 1978.

In an attempt to explore similarities or differences in French and English Canadians, the authors focused on two areas: child-rearing and ethnic identity. They interviewed parents and taped parent-child interactions of 40 sets each of English- and French-Canadian parents of six-year-olds. They also interviewed a sample of first-year high-school students in Quebec.

The authors found that many "seeming" differences between French and English Canadians may be more the result of social-class differences than ethnic ones. Working-class parents (either of French- or English-Canadian origin) were more severe in their reactions to temper tantrums, more restrictive of their children's bid for autonomy and of requests (e.g., having guests over) than middle-class parents. The differences between French- and English-Canadian parents existed but were not as significant. English-Canadian parents tended to be less spontaneous in giving help to a child with a puzzle, reacted more harshly to insolence, and were more restrictive of guests. But the authors felt that they may have wanted to appear in a certain way on the tapes or may have reacted in this way out of fear of losing parental control.

With respect to ethnic identity, language appeared to be a key issue. English Canadians were more likely to identify themselves as Canadians and French Canadians as Quebecers. English Canadians tended to make distinctions between bilingual French and bilingual English reference groups, while French Canadians who attended English schools clearly identified with bilingual reference groups.

Tuition Fees and Opportunities for Participation in Higher Education, Office of the Vice President (Research and Planning) and Registrar, University of Toronto, February 1981.

This paper presented a review of recent studies on the effects of tuition-fee increases on enrolments in higher education. Among the areas touched on in the review are: (1) tuition price elasticity of demand; (2) relationship between rising tuition costs and changes in the enrolment of Grade 13 students in Ontario universities; (3) tuition costs and attrition in the Faculty of Arts and Sciences, University of Toronto; (4) admitted students responses to questions about the relationships of finances to their decisions regarding post-secondary education; (5) inequality of accessibility to Ontario universities: first-year students from Metropolitan Toronto.

The general conclusions reached in this analytic review were that: overall, these studies reinforce the view that the relationship between tuition fees and participation is minimal. Enrollments do not reflect a sensitivity to changes in tuition fees, although they may be more sensitive to changes in the total price of education. This seems to be more characteristic of lower-income groups. Family assistance and summer or part-time jobs are generally among the most important sources of finance for students.

Turrittin, Anton H.; Anisef, Paul; and Mackinnon, Neil J. "Social Inequality, Gender Roles and Educational Achievement: An Attainment Model for a Sample of Previous High School Students." Paper presented at the Annual Canadian Sociology and Anthropology Association Meetings, June 4-7, 1980. Montreal.

In this study the authors showed gender differences in the educational-attainment process. A sample of 694 males and 757 females from a longitudinal study, begun in 1973, of Ontario high-school students was utilized.

Females were found to outperform males in terms of high-school grades; however, the grades received by males had twice the effect on their eventual level of education attainment. Choice of program in high school had a direct effect on the educational attainment of females, whereas socio-economic status was found to indirectly affect their levels of educational attainment. Social-psychological factors, such as self-concept of ability and family encouragement were far more important to females than to males. Family size had no direct effect on males and only a small indirect effect on females through type of high-school programs selected, and self-concept of ability. In terms of area of origin, rural males were more inclined towards technical and vocational courses in high school than urban males. They also tended to have lower self-concepts of ability than did females. Lower occupational expectations played a modest role in educational attainments for males, but not for females. Level of education expectations had a very important effect on educational attainments for females.

The authors concluded that social-background factors play important roles in the educational-attainment process, and that the expectations developed by males and females cause them to operate differently in making and implementing educational plans.

D. Wilkenson, "Education and the Social Mobility of Three Ethnic Groups: A Canadian Case Study." Paper presented at the 1980 C.S.A.A. meetings in Montreal.

This study was undertaken to determine the effects of the educational system on ethnic mobility. One hundred and forty-four students of English, Italian and Finnish origin who had attended high school between 1959-65 in a small town in Northern Ontario were questioned.

The findings showed that the Italians and the Finns were more successful in the educational system than were the English.

218

More specifically, it was found that more than 8 out of 10 Italians and Finns (slightly more females than males in each case) completed high school. But for English students, only 1 out of 2 males and 3 out of 4 females completed high school. In terms of university, Finns and Italians, more than English, attended and graduated from university. However, while for all three groups, more males than females attended university; among the English, slightly more females than males graduated. The reverse was evident in the case of Finns and Italians; there was a 13 to 20 percent difference between male over female graduates.

When income from employment (after completion of education) was examined, the Italians and Finns were more successful educationally, but their incomes were the lowest. The English had greater proportions in managerial and supervisory positions.

The authors concluded that the main barrier to ethnic mobility was to be found in the occupational system, not in the educational system. In fact, the respondents reported little perceived discrimination (from memory) in the educational system.

Williams, Trevor H. (1972). "Educational Aspirations: Longitudinal Evidence on Their Development in Canadian Youth," Sociology of Education, Vol 45(1):107-30.

In this investigation, Williams studied the effects of socio-economic background, parents' expectations, teacher's expectations, intellectual ability, academic achievement, and peers' aspirations on the development of educational aspirations in high school. Utilizing data-bank information on students entering Grade 9 in 1959-60 and followed to Grade 12, Williams selected a sample of 3,687 Grade 12 students.

The findings showed that intellectual ability is a major cause of academic achievement. While teachers' expectations have a major effect on the academic development of girls, peer expectations are relatively more powerful for boys. The author also found that socio-economic background had a minor influence on achievement. Surprisingly, he noted that academic achievement and intellectual ability had little effect on educational aspirations for students in Grade 10. Parental influence had the greatest effect on aspirations; while teacher and peer expectations ranked second and third, respectively, in influence. This was initially the same for girls, but did not hold up from Grade 10 to Grade 12. Peers and teachers gained in influence on girls during this time. However, for boys, parental influence increased, particularly as socio-economic status increased; so did parental expectations. Education for girls does not appear to be as higly valued as for boys.

Losers and Winners

Wolfgang, Aaron, (O.I.S.E.). "Overcoming Handicaps in
      Counselling Immigrant Students," Applied Cross-
      Cultural Psychology, J. W. Berry and W. J. Lonner
      (eds.). (Amsterdam: Swets and Zeitlinger B.V. 1974)
      109-14.

This paper attempts to sensitize school guidance counsellors
to the special needs and sociopsychological difficulties of immigrant students in North America. While many of these students
are handicapped by their language barrier and unfamiliarity with
the new environment, school guidance staff are handicapped by
culturally biased theoretical guidelines. Wolfgang notes that many
immigrant students often resist social interaction and have negative self-images. He suggests that guidance counsellors could
perhaps try to reach these students by inviting them and their
parents to orientation programs in their own languages, and
encourage in them a sense of ethnic pride. Because certain
cultures rely more on nonverbal communication, counsellors could
become more sensitive to appropriate facial expressions, touching
behaviors and other physical cues important to their social relationships with school personnel. Obviously, special training
programs and further research are required.

Zur-Muehlen, Max von (1978). "The Educational Background of
      Parents of Post-Secondary Students in Canada,"
      Statistics Canada, March.

The object of this report was to document to what extent
social-class differences, as measured by parents' educational
attainment, affect their childrens' participation in post-secondary
education. Data was obtained from five basic sources including
the 1968-69 and 1974-75 post-secondary student survey coducted
by the Secretary of State; 1961 and 1971 census data and unemployment data.

The authors reported that post-secondary education increased
tremendously during the 1960s in terms of part-time, full-time and
post-secondary university enrolment. In general, the socio-
economic status of the family was the significant factor in explaining differences in educational opportunities available to
children. Though accessibility to post-secondary education had
remained or increased in favor of students whose parents have
also attended university, the participation rate of disadvantaged
students had also increased. Although greater access to higher
education had occurred, it seemed to be more pronounced for
those enrolled in community colleges than in universities. High
educational attainment, particularly at the university level, was
substantially higher among fathers than mothers. This has implications for the findings which showed that the educational
experiences of mothers appeared to have more influence on their
daughters' educational attainment than those of fathers. But

while parental influence on females' attainment was more significant in the earlier years (1968-69), by 1974-75 the significance
was substantially less.

Male (18-21 years) enrolment rate in full-time undergraduate
studies remained relatively stable from 1968-69 to 1974-75; however, the female enrolment rate increased steadily. The report
showed that part-time students typically had parents with lower
educational attainment. And finally, it also showed that students
from disadvantaged homes were more likely to be unemployed; the
latter being a product of their lower educational attainment.

Zussman, David (1975). "Some Determinants of Post-Secondary
    Education Aspirations," Working Paper, Dept. of
    Secretary of State, Education Support Branch.
    November.

This study was based on a 50 percent random sample of
senior secondary students who were enrolled in Alberta high
schools in 1973-74. It explored the relationship between the
independent variables: father's education, mother's education,
self-rated ability, size of community, parental influence and
gender and students' aspirations to continue schooling after high
school.

Students who rated themselves highly in the self-rated
ability test, were most likely to aspire to continue their education
after high school. However, females were more likely than males
to show a desire to continue. This, however, was contingent on
geographic location in that male students from urban areas were
more likely than male students from rural and middle-sized areas
to want to continue their education after high school. Females,
on the other hand, were more likely to want to continue when
they were from rural and urban areas, than from mid-sized communities. Students who opted for part-time studies rated themselves lower on the ability scale.

There was a positive correlation between father's and
mother's educational attainment and the student's educational
aspirations. The author noted that when predicting student's
desire to continue schooling beyond the secondary level, variables
could be ranked in the following descending order of importance:
self-rated ability, father's education, size of community, and
parental influence.

Index

DATE DUE
DATE DE RETOUR

MAR 2 0 1985			
OCT 19 1986			
APR 2 1 1992			
OCT 2 8 1993			
DEC 1 0 1993			
FEB 2 3 1995			
FEB 0 9 1995			
MAR 1 7 1997			
MAR 1 7 1997			